The Industrial Subscription Economy

A Practical Guide to Designing, Pricing, and Scaling Your Industrial Subscription

by Stephan M. Liozu, PhD

Value Innoruption Advisors Publishing • Crown King AZ • 2022

The Industrial Subscription Economy:
A Practical Guide to Designing, Pricing, and Scaling Your Industrial Subscription
by Stephan M. Liozu, PhD

Published by Value Innoruption Advisors Publishing
PO Box 551, Crown King AZ 86343 USA
www.valueinnoruption.com

ISBN: 978-1-945815-10-2 trade paperback
      978-1-945815-11-9 electronic book

First Printing

Editorial supervision: Kristen Ebert-Wagner (kristen.ebertwagner@gmail.com)
Design and composition: Dick Margulis (www.dmargulis.com)
Proofreading: Janet Werner (www.jbediting.com)

MANUFACTURED IN THE UNITED STATES OF AMERICA

Contents

SECTION 3: SUBSCRIPTION-BASED PRICING

SECTION 4: SCALING & EXECUTING YOUR SUBSCRIPTION OFFERS

SECTION 5: INDUSTRIAL SUBSCRIPTION EXAMPLES

Abbreviations/acronyms used in this book

ACV	Average contract value	**IoT**	Internet of Things
AR	Augmented reality	**IBDP**	Installed base data platform
ARR	Annual recurring revenue	**KPIs**	Key performance indicators
BHAG	Big hairy audacious goal	**LTV**	Lifetime value
CaaS	Communications-as-a-service	**MRR**	Monthly recurring revenues
CAGR	Compound annual growth rate	**MVP**	Minimum viable product
CapEx	Capital expenditure	**NRR**	Net retention rate, Net recurring revenue
CLV	Customer lifetime value	**OpEx**	Operating expenditure
COGS	Cost of goods sold	**PaaS**	Product- or Platform-as-a-service
CRM	Customer relationship management	**PMF**	Product market fit
CVM	Customer value management	**ROI**	Return on investment
DBNER	Dollar-based net expansion rate	**RRR**	Revenue retention rate
EaaS	Equipment-as-a-service	**SaaS**	Software-as-a-service
EBIT	Earnings before interest and taxes	**SLA**	Service level agreement
EBITDA	Earnings before interest, taxes, depreciations, and amortizations	**TAM**	Total addressable market
ERP	enterprise resource planning	**TCV**	Total contract value
EVA	Economic value added	**UX**	User experience
EVC	Economic value to the customer	**WIIFM**	What's in it for me
HaaS	Hardware-as-a-service	**WTP**	Willingness to pay
IIoT	Industrial Internet of Things	**XaaS**	Delivery of anything as a service

Foreword: The Rise of the Industrial Subscription Economy

Robbie Traube

W<small>E LIVE IN EXCITING</small> times. The world is changing, and change is accelerating. Most of that change is triggered by amazing technological developments driven by more empowered consumers. Over the past few years, we've witnessed a transformation as traditional business models are reborn through a transition to flexible consumption business models.

Business model innovation is at the heart of the digital transformation happening all around us. Take, for example, the media, entertainment, and telecom industries, where years of price wars wreaked havoc on the sector. These businesses are now flourishing again, thanks to the introduction of radically different new business models. Both the *New York Times* and the *Financial Times* are examples of resounding transformation successes.

No sector is immune to these changes. Think about the world of smart farming today, where autonomous tractors do their work in the fields but also collect environmental data used to develop smart seeding technology. Who would have thought? At the heart of this business model revolution is the move from product-centric models to consumer-centric ones.

The subscription tsunami

Zuora was founded 14 years ago based on Tien Tzuo's vision to evangelize the shift to subscription-based business models. In fact, Tzuo coined the term

Powering the Subscription Economy® and wrote the best-selling book *Subscribed*. Since then, we've witnessed a large subscription tsunami reaching the shores of the business-to-consumer (B2C), business-to-business (B2B), and, soon, the business-to-government (B2G) markets.

The categories of media, food, gaming, and fitness have been transformed by subscriptions, thanks to companies like Netflix (209 million global paid memberships; Katz, 2021), Doordash (5 million Dashpass members; "Chase Extends," 2021), Microsoft (18 million XBox Game Pass subscriptions; "Microsoft Corporation's," 2021), and Peloton (5.9 million members; "Peloton Interactive," 2021), respectively. Other, more traditional sectors have also jumped on the bandwagon, including insurance, health care, and education. Subscription has become the default way that businesses purchase software. SaaS was worth $640 billion in 2019 (Clayton, 2019) and is estimated at the time of this writing to be worth more than $1 trillion (Taussig, 2020).

Unless you live in a cave or under a rock, you know about subscriptions and have subscribed to a few services online. Consider that there are 200 million Amazon Prime subscribers (Tatevosian, 2021). That tsunami is not done crashing onto new shores. The penetration of the subscription economy is now reaching the land of the industrial world, and the potential is gigantic. Consider the billions of IoT sensors installed over the past 10 years and the amount of data that has been collected. Turning data into insights will generate many opportunities for industrial companies to create value for their ecosystems and for themselves. Consider the two trends of "SaaSification" and "cloudification" in the B2B and the B2G worlds. This is just getting started as well.

The resilience of subscription business models

Companies that have embraced the subscription economy have experienced growth and resilience. Even during the COVID-19 crisis, Zuora's Subscribed Institute found that 8 of 10 companies continued to grow. According to Zuora's *Subscription Economy Index Report* published in March 2021:

> The Subscription Economy has grown nearly 6× (more than 435%) over the last 9 years, and subscription businesses in the Subscription Economy Index (SEI) report have consistently grown five to eight times faster than traditional businesses. In 2020, subscription businesses in the SEI demonstrated revenue growth at a rate of 11.6%, while revenues of its product-based peers declined, changing –1.6%. In Q4 alone, subscription companies in the SEI experienced revenue growth at a rate of 21%, seven times faster than S&P 500 companies' growth rate of 3%.

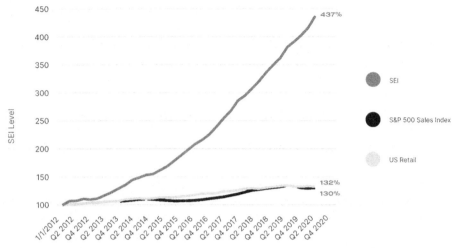

Figure 0.1. The Subscription Economy Index™ versus S&P 500 and US retail sales.

Statistics like these offer a strong motivation for companies to focus on building recurring revenue streams. Embracing the subscription economy and making it a strong innovation priority is a must-do in the context of greater commoditization, sluggish demand levels, and pressure from shareholders.

The five key success factors for manufacturing

The world of manufacturing and the industrial sector in general are different from the B2C and the B2B SaaS worlds. In manufacturing, subscriptions complement product offerings and offer an opportunity to launch parallel business models focused on high-margin recurring revenue streams. The core business is still centered around products, but manufacturers can benefit from experimenting with subscription-based business models at the same time. I see five key success factors for them to be able to succeed in the subscription economy:

1   **Find a balance between one-time and lifetime sales.** Some manufacturing companies have set and communicated recurring revenue targets. They are committed to generating 20 percent to 30 percent of their total sales revenues from recurring business models, including subscriptions. The magic number does not exist. The key is to find the right balance between one-time transaction sales and lifetime recurring sales. By doing both, companies can optimize market penetration and revenue opportunities.

2   **Launch and iterate quickly.** Speed is essential in the subscription world. Traditional innovation cycles are longer in manufacturing and can be measured in years. In the digital world, these cycles have been shortened

to months thanks to access to proven technologies and numerous examples of successful and scaled subscriptions offers.

3 **Leverage data.** Many manufacturers have invested billions in IoT technologies and equipment and have a sea of data at their disposal. The ability to translate data into insights and launch customer-centric digital offers that create value for their end-user base is the next frontier in IoT.

4 **Monetize throughout the subscription life cycle.** Dynamic pricing strategies are essential, from the launch of the subscription to the renewal years down the road. In the subscription world, nothing is static. Agility and automation make the realization of subscriber lifetime value possible. And that requires advanced monetization capabilities.

5 **Culture is king.** Managing two cultures and two types of business models can be quite challenging. Using customer-centricity as your North Star, set a course for a cultural transformation that embraces customer outcomes over product features. This is a critical success factor for manufacturers.

Manufacturers need to continue to excel with their traditional product-centric business models while innovating and launching outstanding new subscription-based business models. They can learn from the best digital natives in the B2C and the B2B SaaS worlds. While different, the pillars of a good industrial subscription business model remain the same: insights, agility, automation for a better subscriber experience.

How this book will help you

I'm excited to see *The Industrial Subscription Economy* come to life. It's full of tips, nuggets, and benchmarks to learn from the best in the B2C and the B2B worlds. The book summarizes many of the reports published over the past few years. Thanks to Zuora's 1,000+ clients and the billions of subscription transactions we manage for them every month, we also have supported this book project, with a chapter from Michael Mansard, Zuora's Principal Director of Subscription Strategy. I encourage you to embrace the subscription wave and the transition from ownership models to usership ones.

Join the subscription economy and get started today.

References

Chase extends partnership with DoorDash to provide DashPass benefit for most Chase co-brand cardmembers. (2021). *Chase Media Center,* May 10. https://media.chase.com/news /chase-extends-partnership-with-doordash

Clayton, A. (2019). History of public SaaS returns and valuations. *Medium.com,* July 10. https://medium.com/@alexfclayton/history-of-public-saas-returns-and-valuations-67e49935a34c

Katz, R. (2021). Netflix statistics: How many subscribers does Netflix have? Worldwide, US member count and growth. *Insider Intelligence,* July 30. www.insiderintelligence.com/insights/netflix-subscribers/

Peloton Interactive, Inc. reports fourth quarter and full-year fiscal 2021 financial results. (2021). *Peloton,* August 26. https://investor.onepeloton.com/news-releases/news-release-details/peloton-interactive-inc-reports-fourth-quarter-and-full-year-0

Microsoft Corporation's (MSFT) CEO Satya Nadella on Q2 2021 results—Earnings call transcript. (2021). *Seeking Alpha,* January 26. https://seekingalpha.com/article/4401205-microsoft-corporations-msft-ceo-satya-nadella-on-q2-2021-results-earnings-call-transcript

Tatevosian, P. (2021). Amazon reaches 200 million Prime members: Here's why that's a big deal. *Motley Fool,* April 27. www.fool.com/investing/2021/04/27/amazon-reaches-200-million-prime-member-milestone/

Taussig, A. (2020). Firehose #182: Subscription addiction. *Firehose,* November 30. www.firehose.vc/p/firehose-182-subscription-addiction

Zuora. (2021, March). *Subscription Economy Index Report.* Available at www.zuora.com/resource/subscription-economy-index/

About Robbie Traube

Robbie Traube is Chief Revenue Officer at Zuora, where he leads the global go-to-market teams. Robbie has an extensive career in the software industry, with long experience at Adobe and Omniture. He holds an industrial engineering degree from Nottingham University and an MBA from Cass Business School at City University in London.

Powering the Subscription Economy is a registered trademark of Zuora, Inc.

Introduction

DIGITAL TRANSFORMATION IS ALL around us. Technology at home and in business has become a way of life, and it'll only get better from here. With technology come new business and revenue models that challenged us for a while but then became the new normal. Subscriptions have become the new way of doing business in many areas of our lives and, to a certain extent, in how we conduct business. The categories of media, food, gaming, and fitness have been more recently transformed by subscriptions. Other, more traditional sectors have also jumped on the bandwagon: insurance, health care, and education. Imagine that you can now buy a subscription for cosmetics and toilet paper:

> A Japanese startup will soon launch a subscription service for toilet paper made from bamboo with an eye to environmentally conscious consumers. Okaeri, based in Nagano Prefecture, will next month begin to deliver Bamboo Roll toilet paper made from 100% bamboo pulp and packaged in recycled cardboard.... An 18-roll package of Bamboo Roll will be priced at 1,800 yen ($17), which is pricier than conventional toilet paper. (Nikkei Staff Writers, 2021)

Recently, Taco Bell entered the subscription dance with their Taco Lover's Pass (Coley, 2021), joining other restaurant businesses such as Panera Bread, Urban Plates, and Coolgreens.

According to LightSpeed, "Subscription has become the default way that businesses purchase software. The SaaS ecosystem was worth $640B in 2019, up from next to nothing just 15 years ago, and is likely worth over $1T today" (Taussig, 2020).

In 2018 I attended the Subscribe Zuora show in San Francisco. It's where I caught the bug. Most of the stories during the show were B2C, heavily focused on media, entertainment, and B2B SaaS. Since then, the subscription tsunami has reached other shores. Imagine what has happened in just three years:

- "83% of retail leaders said converting one-and-done buyers into recurring customers is very important for their overall retail strategy" (Alvo, 2019).
- "IDC expects that by 2022, 53% of all software revenue will be purchased with a subscription model. Even the car subscription market is set to grow by 71% by 2022" (Subramanian, 2021).
- "78% of international adults currently have subscription services (71% in 2018). And 75% believe that in the future, people will subscribe to more services and own less physical 'stuff.' Subscription businesses have consistently grown 5–8x faster than traditional businesses, according to the SEI report. In 2020, they demonstrated revenue growth at a rate of 11.6%, while revenues of product-based peers declined, changing −1.6%." "The Subscription Economy has grown nearly 6x (more than 435%) over the last 9 years, according to Zuora. The subscription management platform provider has published two reports which examine the growth of subscription services" (Kalim, 2021).
- "Subscription (i.e., XaaS, pay-as-you-go) business models are quickly becoming the standard for most organizations to deliver content or services. Most senior finance executives believe about 40% of their organizations' revenues are recurring, and 70% of business leaders expect subscription business will be key to their future. According to Gartner, all new entrants and 80% of historical vendors will soon offer subscription-based business models" (Rao, 2020).
- "'SaaS has not killed the software market but is growing rapidly and pressuring legacy providers to include SaaS options or risk losing market traction,' explains Laurie Wurster, research director at Gartner. Gartner predicts that by 2020, all new entrants and 80% of historical vendors will offer subscription-based business models, regardless of where the software resides. 'What began as a trickle a few years ago has become a stampede of vendors wanting to make a move to a subscription business model'" (Petty, 2018).
- "[Subscription] services, which include streaming platforms, subscription boxes, product subscriptions, media and publications and memberships, saw an 84% increase in subscribers throughout 2020, with each segment experiencing record numbers, according to the Subscription Trade Association" (Williams, 2021).
- "Attracted by the value creation potential, PE-owned software companies are moving faster to make the transition. In [their] signature research, [West-Monroe reports that] PE-backed companies have been more proactive in the adoption of subscription software models than non-PE-held companies: 40% of PE respondents said that between 50% and 70% of their technology portfolio now operates on a subscription basis; by contrast, 50% of corporate buyers said that less than half of their technology portfolio revenue currently comes from subscriptions" (Moogimane, 2021).

Are you convinced, or should I keep going? The speed and intensity of change have been dramatically impacted by the COVID-19 crisis. But the transformation began a decade ago. It just recently accelerated and is reaching new horizons like manufacturing.

Zooming in on the car business

Look at the car business and at how many companies are now talking about mobility and software instead of just cars, services, and parts. This is a revolution. Here's a powerful quote from Volkswagen's Chairman Herbert Dies: "Software will account for 90% of future innovations in the car" (Charette, 2021).

> "Once, software was a part of the car. Now, software determines the value of a car. The success of a car depends on its software much more than the mechanical side. Nearly all vehicle innovations by auto manufacturers, or original equipment manufacturers (OEMs) as they are called by industry insiders, are now tied to software." (Manfred Broy, emeritus professor of informatics at Technical University, Munich, and a leading expert on software in automobiles, quoted in Charette, 2021)

Further, internal, and external vehicle communications have exploded in the past decade. In 2008, an estimated 2,500 data signals were being exchanged among the ECUs in a luxury car. Volvo's Antinyan says that today more than 7,000 external signals connect the 120 ECUs in Volvo vehicles, and the number of internal vehicle signals being exchanged is two orders of magnitude greater. Consulting firm McKinsey & Company estimates this information can easily surpass 25 gigabytes of data an hour (Charette, 2021).

Of course, you can expect Tesla to be at the forefront of this revolution. Tesla is out with its new driver assistance called "Full Self Driving" even though it is essentially a Level 2 autonomous system. The company is offering the system for $199 a month or $99 per month for customers who previously bought Tesla's Enhanced Autopilot package. One of the biggest bulls on the FSD upside for Tesla is New Street Research analyst Pierre Ferragu. He thinks Tesla will make roughly $7K in profit from selling a car and almost $23K from selling FSD subscriptions on the same vehicle by 2030. If Ferragu is correct, the entire industry is expected to move toward an autonomous subscription service model (Schultz, 2021).

Porsche is another good example. For $474 up front—or $12 a month—Porsche HQ will remotely switch on what it calls the intelligent range manager, an over-the-air software update that limits the maximum speed and tweaks the car's navigation system to stretch how far it will travel on a single charge. Most major automakers are fleshing out a strategy for selling upgrades via over-the-air software updates, and a rash of them will begin popping up in the wild in the next few months, beginning with luxury vehicles. "If you don't have digital experiences, you are not on the radar screen," Kjell Gruner, CEO of Porsche Cars North America, recently told Bloomberg. "You're irrelevant" (Stock, 2021). Even the big car rental companies—Hertz, Sixt, and Enterprise—are getting in on the action. Most of these subscriptions are only available in specific cities and are still in the pilot phase. Mercedes-Benz first rolled out its Collection subscription service in Atlanta in 2018 with the goal of appealing to customers who want to have access to a fleet of fancy cars but don't necessarily want to own one. The program offered subscribers access to 30 models for a monthly fee, which included insurance, 24/7 roadside assistance, and vehicle maintenance (Hawkins, 2020).

Many industrial companies have gotten started with subscription

Some of the industrial pioneers have worked on digital transformations for many years. Part of their transformation is about leveraging the data they acquired and turning data into monetized subscription offers. It takes a while to get there, but it's the real challenge. The issue is not about having data! "By 2025 the number of IoT connections will be 36.8 billion, more than double the 17.7 billion in 2020, according to Juniper Research. Experts at World Economic Forum are projecting an estimated $3.7 trillion in value creation in 2025, for the manufacturing sector alone, by optimizing these burgeoning data stores" (Shoreman, 2021).

> There is certainly no shortage of data to drive operational insights. IDC projects the five-year compound annual growth rate (CAGR) for all data captured and consumed globally to hit 26% through 2024. Moreover, the firm says the amount of data created over the next three years will outpace what was created over the last three decades. From 2010 to 2020, worldwide data ballooned from 1.2 trillion gigabytes to 59 trillion gigabytes— an astounding 5,000% leap. (Shoreman, 2021)

Recently, the focus has been much more on extracting value through the data and on making an impact on the bottom line. According to Colin Parris, GE's CTO, many companies are continuing their digital investments, with a few "doubling down" on their strategies. "There are a couple of realities surfacing here: In addition to productivity, people are asking for real visibility not only into performance, but also the financial impact," he says. "COVID-19 has emphasized the need to look at financials to understand base cost versus variable cost. Digital could enable leaders to make much more intelligent decisions. This is becoming more vital than ever" (Fretty, 2020). This remains the challenge. Collecting data is one thing. Creating value with insights for the eco-system is another thing.

Many organizations are struggling to get business value from their ana-lytics. According to Gartner, through 2022, only 20 percent of analytic insights will deliver business outcomes. When it comes to AI, Gartner says 80 percent of projects this year will remain "alchemy, run by wiz-ards whose talents will not scale in the organization." Setting up analytics projects or an analytics organization is one thing but deriving value from analytics is another. And with the COVID-19 pandemic disrupting econ-omies around the globe, companies will likely take a close look at ROI when it comes to analytics and data science groups. "It's not about ana-lytics. It's not even about insights. It's about impact. If you're not making an impact, you're wasting your time," says Mike Onders, chief data officer, divisional CIO, and head of enterprise architecture at Cleveland, Ohio-based KeyBank. (Olavsrud, 2020)

In this book, I want to give the audience lots of case studies and success stories from companies who've managed to pull ahead. Here are some quick examples from the best and how they project value for their digital projects:

SKF case study. SKF was one of the early adopters of technology with SKF Insight ("Condition Monitoring," n.d.), a way to turn its industrial products into digital services. The journey began with hardware equipped with sensors installed into bearings that are powered by the kinetic motion of the machines themselves. Those systems transmitted real-time data about the performance of industrial machines as well as the components of energy and transportation systems. In 2013 they piloted this concept in a couple of verticals. By 2015 SKF provided 45 different iPad apps to allow managers to monitor the maintenance, speed, and reliability of up to 8,000 kinds of smart objects. SKF coined this con-cept knowledge-as-a-service (KaaS), as more than a half-million machines were already connected to the SKF Cloud. Fast-forward to today, and SKF is a leader in remote condition-based monitoring (Sinfield et al., 2015).

Honeywell Forge case study. "In offering Honeywell Forge, Honey-well can take advantage of its 'large install base,' which includes 25,000 engines, 20,000 braking systems, 30,000 APUs, 20,000 flight management systems, 300 services and apps, 10,000 satcom terminals, and more than 1,800 aircraft with JetWave, according to the company. 'We took a look and talked to the airlines, and we see that there are over $25 billion lost in flight delays,' [John] Peter-son, [VP and GM of software and services at Honeywell Connected Enterprise] said. 'There's $10,000 per hour [spent] on grounded aircraft due to unforeseen situations.' In designing Forge, Honeywell saw an opportunity to reduce 'the amount of waste in terms of delays, cancellations and groundings,' he said. [...]

The Honeywell Forge data analytics tool allows airlines to save up to $200,000 per aircraft per year in fuel costs and up to $40,000 per aircraft per year in maintenance costs" (Wolfe, 2019).

Bosch case study. Bosch announced that they "sold 10 million connected power tools, home appliances, and heating systems, and ha[ve] added about €300 million in revenue by adding artificial intelligence (AI) to its product line since setting up an AI division three years ago. Its AI and IoT strategy [were] a bright spot in a tough set of financial results, capping a grim year for the wider industrial sector, and for the automotive market. [...] The Bosch Center for AI (BCAI) was established almost four years ago, in early 2017. It employs 270 specialists, and is 'bearing fruit,' the firm said, adding €300 million to the company's top line over the past 12 months. The unit is engaged in 180-odd projects in the mobility, manufacturing, smart homes, and agriculture sectors" (Blackman, 2021).

ABB case study. ABB is very active in marketplaces and subscriptions. By 2020, they had launched 173 digital projects that were proposed by the business units (Bossart, 2020). These investments, funded 50/50 between the business lines and digital factories, resulted in 66 MVPs. Of these MVPs, 60 percent resulted in new business models (like subscription pricing) and 30 were fully released for sales to customers (45%).

Bridgestone case study. "Over the past few years we have launched the Digital Garage, which is a partnership between R&D, Marketing, and IT. It's an open innovation platform and ecosystem where we are incubating new potential services that we can bring to our customers" (Michael Johnson, Vice President of IT and CIO of Bridgestone Europe, Middle East, and Africa [EMEA], quoted in Cambier-Unruh, 2021).

Here are just a few examples of digital capabilities that Bridgestone is leveraging into successful service-based subscriptions:

Sensorization. Bridgestone's traditional expertise in creating "things" has been augmented by the evolution to next generation smart devices, enabled for IoT. External valve-mounted sensors on tires can measure pressure, temperate, and tread depth. "Smart tires" optimize tire life, improve safety, and fuel efficiency, and prevent breakdowns, all while replacing time-consuming manual inspection processes. Firestone (a Bridgestone brand) offers this technology to enterprise customers ranging from truck fleets to mining and agricultural vehicles, to tires used in aviation.

Cloud. Cloud computing allows Bridgestone and their customers to store and manage vast quantities of data on tire performance and more. Fleet managers can collect vehicle data via a centralized router, then use an app to generate fleet inspection reports and repair alerts. Bridgestone also reduces their own manufacturing costs by managing workloads in the cloud much more efficiently than they could using traditional infrastructure.

AI-Based Data Analytics Capabilities. Bridgestone uses machine learning and AI-based analytics to process the data collected from its IoT-enabled products. Analytics drive Bridgestone's proprietary service delivery platform for roadside assistance, REACH, which uses web and mobile applications to centralize communications between fleet managers, drivers, dealers, and service technicians with real-time updates and GPS support.

Digital Customer Experience. Of course, both individual and enterprise customers can purchase and manage their subscriptions online, but the digital customer experience does not end there. Services like Intellitire are seamlessly integrated with other products in the Bridgestone ecosystem, like the Toolbox Total Rim and Tire Management system.

Digital Partnerships. Bridgestone uses SaaS within their partner ecosystem to optimize the end-to-end supply chain and develop APIs to be able to move data around that supply chain. These digital partnerships help them reduce inventory and working capital, which results in faster execution and speedier times to market. Digitization has helped not only with large partners like Tata Consultancy Services (TCS), but also with smaller, niche, boutique companies that bring specific capabilities and an entrepreneurial innovative mindset. (Cambier-Unruh, 2021)

This was just a teaser. Section 5 in the book offers another 25 subscription case studies. I picked the best 25 out of the 100+ I collected and studied.

Why this book?

We all know that traditionally the industrial sector lags behind other sectors in adopting technologies and innovations. Once they catch up, though, things can go very fast. I came up with this book concept to accelerate the change process and to boost capabilities in industrial teams so they can maximize their chances of success. I designed this book as a cookbook of recipes, tips, best practices, and case studies. The goal is to embrace what others have done and written about and to accelerate. You won't find a lot of theory in this book. It's practical, concrete, and focused on actions. It also aims to fill some of the knowledge gaps that aren't often discussed in other subscription-related books. For example, you'll find a chapter dedicated to bringing channel partners on board. Another one focuses on bringing your financial experts on board to anticipate resistance when pitching OpEx-based business models internally. The book is based on 18 months of research. During this period, I've collected over 175 subscription-related papers and more than 150 blogs on the subject. I've used many of these to support my key findings and recommendations. Consider this a time-saving approach for you. You can read the references and read more about the specific topics. It is, in essence, a panorama of what's been published about subscription and industrial subscriptions since 2018 or so.

As with previous books, I've recruited the best brains in the business to write some chapters and lots of shorter contributions in the form of Lightning Strikes. Obviously, I have a lot of experience in the business, but there are better experts than me. It's essential for you to hear different voices and to learn from experts who have specific areas of experience. Here are the contributors:

- Robbie Kellman Baxter
- Guneet Singh Bedi
- Mark Burton
- David Burns
- David DiMillo
- Nizard Djemmali
- Steven Forth
- Ajit Ghuman
- Mrinal (MG) Gurbaxani
- Matt Johnston
- Vivek Joshi
- Ron Kermisch
- Felix Krohn
- Michael Mansard
- Peyton Marshall
- Ash Maurya
- Scott Miller
- Holger Pietzsch
- John Porter
- Kyle Poyar
- Emilie Saule
- Alex Smith
- Robbie Traube
- Maciej Wilczyński

I thank all the contributors for their time, passion, and willingness to share widely. Please connect with them on LinkedIn and share some feedback.

Book structure

This book has 24 chapters organized in five sections. Section 1 focuses on setting the stage and why now is the time to invest in recurring business models and subscriptions. The sense of urgency has never been so high. I also make the case that industrial companies are in the best position to win if they avoid the mistakes and myths that are typically seen when adopting transformative innovations. Section 2 focuses on subscription business modeling and how to get started. I focus on how to get started and what to do first. In this section I also cover the transition to SaaS and to EaaS. Section 3 is dedicated to the topic of pricing. This is a rich section, as it covers similarities between subscription pricing in B2C and B2B, best practices for designing subscription pricing, mistakes to avoid when pricing in the industrial world, outcome-based pricing and EaaS pricing, and two essays on how to conduct pricing research if you have the time and budgets. Section 4 highlights the topic of scaling your subscription business model, with a focus on execution. Lots can happen before and during scaling. Robbie Kellman Baxter discusses barriers to scaling your subscription. Other chapters cover the topics of working with channel partners, convincing your finance teams, and organizing your sales team for success. This is also a rich section. The last section presents 25 industrial subscriptions out of the 100+ I've collected. Emilie Saule begins this section by showing some statistics related to our findings from the research process. I couldn't squeeze 100 case studies into this book, so I've created a supplemental e-book that can be purchased at the Value Innoruption bookstore, www.valueinnoruption.com/shop/.

Final thoughts

Thank you for buying this book. It represents almost two years of work. I'm very proud of the outcome. Of course, I could have included much more—but no one buys a 500-page book! I'm happy to share with you some of the sources and papers I've collected as a result of two years of research. Not everything is relevant to the industrial sector, so I've done the refining for you. The key is to read the book, note what's relevant to you, and put yourself into action mode. Again, you don't have to reinvent the wheel. Many companies have made the mistakes that allow us to go faster and scale better. Please resist the not-invented-here syndrome that many engineering-focused companies suffer from. Trust the experts, be agile, and execute. Also remember that in industrial work, digital complements the core and eventually becomes part of that core. Product, hardware, and equipment will still be important. The complementary of the physical and the digital is what makes us strong. Let's not lose sight of that.

References

Alvo, G. (2019). Subscriptions increase incremental spend by 60%. *CFODive,* December 16. www.cfodive.com/news /subscriptions-increase-incremental-spend/569170/

Blackman, J. (2021). Bosch counts upside of AI, IoT—Even as sales slide in COVID-ravaged industrial sector. *Enterprise Insights,* February 5. https://enterpriseiotinsights.com/20210205/channels/news /bosch-counts-upside-of-ai-iot-in-covid-ravaged-industrial-sector

Bossart, F. (2020). ABB's digital lighthouse program: Igniting transformation. LinkedIn, July 17. www.linkedin.com/pulse /abbs-digital-lighthouse-program-igniting-franziska-bossart/

Cambier-Unruh, F. (2021). Where the rubber meets the road: Bridgestone turns tech investments into recurring revenue. *Subscribed,* May 4. www.subscribed.com/read/news-and-editorial/where-the-rubber -meets-the-road-bridgestone-turns-tech-investments-into-recurring -revenue

Charette, R. N. (2021). How software is eating the car. *IEEE Spectrum,* June 7. https://spectrum.ieee.org/software-eating-car#toggle-gdpr

Coley, B. (2021). Taco Bell tests new "Taco Lover's Pass" subscription service. *QSR,* September 13. www.qsrmagazine.com/fast-food /taco-bell-tests-new-taco-lovers-pass-subscription-service

Condition monitoring. (n.d.). *SKF.* www.skf.com/group/industries/railways /products-and-services/condition-monitoring

Fretty, P. (2020). Digital transformation isn't just possible today, it's crucial. *IndustryWeek,* July 7. www.industryweek.com/technology-and-iiot/article/21135888 /digital-transformation-isnt-just-possible-today-its-crucial

Hawkins, A. J. (2020). Mercedes-Benz reportedly pulls the plug on its subscription service after poor sales. *The Verge,* June 29. www.theverge.com/platform/amp/2020/6/29/21306823 /mercedes-benz-collection-subscription-service-cancel-sales

Kalim, F. (2021). The subscription economy has grown over 435% in 9 years (and the uptick is expected to continue). *What's New in Publishing,* March 5. https://whatsnewinpublishing.com/the-subscription -economy-has-grown-over-435-in-9-years-and-the-uptick-is -expected-to-continue/

Moogimane, D. (2021). 10 priorities for software companies transitioning to a subscription business model. *WestMonroe,* April. www.westmonroe.com/perspectives/point-of-view /software-companies-transitioning-subscription-business-model

Nikkei Staff Writers. (2021). Sustainable toilet paper: Bamboo rolls offered by subscription in Japan. *Nikkei Asia,* February 13. https://asia.nikkei.com/Spotlight/Environment/Sustainable-toilet -paper-Bamboo-rolls-offered-by-subscription-in-Japan

Olavsrud, T. (2020). Transforming analytics into business impact. *CIO,* September 1. www.cio.com/article/3572642/transforming-analytics -into-business-impact.html

Petty, C. (2018). Moving to a software subscription model. *Gartner,* May 30. www.gartner.com/smarterwithgartner /moving-to-a-software-subscription-model

Rao, R. (2020). Strategies and practices for transformation to a subscription business model. *Forbes,* August 3. www.forbes.com/sites /forbestechcouncil/2020/08/03/strategies-and-practices-for -transformation-to-a-subscription-business-model/

Schultz, C. (2021). Tesla roundup: Driver assistance service unveiled, Model 3 deliveries said to be pushed back. *Seeking Alpha,* July 19. https://seekingalpha.com/news/3716498-tesla-roundup-driver -assistance-service-unveiled-model-3-deliveries-said-to-be-pushed -back

Shoreman, J. (2021). The secret to data-driven business lies with continuous intelligence. *Forbes,* July 19. www.forbes.com/sites/forbestechcouncil/2021/07/19/the-secret-to-data-driven-business-lies-with-continuous-intelligence/amp/

Sinfield, J., Calder, N., & Geheb, B. (2015). How industrial systems are turning into digital services. *Harvard Business Review,* June 23. https://hbr.org/amp/2015/06/how-industrial-systems-are-turning-into-digital-services

Stock, K. (2021). Your car is about to be a software platform, subscriptions and all. *Bloomberg,* May 1. www.bloomberg.com/news/articles/2021-05-01/your-car-is-about-to-be-a-software-platform-subscriptions-and-all

Subramanian, K. (2021). Software subscriptions are eating the world: Solving billing and cash flow woes simultaneously. *TechCrunch,* May 13. https://techcrunch.com/2021/05/13/software-subscriptions-are-eating-the-world-solving-billing-and-cash-flow-woes-simultaneously/

Taussig, A. (2020). Firehose #182: Subscription addiction. *Firehose,* November 30. www.firehose.vc/p/firehose-182-subscription-addiction

Williams, A. (2021). What's happening to subscription services? *Jabil.* www.jabil.com/blog/subscription-services-for-cpg.html

Wolfe, F. (2019). Honeywell Forge can lead to significant savings for airlines, company says. *Aviation Today,* November 15. www.aviationtoday.com/2019/11/15/honeywell-forge-can-lead-significant-savings-airlines-company-says/

SECTION 1

SETTING THE STAGE FOR THE INDUSTRIAL SUBSCRIPTION ECONOMY

The New Reality
and Sense of Urgency
for Industrial Companies

I'M AN INFORMATION ADDICT. I read everything that's published in the industrial world. I stay up to date on bold moves, mistakes, and transformations that industrial companies make, the pressure on many fronts. First, industrial companies must diversify their portfolio through SaaS expansion or software-firm acquisitions. Second, they're under pressure to make digital transformation work to show impact. Third, they have to capture the vast potential of the aftermarket business and focus on recurring business revenues. They have their work cut out for them.

The unfilled promises of digital transformations

Each year, vast amounts of investments are allocated and spent to support digital transformations. In 2019 alone, according to IDC ("Businesses Will Spend," 2019), $1.18 trillion in investments were made in technologies and services to enable digital transformations. IDC also predicted that $6 trillion would be invested between 2018 and 2022. That's a massive amount of cash.

In contrast to these staggering numbers, consider the following statistics:

- "Only 6% of companies have managed to create financial impact from their digital investments" (Accenture, 2019).
- "Only 30% of transformations met or exceeded their target value and resulted in sustainable change" (Forth et al., 2020).
- "Fewer than 15% of business (digital) ecosystems were sustainable in the long run... leading to more than $50 billion of capital is lost every year" (Pidun et al., 2020).

- "Only 14% of manufacturers surveyed say they have created go-to-market IoT strategies" (PwC/MAPI, 2017).
- "Eighty-four percent of companies were stuck in pilot mode for over a year and 28 percent for over two years" (de Boer & Narayanan, 2018).

So, what's really happening with digital transformation programs? Why don't we see higher success rates? Originally, management and digital consultants focused on the technology side of digital transformation. They promised trillions of dollars in created and delivered value to the economy. More recently, and realizing that business model innovation and cultural transformation are equally important to digital journeys (Napier et al., 2020), they restated their forecast and published much more content on go-to-market strategies, cultural mindsets, and digital human capital. With trillions of dollars invested, a new normal post-COVID-19 pandemic, and an increased sense of urgency from boards of directors (Goasduff, 2020), industrial companies have had to change their approach to begin realizing the promises of their digital efforts. This is what I call digital transformation 2.0. The new normal will be much more practical, realistic, and focused on impact. This is what was lacking in digital transformation 1.0, especially considering the poor record of success. Here are eight considerations for manufacturing leaders to think about as they redesign their digital programs:

Focus, focus, focus. Focus is the name of the game. Many digital transformations were well financed but had no clear pipeline of innovation. As a result, digital teams were "chasing" opportunities and creating busywork that brought little value. This is a typical case of capital chasing opportunities, as we witnessed during the internet bubble of the earlier 2000s. In the past three to five years, industrial firms have poured billions in digital transformations, trying to strike gold. For many of them, the lack of focus led to failures and false starts. Most did not fulfill the promises of their digital transformations. The next two to three years will be about focus, impact, and profitable growth.

Keep it simple, stupid. Global digital transformations can no longer be complex organisms with multiple entities, dozens of work streams, and hundreds of projects running in parallel. Many of them are set up as parallel organizations suffering from lack of leadership, accountability, and a certain level of disconnect with the core business. The future is more about agility, fluidity, and clear accountability to business stakeholders. Removing that unnecessary complexity is a necessary step to match the level of market dynamism and to scale successfully.

Forget about legacy versus digital business. Digital transformations need to focus on true innovation around the core business and generate growth for that core market's verticals. This is a hard lesson to learn, but a necessary one. The implication of this is greater integration and coordination between the core legacy entities and the digital business. There can't be that great divide between the two organizations. It's no longer us versus them.

Prioritize better and faster. The times for me-too commodity digital projects, pet projects, theoretical ideas, unrealistic futuristic dreams, and boil-the-ocean programs are over. These opportunities need to be killed before they enter the innovation pipeline. They create complexity and burn cash resources. The digital future is about true innovation and executable opportunities. The proof of the pudding is in the eating! We must return to the basics and focus on customer pains, customer problems, true differentiation, willingness to pay, and pricing power. This implies that digital teams must do their homework early in the process and kill projects if they don't meet the impact requirements.

Address the internal typical organizational bottlenecks. Some of the behaviors we see in digital transformation teams must be addressed and fixed as soon as possible: "We should go at it alone," "not invented here," "I know better than the best in the business," "We can build this software ourselves," and "We can manage subscriptions manually." Enough already with these! The wheel has already been invented. IoT has been around for 20 years. The focus on speed, automation, experience, and impact requires partnership, open innovation, and working with established commercial partners.

Digital opportunities begin with new business models. True digital innovations must be thought of as new business models, not business as usual. They should focus on the attractiveness, feasibility, and viability of the opportunities. A digital transformation might include a dozen new business models to be managed as a dynamic portfolio. This also implies a requirement to look at commonalities among business models and approach the portfolio with a platform mindset. That's essential for very large industrial companies with many divisions serving many types of verticals. The temptation will be for every division to do their own transformation instead of pooling resources and investing in some very critical corporate resources and systems.

Monetize and leverage data. Successful digital transformations are first and foremost data transformations focused on customers and ecosystems. The management and leveraging of data cannot be an afterthought or part of the 28 other projects running as part of digital transformations. Do you have a robust and long-term data strategy? Are your data projects well financed? The future of digital is to extract, integrate, and mine data. This is the core of your innovation pipeline. Monetizing and extracting the value of your data is equally essential. This is often overlooked.

Solve your internal inefficiencies now. The COVID-19 crisis is a test of your internal digital capabilities. It's an opportunity to test your communication capabilities, your IT infrastructure, your collaboration tools, and your bandwidth. But it's also a test of your digital mindset among IT and engineering teams. Your ability to drive internal digital transformations is a make-or-break point in your overall digital transformation. Take a realistic look at how you're doing in this crisis and make sure you modify your roadmap accordingly.

This crisis offers new beginnings and opportunities. Digital isn't dead. It's resetting, like many other processes and functions in business. Digital transformation 2.0 is focused, less complex, customer-centric, profitable, differentiated, automated, and grounded in data monetization. Digital transformation 1.0 is dead. Long live digital transformation 2.0!

Harness the power of recurring business models

Some experts call it digital transformation. Others refer to servitization strategies. And a few more call it business model diversification. They all refer to the same outcome: recurring revenues. During the COVID-19 crisis, companies that have successfully invested and executed recurring business models have proved more resilient than those who haven't. The latest Zuora Subscription Economy Index shows that companies using a subscription business model grew five times faster in 2020 than the average S&P 500 growth. Many of these companies have realized that, while their customers did not have the capital expenditure (CapEx) to acquire new equipment, they were interested in maintaining existing assets, in leveraging their installed based, and in launching service innovations on their own. In the manufacturing and high-tech world, suppliers are increasingly offering more aftermarket services, such as maintenance, spare parts, and other value-added services. They have done so in response to customer demands for more outcome-based servicing agreements, for extension of existing asset lifetime, and/or for assistance in transitioning to recurring business models themselves.

The benefits of recurring business models
The benefits of investing in a recurring revenue strategy for suppliers include the following:

1 **Greater predictability for everyone.** One-time transactions come and go and are subject to high levels of pricing competition. Signing longer-term recurring agreements with customers allows for more stability for suppliers and better predictability for customers. Recurring pricing strategies offer more transparency to the customer for a period of three to five years on average.

2 **Higher margins.** The value of recurring transactions is generally lower, but they are also traditionally high in profit. Deloitte reports that aftermarkets parts and services deliver over 50 percent of a manufacturer's profit (Deloitte Insights, 2020). Another analysis conducted by McKinsey in 2017 across 30 industries found that the average earnings before interest and

taxes (EBIT) margin for aftermarket services was 25 percent, compared with 10 percent for new equipment (Ambadipudi et al., 2017).

3 **Diversification in business models.** The COVID-19 crisis created a sense of urgency for business model diversification and accelerated the transition to the cloud and to SaaS models for many suppliers. The crisis forces companies to reevaluate their strategies and business model portfolio to help mitigate the high level of uncertainty. As customers face a severe cash crunch, suppliers can transition them from traditional CapEx to operating expenditure (OpEx) models and continue transacting.

4 **Alignment with customers' value metric.** As more and more companies move to recurring business models, they expect their suppliers to make the same transition to align the suppliers' pricing mechanisms with their internal value metric. For example, a customer moving to a SaaS model will expect their suppliers of software and cloud services to also sell to them using a similar subscription model or a model based on usage.

5 **Reinforcement of customer relationships over time.** The transition to a recurring business model allows for more customer touchpoints and numerous possible transactions during the relationship. As a result, suppliers develop greater intimacy about customer behaviors and product usage. They can in turn introduce additional services or digital innovations to delight the customers even more.

6 **Focusing on customer lifetime value.** The main benefit of recurring revenue models is to extract greater value from customers and markets over time. There are lots of opportunities to innovate, to upsell, and to cross-sell to maximize customer satisfaction and retention over time. The end goal of a recurring business strategy is to capture as much of the customer lifetime value as possible.

Types of recurring revenue sources

There are multiple sources of recurring revenue. The goal is to maximize the number of sources through a diversified portfolio of recurring business models.

1 **Internal efficiency opportunities.** Selling recurring opportunities internally through intercompany mechanisms to test the value propositions and pricing models.

2 **Aftermarket services and parts.** Selling traditional services including maintenance, repair, diagnostics, monitoring, and others in the form of recurring service agreements.

3 **Software-as-a-service (SaaS).** Launching new software in the form of subscriptions or transitioning existing software from perpetual licenses to SaaS.

4   **Connected products and services (PaaS, EaaS, HaaS, DaaS).** Transitioning from one-time transactions to monthly or annual subscriptions to product, equipment, hardware, or devices.

5   **APIs and data.** Selling subscriptions to APIs or other data-related services or offers. These can be stand-alone offers or included in a digital bundle.

6   **Digital platforms and marketplaces.** Extracting value from marketplaces or platform by collecting transaction fees, entry fees, subscriptions to offers within the ecosystem.

Companies that have embraced the recurring business model have set corporate recurring revenue targets as part of their corporate strategic plans. What's the magic number? Anywhere from 15 percent to 25 percent of total sales is a good and challenging target, according to experts.

The pillars of a recurring-based strategy

What are the critical success factors for a solid recurring-based strategy? Here are five of them:

1   **A dedicated strategic priority and not an afterthought.** Top executives must realize the benefits of recurring business models and the need to leverage customer relationships. They must make it a priority to leverage the existing installed base and to diversify their business model portfolio. Having an informal network of managers or one initiative around the installed base isn't enough. It must be at the top of the strategic agenda.

2   **Build and operate a service-focused organization.** The champions in recurring strategies have established dedicated business units for their recurring businesses with dedicated processes, systems, and talent strategies. There is no digital transformation or recurring business model without a strong service orientation.

3   **A shift from cost to value orientation.** A customer value management orientation is also required. Recurring opportunities are studied from a customer value perspective and priced based on a quantified value proposition. Customer success teams work with value engineering teams to deliver the promised value to customers. Costs are still critical but not the heart of the recurring value and pricing strategies.

4   **A shift from a product-based mindset to a usage-solutions mindset.** The product is no longer at the center of the business model: the customer and/or subscriber is. This requires a focus on customer processes, desired outcomes, and jobs-to-be-done. Technical teams are organized around customer needs and pains. Priorities are set to deliver outstanding value and experience.

5 A pipeline of digital and service innovations. Greater customer-centricity and intimacy generate a tremendous amount of customer data that can be turned into service and digital innovations. Recurring business models require a focus on retention, renewal, and increased customer value over time. It's a way of life!

Concluding thoughts

The transition to recurring business models can be powerful for a company that makes it a part of the strategic agenda. The focus of digital transformations should be the design and launch of high-margin and differentiated recurring innovations. That requires an electro-shock internally to change the culture and put the customer at the center of the business model. Many companies have begun this transition and reaped the benefits of recurring business models. For the laggards, it's not too late to get started! Recurring revenue business models, also known as subscription or usage-based models, are opening up new opportunities across many industries—even in sectors where they haven't traditionally been. For example, the subscription model has taken root in industrial sectors, like heavy equipment manufacturing, and in specialty markets such as medical devices and smart agriculture. A survey of senior finance executives by CFO Research, in collaboration with Salesforce, showed that recurring revenue models are well established and growing. More than half (53%) of the CFO Research/Salesforce survey respondents said at least 40 percent of their organizations' revenues were recurring, that is, sold via a subscription- or usage-based model (Marletta, 2019). The pressure's on. How far are you in your transformation?

References

Accenture. (2019). *Your business as-a-service: Putting the right pieces in place.* www.accenture.com/_acnmedia/PDF-119/Accenture-As-a -Service-Business-Acceleration.pdf

Ambadipudi, A., Brotschi, A., Forsgren, M., Kervazo, F., Lavandier, H., & Xing, J. (2017). *Industrial aftermarket services: Growing the core.* McKinsey & Company, July 27. www.mckinsey.com/industries/advanced-electronics/our-insights /industrial-aftermarket-services-growing-the-core

Businesses will spend nearly $1.2 trillion on digital transformation this year as they seek an edge in the digital economy, according to a new IDC spending guide. (2019). *BusinessWire,* April 24. www.businesswire .com/news/home/20190424005113/en/Businesses-Spend-1.2 -Trillion de Boer, E., & Narayanan, S. (2018). Avoid pilot purgatory in 7 steps. McKinsey & Company, April 16. www.mckinsey.com/business -functions/people-and-organizational-performance/our-insights /the-organization-blog/avoid-pilot-purgatory-in-7-steps

Deloitte Insights. (2020). *The rise of aftermarket services.* www2.deloitte.com /content/dam/Deloitte/us/Documents/manufacturing/us -aftermarket-services-mfg.pdf

Forth, P., Reichert, T., de Laubier, R., & Chakraborty, S. (2020). *Flipping the odds of digital transformation success.* Boston Consulting Group, October 29. www.bcg.com/publications/2020 /increasing-odds-of-success-in-digital-transformation

Goasduff, L. (2020). COVID-19 accelerates digital strategy initiatives. *Gartner,* November 6. www.gartner.com/smarterwithgartner /covid-19-accelerates-digital-strategy-initiatives

Marletta, G. (2019). Recurring revenue rising. *CFO,* February 27. www.cfo.com/cash-flow/2019/02/recurring-revenue-rising/

Napier, L., Libert, B., & de Vries, K. D. (2020). Changing culture is central to changing business models. *MIT Sloan Management Review,* November 30. https://sloanreview.mit.edu/article /changing-culture-is-central-to-changing-business-models/

Pidun, U., Reeves, M., & Schüssler, M. (2020). Why do most business ecosystems fail? Boston Consulting Group, June 22. www.bcg.com/en-us /publications/2020/why-do-most-business-ecosystems-fail

PwC/MAPI. (2017, July). *Monetizing the industrial internet of things.* www.pwc.com/us/en/industrial-products/publications/assets /pwc-monetizing-the-industrial-internet-of-things.pdf

Industrial Natives
Have the Advantage

ABOUT THREE TO FIVE years ago, digital transformation consultants agreed that the industrial world would be shaken up by "digital natives." These digital natives were fast, agile, well funded, and unstoppable. They were and still are formidable competitors: Google, Amazon, Palantir, Alibaba, Tesla, Space X, and Microsoft. They knew how to get, integrate, and extract value from data. That triggered a gold rush with industrial companies to start their own digital transformations to get ready to compete in this data-rich new world (Liozu, 2019). These data and digital unicorns were going to disrupt the traditional ecosystems of what they called the industrial natives. In contrast, these companies were slow, very bureaucratic, and highly product-centric. This battle between digital and industrial natives was promised to be ferocious and epic. Lots of very reputable industrial companies began early and rushed to become digital players. They were too early, rushed through the process of transformation, and lost some technological bets. The same consultants that were paid billions in digital transformation services quickly concluded that culture was critical in the digital transformation process and that digital was mostly about business model innovation and the ability of industrial firms to become ambidextrous organizations, meaning managing legacy businesses while innovating in digital. What a shocker! The same conclusions were reached by management scholars during the 1900s' industrial revolution!

Since then, we've witnessed the emergence of a third type of player. They're neither digital natives nor industrial natives. They're in the middle, morphing their DNA to become what I call *in-digital players*. They have the traits of industrial companies and are mutating to become more like digital players. These companies have the following characteristics:

1 They have a strong legacy of success and astounding customer relationships. large installed bases, long-lasting contractual relationships, and a strong

customer co-development mindset. I cannot repeat it enough: knowing and leveraging the industrial base is the most powerful differentiator that an industrial company has. I invited Vivek Joshi to give us more insights on how to leverage an installed base. Read the Lightning Strike section of this chapter.

2   Some of these companies have been around for over a century, and others, for decades. They don't intend to disappear, and they're now fighting back against digital natives that have great access to capital but poor success records.

3   They have product, software, systems technology in their DNA. They're a force of engineering and can quickly mobilize some of the most diverse and talented engineers in the world to solve customer problems. And with decades of engineering capabilities, they have deep domain knowledge that's impossible to develop overnight.

4   They're patiently making digital part of their renewed selves while navigating the need to migrate at the market pace and to educate players in their established ecosystems. They've learned from their initial efforts and from successes of digital natives.

5   They're pragmatic and focus on leveraging their strong position in their legacy markets. They focus on making their core business even stronger and adding technology and digital solutions as part of their overall value propositions.

6   They've acquired some of the best digital, analytics technology, and software companies in the world to leapfrog in their development of integrated systems using AI, data analytics, and cybersecurity.

7   They know hardware inside and out. That means that adding software and edge analytics to their toolbox creates a powerful combination. Because these companies design hardware and equipment, they can add smart components by design instead of doing that later once they're installed.

8   They now have boards of directors and investors pushing them to invest more and go faster. That's a major difference from years ago, when most boards didn't yet realize the potential of digital transformations.

These in-digital natives include companies like Thales, Siemens, Honeywell, Sandvik, Airbus, Michelin, Schneider Electric, ABB, Toyota, Medtronic, Stanley Black & Decker, and others. They're strong and profitable players in their market spaces. They've acted deliberately and patiently over the past five to eight years, not rushing to make the wrong digital investments and pour billions into shiny and promising technologies. Their CEOs have managed to focus on the difficult balance of profitable growth, growth from digital, and cash-flow control. Some of the CEOs of digital natives regularly mock their industrial CEOs for how antiquated and slow they are. But I'd like to encourage you to imagine the future, and I can guarantee these in-digital players won't go anywhere. In a few years, digital will be the new normal! I had the privilege to work for one of them for five years, and I can assure you that the metamorphosis is going very well and the future is bright. Pay attention to the transformation of these industrial champions as they continue to be stable, sustainable, and profitable. Of course, some will make mistakes and stumble along the way. But this will happen to digital natives as well, especially as we read current stories about WeWork, Uber, and other failed unicorns. Consultants might disagree with my position, but I predict that their next round of content in the digital space will focus on the emergence of unstoppable in-digital companies that are making the world more secure and connected. If you're working in an industrial company today, learn about these champions and embrace their best practices and how they are transforming their culture at a pace that makes sense for their customers, their employees, and their shareholders. Be an agent of change by scanning the B2C world and by identifying the best-practice nuggets that can be adapted and integrated into your unique DNA.

Lightning Strike: Industrial Original Equipment Manufacturers Are a Unique Breed of Corporation with Their High Focus on Existing Customers

Vivek Joshi

Consider this—our analysis shows that industrials, on an average, add less than 3 percent of new customers every year. On the other hand, more than 70 percent of new equipment sales are to existing customers, with 90 percent of those returning customers having had frequent aftermarket interactions with the OEM.

In other words, an OEM's installed base is a gift that keeps on giving, in terms of both aftersales revenue and deepening customer loyalty.

When I say this to our customers the first time I meet them, they nod vigorously in agreement. Then, I ask, why aren't you getting many gifts?

(Cue the sound of crickets chirping...)

This has been one of the confounding observations I've dealt with over the past few years of working with some of the world's top industrials at Entytle. It isn't as if we're working with a self-selected group of customers. Multiple reputable industry sources also confirm that this is a problem that is endemic to most OEMs.

As we began digging into the cause of this situation, some points emerged:

1   OEMs by nature need to track equipment sold 20 years ago (or more) while designing and building what should last the next 20 years. Only a very small group of industries need to think on this time horizon (construction,

utilities, etc.). Such a long equipment life cycle means that OEMs simply lose track of their installed base as their tracking tools and their people churn at a rate many times faster than the equipment.

2 Their view of their installed base is seemingly limited to a list of customers and the products they bought, which is invariably not trusted by customer-facing employees because of data quality and completeness issues.

This is a huge problem for most OEMs, as it hinders their ability to systematically and scalably serve every customer in their installed base. The problem is exacerbated by some megatrends impacting the OEM market (Figure 2.1):

- looming generational change in the supplier and customer workforces
- changing expectations from B2B buyers
- irreversible changes wrought by COVID-19 vis-à-vis remote work requiring collaboration
- a business-model change from an equipment manufacturer to a software and analytics provider to their customers
- the challenge of perceived required investments in multiple new, potentially industry-disruptive, technologies (IoT, additive manufacturing, AI, electrification, AR/VR, etc.)
- the first underpinnings of the ubiquitous subscription economy making inroads in the equipment sector, where equipment uptime would determine revenue instead of one-and-done equipment deals

This is a lot of change for an industry that moves very cautiously. However, these changes are here to stay, and to make this transition easier, OEMs need to find a way to engage with each and every one of their customers and their installed assets. Without a clear connection to their customers, they risk being an afterthought to them—and worse, they open the door to a well-funded startup to get between them and their customer and disrupt that relationship. To do so, they need to have a really good idea of their installed base.

So how do they go about doing this? After all, if it were easy, we wouldn't be talking about this. From our experience working with some of the largest OEMs in the world, here are 10 suggestions to jumpstart your installed base strategy.

1. Don't "boil the ocean"

It can be overwhelming when you realize that getting a true picture of your installed base requires gathering data from multiple sources, including "paper." Industrial OEMs view every undertaking as a multiquarter/multiyear project, which is a direct outcome of the way they're accustomed to developing new products as well as the way every vendor stretches tool implementations into three-to-five-year implementation cycles. Ask yourself these questions first:

Trends	Examples
Generational change on the supplier & customer workforces	The Bureau of Labor Statistics shows that machinery OEMs have a workforce with 29% over age 55, indicating that almost a third will retire in less than 10 years (US Bureau of Labor Statistics, 2021). This will be compounded by another 5% of the manufacturing workforce that will be rehired in the post-COVID recovery (Daniel, 2021).
Changing expectations from B2B buyers as they are forced to adapt to their own consumer needs	PWC study showed that 65% of B2B buyers prefer to research online and 86% prefer to reorder online instead of via phone (PwC, n.d.).
Pandemic-driven changes & the anticipated needs of a post-pandemic boom	49% of employees want a hybrid work environment, and 79% of CEOs expect to provide hybrid environments for jobs where it is possible, according to a study by Robert Half (Schawbel, 2021).
Business model change from an equipment manufacturer to data & analytics provider to their consumers	Car and truck manufacturers license data to telematics service providers, who then resell to customers. McKinsey estimates this to create $250 to $400B in revenue for the ecosystem by 2030 based on current trends (Bertoncello et al., 2021).
Challenge of perceived required investments in multiple new, potentially industry-disruptive technologies	Daimler and Volvo, two competitors, had their R&D budgets stretched so thin that they joined forces to collaborate on fuel-cell development rather than each investing independently (and at higher cost) (Daimler, 2020).
Subscription economy models	Kaeser Kompressoren switched from making air compressors to providing "air as a service."

Figure 2.1. Industry megatrends.

- **What use case, or problem, am I solving?** I recommend beginning with an acute problem that needs to be solved ASAP. The chances of getting executive buy-in are much greater when the problem is acute or if there's a budget available.
- **To what degree of accuracy?** You could plan on reaching the highest level of accuracy (i.e., down to the BOM) or keep it simple at the location + equipment + parts level—your choice determines how wide and deep you need to traverse through your installed base

- **Therefore, what's the minimum installed-base data required?**
Put simply, should you begin with common equipment spanning multiple divisions, or focus on one division first? I advise doing the latter, as it's easier to get things done within a division than to work with multiple divisions.

2. Define a minimum viable IB use case

- **Use-case-specific.** Say you want to run an equipment upgrade campaign *or* add an IIoT part to existing equipment. Maybe it's an excess inventory campaign or a product maintenance toolkit you'd like to sell. Get specific!
- **Tight deliverables and scope.** Who's involved? Who's driving the IB strategy? Who's closest to the outcomes, and who's sponsoring it? What's the scope for each individual and team? All these factors matter.
- **Tight timelines.** This is a no-brainer. Industrials are prone to stretching projects for years and eventually losing interest as funding is reallocated. Avoid that trap.
- **Defined success criteria.** What does success look like to you and your team? Is it more parts sold, more customers engaged? More warranties sold? A good IB strategy can be driven by a robust installed-base data platform that can yield up to 10 times your ROI, so get real with the numbers.

3. Deploy a robust data-quality engine

- **No need to go "whole hog" for a master data-management tool, yet.** MDM projects are known to expand rapidly and yield slow results, and they're highly susceptible to being rendered outdated and obsolete with evolving data needs. Define data-quality metrics—and remember, perfect is the enemy of good.
- **Implement governance processes to ensure no backsliding.** Enterprises are typically good at governance when it comes to process; however, a well-defined governance model will go a long way toward ensuring success.

4. Build an agile process for fast iterative development

- **Two-week sprints with defined goals.** A sprint is typically a two-week unit in the iterative development world. It's not long enough to lose track but short enough to see actual progress.
- **Short overall release cycle (quarterly?).** Have specific, achievable quarterly goals that help you showcase actual outcomes and results to the broader org. For example, OEMs typically focus on one division + one product line in the first quarter and then expand rapidly.
- **Multifunctional—it can't be the province of IT alone.** Today's IT org is entrusted with way too many projects, and it's no surprise that many of those end up in an "enterprise tool graveyard." An IB strategy stands

a better chance of success and survival if actual end users and beneficiaries along with IT are involved. As part of this multifunctional approach, it's critical to have a business leader take ownership of the project and the results—and it needs to be someone with standing in the organization to get things done. In most successful IB projects, there's typically an overweighting of executive engagement—make it a critical priority for a high-capability executive for a short period of time.

5. Get quick wins in the field

- **Data is only as good as its use.** "Perfect is the enemy of good." Design a use case, execute, iterate, and usher in incremental success. This is what works for all of our customers, every single time.
- **Quality and other issues get sorted-through fast with end users.** Loop them in early; your sales reps and sales managers (whom I like to call actual data handlers) are the ones who know every single challenge with your current data. They will happily jump on the opportunity to remedy the situation.
- **Quick wins inspire confidence engendering adoption.** After all, success has a compounding effect. A successful IB strategy quickly expands across the org. I wish I could name names, but it's satisfying to see OEM executives grow individually in their careers and as teams when they execute an IB strategy just the right way.

6. Expand aspirations via use-case roadmap

- **Use early successes to define what's possible.** Some use cases are just not meant to be, as they lack executive sponsorship. Begin with what the org cares about the most and lay out a roadmap for the next iterations.
- **Break down into manageable, everyday workflows.** The single most important piece of advice I can give here is to ensure that any IB strategy is made part of the user's regular workflows. Define how the team would use IB data daily (review the up-to-date customer data before placing a call, *or* have IB data on the screen when talking to customers over a call), weekly (review possible opportunities to upsell/cross-sell), monthly (review territories), quarterly (review IB growth as part of quarterly reviews and account planning process/template).
- **Roadmap outlines expectations and aspirations.** Tie expectations to users' goals and aspirations. After all, this is what high-performing sales teams do. A roadmap they can refer to and incorporate in their quarterly goals works best for everyone.
- **In general, solving your IB will not be a one-time development effort that can then be not invested in moving forward.** There will be new use cases in the future that you haven't thought about today, new

analytics technologies that are currently not foreseen, new data sources and new consumers of data and insights. You'll need a solution that evolves to meet these future needs—through having either a dedicated internal team or an external partner who's evolving the solution and capability to meet future needs.

7. Expand data sources

- **Simple data sets → complex data sets.** Start with the simple stuff. You'd be surprised how many insights can be gained from the simplest of databases. It's easy to fall into the "we will do predictive sales analytics" trap. Even a simple mapping of location-equipment-parts-service-warranties-contacts gives you enough insights to launch a major campaign or two.
- **Few data sources → more data sources.** Integrating all your tools is nice to have, not a mandate. Often, industrial OEM data is duplicated across different systems and within the same tools. Our experience with industrial data over the years tells us that approximately 35 percent of records are duplicates in some way. Begin with a few tools that you have the most confidence in, and then integrate the less-used ones.
- **Structured data → unstructured data.** Begin with structured data, such as contact names, equipment database, parts database, and locations, and then move to the more inaccessible data, such as BOM, documents, and engineering drawings.

8. Democratize access to IB data

- **Have more people access data—in a controlled environment.** The more people access a tool, the more it gets used and the more it evolves for the greater good of the org. However, a fair degree of control is needed. You need to have governance in place that allows users to edit data but provides an approval and audit mechanism as well. Access to specific territories or geographies should be able to be controlled.
- **Get feedback, repeat agile loops.** Each user who interacts with the IB data will provide specific feedback and have specific asks that help them get better at their jobs. This is a sales-enablement opportunity at its finest. Incorporate those changes iteratively so that everyone feels included and heard.
- **Shine the light on data-quality and process issues.** I left this for the latter part of the list because it's not easy to fix decades of data and process challenges. At best, a good IB strategy can shine the light on recurring data governance issues; however, it can't fix the root cause itself—not till we get rid of archaic ERP systems that were designed as data-entry tools rather than user-friendly systems that allow easy access to the right data and insights and thus prevent the workarounds that resulted in poor data quality historically.

9. Create evergreen data refresh processes

- **Cannot be a one-and-done.** I referred to the "enterprise tool graveyard" earlier. Don't let an IB strategy be relegated to that realm. Your IB data represent your customers, and the health of your IB data represents how much you value your customers and their repeat business. The biggest differentiator between companies that enjoy high aftermarket growth year after year and those that don't is the loyalty of their customers. Having a complete, updated picture of customers always is not a wish-list item; it's a mandate in the next economy.

- **Update frequency based on business cycle.** This may sound a bit counter to what I said above, but there are practical challenges to constant updates to your IB data. You may choose to align your IB data refresh and strategy overhaul with your business cadence so that you don't hit major hurdles or distractions from core work.

- **Automate data flows.** This is a by-product of a good IB strategy. Automating data flows becomes a no-brainer, just as automating assembly lines is, and a good IB strategy would inform you which tools, systems, and sources need to be integrated for optimum results. This isn't just about data flowing into an IB database or tool; it's also about unified data, updates, insights, and opportunities automatically flowing to other enterprise systems for use in other workflows.

10. Remember item 1!

About Vivek Joshi

Vivek Joshi is a co-founder and CEO of Entytle, Inc. He brings significant leadership experience to Entytle based on his roles in various industries, spanning private equity, high technology, diversified industrial manufacturing, and health care. He previously was founder and CEO of LumaSense Technologies Inc., a global sensor and instrumentation company based in Santa Clara, CA. Vivek's experiences span leadership roles at General Electric, Sun MicroSystems, Webvan, and Johnson & Johnson. He also was an investor at Shah Capital and a consultant at Booz Allen Hamilton. Vivek has an MS in Chemical Engineering and an MBA from the Darden School of Business at the University of Virginia, Charlottesville, and a B.Tech in Chemical Engineering from IIT, Mumbai.

About Entytle

Entytle, Inc. is a provider of Entytle Insyghts, the world's first installed base data platform (IBDP) for industrial OEMs to unify, organize, and analyze their customers' information while significantly improving available data quality. Insyghts, a SaaS platform, incorporates purpose-built AI/ML analytics to identify sales and service opportunities to increase wallet share from the OEM's installed base. Entytle is trusted by industry leaders including Johnson Controls, Baker Hughes, Peerless Pump, Dematic, ColeParmer, and many more who use Entytle to drive organic growth at scale. Learn more at www.entytle.com/.

References

Bertoncello, M., Martens, C., Möller, T., & Schneiderbauer, T. (2021). *Unlocking the full life-cycle value from connected-car data.* McKinsey & Company, February 11. www.mckinsey.com/industries/automotive-and-assembly /our-insights/unlocking-the-full-life-cycle-value-from-connected -car-data

Daimler. (2020, November 2). Fuel-cell joint venture. Volvo Group and Daimler Truck AG sign binding agreement. www.daimler.com/company /news/fuel-cell-joint-venture-volvo.html

Daniel, S. (2021). *We are where we are supposed to be.* LinkedIn, June 17. www.linkedin.com/pulse/we-where-supposed-stephen-daniel/

Liozu, S. (2019). Gold rush or fool's gold? 10 digital transformation myths. *IndustryWeek,* August 14. www.industryweek.com /technology-and-iiot/article/22028079 /gold-rush-or-fools-gold-10-digital-transformation-myths

PwC. (n.d.). *Manufacturing is ready for e-commerce. Seven things to consider before diving in.* www.pwc.com/us/en/industries/industrial-products /library/manufacturing-e-commerce.html

Schawbel, D. (2021). *Hybrid working is here to stay. But what does that mean in your office?* World Economic Forum, May 25. www.weforum.org/agenda/2021/05/hybrid-working-your-office-future/

US Bureau of Labor Statistics. (2021). *Labor force statistics from the Current Population Survey.* www.bls.gov/cps/cpsaat18b.htm

3

Important Myths
to Understand before
Thinking about Subscriptions

DON'T BELIEVE EVERYTHING YOU read when it comes to digital transformations and industrial subscriptions. Unless you've done both very successfully, it's very conceptual and theoretical. I'm still looking for outright and clear success stories. Granted, things are getting better, and we're collecting an enormous amount of data. What to do with the amassed data remains a critical question. This book is not intended to focus on the rosy side of the business transformation. I want to give a realistic panorama of what's happening, what needs to be done, and how to get things done.

10 myths about industrial digital transformations

Data is the new gold. The current digital revolution is a gold rush. Thousands of firms are launching comprehensive and expensive digital transformations with the hope of finding a significant gold vein. As in any gold rush, there will be winners and losers. A tiny fraction of these organizations will show significant success from their digital transformations. Others will learn from the process and still benefit internally from large-scale digital investments. Right now, though, we're still in the midst of the rush, and everything looks shiny indeed.

As in any gold rush, there are beautiful stories and anecdotes of companies' striking gold. For every one of these stories, there are dozens of failures and false starts reinforced by a series of myths. Here are several myths that I've found in working and interacting with industrial peers.

1   **A digital transformation is an externally focused transformation.** In a way, this is true. Digital transformations that are focused on delivering digitally drive innovation to customers and markets. This is true

at least on paper and in the strategy-building process. However, a digital transformation won't succeed without the right digital tools internally. This implies that for the sake of execution and value capture, an internal digital transformation must also happen. This is a duality that is hard to grasp at the executive level. It's much jazzier to invest in an IoT platform than to deploy an internal sales-enablement platform.

2   **A digital transformation is a technology transformation.** This is the most prevalent myth in industrial markets. Most digital transformations are led by engineering and technology folks who have very little knowledge of marketing and business models. As a results, firms fall into the 90/10 trap: 90 percent of investments, attention, and resources are in IT and technology, and 10 percent are in marketing. This is deadly. A digital transformation is first and foremost a strategic and business model transformation. It needs to be led by strategy and marketing. In practical terms, it means that your chief digital officer must be a marketing expert. Then, there needs to be a balance of investments: 50 percent in marketing and 50 percent in technology.

3   **You can execute a digital transformation at the same speed at which you'd deploy innovation in your legacy business.** Speed is the new currency of business. In the digital space, that speed is supersonic. Nimble startups and digital natives go to market fast and take many more risks than industrial natives. I often say that 90 days is what it takes for an industrial native to get a workshop organized. Ninety days for a startup is what it takes to conduct a go-to-market sprint.

4   **A digital transformation on top of a broken business model or strategy will save the business.** There are probably good ways to turn a business or a division around in the event of a broken business model or disrupted strategy. A digital transformation isn't one of them. It requires large investments and a significant portion of organizational bandwidth. Without cash and resources, it's a lost cause, and it will distract the organization from fixing the structural issues in the core business.

5   **You can digitally transform without marketing maturity and customer intimacy in the core business.** Simply said, if you don't have the right marketing and customer maturity in the core business, you won't have it to be successful in your digital transformation. Most industrial natives lack deep customer intimacy and lag behind in digital marketing investments. Many still rely on channel partners to manage the customer relationship. Without customer data, it's hard to develop digital innovations. It's imperative to invest quickly in the right marketing tools and to gather the customer intelligence residing in people, laptops, static PowerPoint slide decks, and forgotten SharePoint sites. And, by the way, if your core business suffers from a deep gap between sales and marketing, your digital transformation might be rocky.

6 **You can package current digital pilot projects into a transformation.** A digital transformation is a comprehensive set of transformational programs and investments carefully designed to support a strategic agenda. It isn't the packaging of a few connected products and software into a digital umbrella. A digital project or two does not translate to a deep digital transformation. I've visited dozens of websites of industrial firms, and I find this is often the case. Some industrial groups have also acquired a few software companies and have called themselves "digital champions." Finally, there's a perception that opening a digital factory, or an incubator, can be called a digital transformation. It's part of it, but it can't be the whole of it.

7 **You can make money and produce industrial unicorns overnight.** Every industrial company wants to become the go-to platform for their industrial ecosystem. They often underestimate the time needed to reach the status of platform unicorn. They often refer to Uber, Airbnb, and Amazon to qualify their aspirations. They forget to mention that these businesses have been around for over 10 years and have lost significant sums of money in getting there. And they still do today. In digital, competition is fierce, and many of the value chains have already been commoditized. Executives cannot have the same earnings before interest and taxes (EBIT) and cash-flow requirements that they apply to the core business. It will take exploration, experimentation, and losses along the way.

8 **You can take people from your core business and turn them into digital champions overnight.** Naming divisional and functional digital champions and digital product owners is a first step. The next step is to invest heavily in upskilling and reskilling them as soon as possible. This means that your digital academy or other digital learning infrastructure needs to be in place before you begin your digital transformation, not two years into the transformation. People don't acquire skills magically overnight. Reading a book and attending a conference won't cut it. You need sustained action learning. By the way, the HR strategy of plugging holes with available people and B-players is also a bad idea. Digital transformations require the best of the best dedicated to their journey.

9 **If you're a product-driven company, you'll have an easy time becoming solutions-oriented in digital.** If you've been a product-centric industrial organization for decades, your organizational mindset is that of a product company. You might have some service departments embedded in your product divisions, but chances are they're fragmented and not coordinated. A digital transformation requires a service mindset. If you lack that, you can't hope to go from product-centricity to solution-centricity in a couple of years. It'll take a decade. If your organization is already organized for services and complex system delivery, then you have a greater chance of success. You need to crawl before you can run. The

sequence is from products to services to connected services and products, and to product-as-a-service (PaaS). That transition takes time.

10 You can scale your digital innovation and startups with a traditional legacy back office. Do you think your IT, finance, and sales team will embrace your digital innovations and programs with open arms? Think again. Someone needs to worry about the integration of all these innovations and technologies in the core infrastructure and back office. This is where many digital projects get stuck or killed altogether. Culture does matter. Running a digital transformation as a shiny and trendy project managed by young folks in jeans and flip-flops reinforces silo thinking, generational cleavages, and turf wars. You think I'm kidding? Try to convince IT to integrate an open-source IoT digital platform into a highly secured optimized IT network. Similarly, try to get finance controllers to change their KPIs for success for a SaaS opportunity that will be cash-flow negative for five years!

Most consulting and industry reports note that 85 to 90 percent of firms have begun some type of digital transformation. The gold rush is a reality! Before jumping on the bandwagon and committing significant investments to a digital transformation, though, I strongly recommend candid C-suite discussions around these 10 myths. Most of these potential issues can be avoided in the design phase of the transformation, even if you've already gotten started. I recommend beginning by reinforcing the core and back office with the right digital tools while exploring digital innovations in the market. The key to success is in the design and roadmapping of your transformation.

10 myths about the industrial subscription business model

The subscription economy is real. There's no doubt that some industries have shifted to consumption business models (usage and subscription models). Consultants and software vendors are quick to conclude that ownership is dead, and that usership is the way of the future. They're claiming that every single piece of hardware, equipment, and software can be sold using a recurring model consisting of subscription, usage, or outcome-based components. In theory, everything can be transferred to a flexible consumption format. In practice, I don't believe this is true. I've worked with industrial and manufacturing companies for the past 30 years. This long and deep experience allows me to see through the confusion and the myths of the subscription trend. I agree that there's room for subscription business models in manufacturing and that it's essential for industrial businesses to set a target for the portion of sales moving to a recurring model. Here are some of the most common myths I read and hear about:

1 One hundred percent of your business will move to recurring. Thinking that all equipment can be sold in the form of long-term subscriptions is irrational. Some of these pieces of equipment last for 20 or 30 years and need to be maintained and depreciated. Subscription contracts are traditionally two to five years maximum, renewable over time. Should a customer decide not to renew, will they really dismantle assets on their production line after two years and switch to another supplier? The concept of switching costs might limit the use of subscription in some industries.

2   **Hardware and equipment ownership will disappear.** Semifinished goods manufacturers selling parts, single components, and semiassembled components might not be able to sell these in a subscription format. Much of the manufacturing output is being integrated and absorbed into the value and supply chain. Only finished products might be able to move to a PaaS model (product-as-a-service).

3   **Subscription is for every one of your customers.** A large portion of your customer base has no interest in a flexible consumption model, including subscription. They want to acquire the product or software and do things on their own. They want control over the acquired assets. With subscriptions, much of the control and data are shared with vendors.

4   **It's easy to scale subscription offers.** This isn't the case. Assuming you've done the development work correctly, you'll be facing headwinds in the scaling of the business. Most of the battles will be internal. You'll have to do a lot of convincing and collaborating with IT, finance, legal, HR, and sales, among others. You'll need a strong back office with the right tools and systems. Be ready for a marathon.

5   **Once you've launched your subscription offer, you're done.** Launching is just the beginning. In the subscription world, the customer is at the heart of the business model. Customers are fickle! They want innovation, experience, freedom, and affordability. The success of a subscription business model comes from flexibility to make changes and adapt to changes in customer needs.

6   **Subscriptions offer quick sales and a fast route to profit.** A subscription business will have a short-term negative impact on sales growth, profit, and cash flow. In the B2C and SaaS worlds, this is known as the swallow-the-fish concept. You'll face resistance from the finance and business leaders who expect quick sales growth and profit. Companies must be ready to see negative trends up front for longer-term positive trends. Finally, many subscription-based startups don't survive. They lose too much money and burn through cash quickly.

7   **You can apply B2C and SaaS KPIs to your subscription.** Some of the KPIs used in the B2C and the SaaS world cannot be applied to the manufacturing world. For example, the rule of 40 states that if your growth rate minus your earnings before interest and taxes (EBIT) losses exceeds 40, you're in good shape. Imagine you have 100 percent growth, and you make a 60 percent EBIT loss: how well would this fly with your management? Some

of the traditional SaaS KPIs are acceptable. In reality, they'll be blended with traditional manufacturing KPIs.

8 **Free is the way to go.** Freemium and free-trial concepts are well accepted in the B2C and SaaS worlds. Subscriptions that include hardware and products might not survive the financial and business review process. Manufacturing and industrial companies traditionally try to recoup R&D and variable costs from the first sale. As a result, there's a need to focus on differentiated and attractive subscription offers that customers are willing to pay for from the get-go. Easier said than done.

9 **Your salesforce will jump onboard right away.** You can't imagine how much time you'll spend redesigning your sales process and conducting change-management activities to bring your salesforce on board. I've worked with several industrial companies that had to completely redesign sales enablement for the subscription side of their business. We do a deep dive on this topic in section 5. For now, note that it'll take time and efforts to get to market.

10 **Technology is fully proven and easy to deploy.** You'd think that technologies in the areas of IoT, predictive maintenance, augmented reality, and subscription management are proven, easy to plug in, and operationalizable in 90 days. Think again. The IoT is over 20 years old, but it isn't as easy as you might think to deploy in collaboration with customers. Subscription billing platforms also require some work. Nothing is simple and easy in the technology world. You need to expect delays and technical issues despite a relatively high adoption rate for these technologies.

The subscription economy is here to stay. The tsunami will reach the B2B and industrial shores. However, the wave won't be as strong as it was with the B2C and B2B SaaS sectors. The manufacturing sector will benefit from the opportunity offered by the subscription business model. Software vendors and consultants offering subscription solutions to the manufacturing world must adapt their offerings to be right-sized, right-engineered, and scalable at the speed of B2B. The speed and rate of adoption will be different.

4

A Lot Could Go Wrong with Your Subscription Program

Y OU GOT IT. SUBSCRIPTIONS are the way to go. They'll keep growing across many sectors and will be here for a while. Here's a reality check. A lot could go wrong with the design, launch, and management of your subscription project. I don't want to be a "party pooper," but I do want to show examples of failures, and causes of failures, and introduce to you the concept of subscription fatigue, which is being discussed more and more in the B2C world.

Subscription fatigue

Recently, Robbie Kellman Baxter (2021) wrote a good post on LinkedIn discussing subscription fatigue. She states that many people are beginning to complain of fatigue as more and more households subscribe to new services and have trouble keeping up with them. Robbie points out that "they might feel that the subscription pricing isn't justified by the offer (a product/market fit problem). Or maybe they feel bad about fact that they aren't taking advantage of all the great value their subscriptions provide—too many unread *New Yorkers*, uneaten Blue Apron kits (subscription guilt). Or maybe they're just angry that it's so darn hard to find the cancel button." I admit that I've experienced such fatigue. I already subscribe to Netflix, Hulu, and Peacock. Now, I'm bombarded with additional potential content site from Paramount, Discovery, and more. How many subscriptions can one get? The plethora of options has a downside: nearly half (47%) of US consumers say they're frustrated by the growing number of subscriptions and services required to watch what they want, according to the 15th edition of Deloitte's annual Digital Media Trends survey (Westcott et al., 2021). An even bigger pet peeve: 57 percent said they're frustrated when content vanishes because rights to their favorite TV shows or movies have expired (Spanger, 2019). And this phenomenon is not unique to the B2C world.

Subscription fatigue is being discussed in the B2B SaaS world as well. B2B customers are being attacked by numerous startups promoting the outstanding benefits of SaaS software to replace legacy on-premise software or as new services to subscribe to.

So, we begin seeing some cracks in the subscription economy. The subscription experts are beginning to notice and write about it (Campbell, 2020). It's inevitable to happen as more and more transition to a full consumption model or a hybrid one. Here's what's being written about it:

- **Expressed concerns about subscription.** "Despite the increase in subscription service adoption for household staples, we did notice a decrease in satisfaction with these services. In last year's survey, nearly a quarter (24%) affirmed that they had no complaints about subscription services for household staples. This year, the percentage of fully satisfied customers have fallen to just 10% of users. This means subscription services for household staples have seen a 58% drop in fully satisfied customers year-over-year. 34% say their biggest dislike about subscription services is that they are difficult to cancel, while 33% say their biggest dislike about subscription services is that they are more expensive" (Williams, 2021).
- **Customers are overwhelmed.** According to a Deloitte survey, the average American subscribed to 12 paid media and entertainment services pre-pandemic. Among those age 25 to 40 who averaged 17 subscriptions, 40% reported feeling overwhelmed by the number of their subscriptions and intended to reduce them (Westcott et al., 2021).
- **More customers are hitting the cancel button.** "Research from Emarsys shows that only one in fifty UK shoppers have kept their subscription services for more than a year. This means that 98 percent cancel their services within the first twelve months of subscribing. The average consumer in the United Kingdom even cancels their subscriptions in less than half a year—an average of 5.3 months" ("Most Brits," 2021).
- **Auto subscriptions are not scaling well.** "Subscriptions have been a mixed bag for the auto industry. Ford walked away from its service last fall following low demand. Cadillac shut down its service Book in 2018, only to resurrect it several months later with fewer options. […] Other automakers have had some success. BMW, Porsche, Audi, Volvo, Nissan, and Jaguar are still offering some variation of a subscription service" (Hawkins, 2021). But in general, the sales numbers for car subscriptions are not what the industry expected.

Serious tests for subscription models

Designing, launching, and scaling a subscription isn't easy. Many companies succeed, but many fail. The complexity arises because this is a completely new business model that requires internal and external transformational work. A lot could go wrong along the way, especially in the B2B and industrial sectors.

1 **Do customers really need the subscription, or are they getting value from it?** That's question number one. What does the customer need, and what problem does the subscription offer solve? This concept of customer problem is essential for any innovation. The heart of the subscription value proposition needs to address customer pains and gains. Remember that customers have choices, and that they're considering several options. In the B2C world, the space is crowded, and some markets are saturated with subscription offers. In industrial IoT, this is the case as well. With over 800 commercially available IoT platforms, how do you stand out from the crowd? How will you create more value than another IoT platform vendor? Bottom line: you must go deeper in the customer operations to do better research than your competitors. You must uncover unmet needs and new ways to frame the customer's problem. I invited Ash Maurya to write a short essay (presented at the end of this chapter) about why it's important to love the problem, not your solutions.

2 **Does the subscription support the customer's business and operations?** If your subscription creates tremendous customer value compared with the existing situation or competitors, you can enjoy a long-term relationship with your customers. You might be able to avoid the expense-reduction cut when things aren't going well. In both the B2B and the B2C worlds, when times are tough, customers cut unnecessary expenses. How is your subscription considered? Is it a discretionary spend, or a critical one?

3 **Can you clearly demonstrate the value you bring to your customers with your subscriptions?** You can't wait until renewal time to engage your customers on the value you've created for them. Value selling must be ongoing and based on real, realized value numbers. The subscription business model requires putting the subscriber, not the product, at the heart of the relationship. You must communicate constantly with your customers and demonstrate value.

4 **Do you use the right value metric?** Have you considered aligning your pricing metric with the customer's value metric? The cost of your subscription in your customer's P&L must be aligned with their revenues. The more they sell, the more you make. But if things slow down for the customers, and your cost increases or stays stable, you might be on the chopping block.

5 **Should all customers move to the subscription model?** I often get this question, and it's a tricky one. Not every customer wants a subscription. Some consider subscriptions too expensive; others want to keep ownership of the product or software. So, don't push subscriptions to customers

who are cash-rich, not interested in OpEx models, or not willing to let go of the control to own the asset. Therefore, I always recommend conducting a thorough segmentation analysis and focusing on the pockets of customers who see value in recurring business models.

6 **Are you dynamically optimizing your subscription prices?** In the recurring world, prices need to be dynamically managed. Chances are that your pricing structure at the time of launch won't stay valid very long once you scale. You'll learn a ton from your customer usage. You might have to modify your price metrics, your tier levels, your discount structure. Failure to do so can be deadly for your subscription business. Customers will drop like flies if they see your offer as too inflexible and too expensive.

7 **How good is your subscription customer experience?** This is a sore subject for industrial companies. They're not known for outstanding user experience (UX). It's one of the pillars of the subscription economy: simplicity, transparency, and empowerment. Customers don't want to call their providers each time they want to modify or interact with their subscription.

8 **Have you test-driven your subscription to overcome pain points?** Selling via a subscription model can also necessitate IT modifications. Traditional systems, for example, have trouble handling product and offer bundling. When a subscription product or service is sold with upgrades or add-ons, a traditional system may create a new SKU for each change to the bundle, producing a dizzying array of pricing, bundling, and distribution combinations. CFO.com recently published a good report on the topic of recurring revenue pain points. They report that a traditional order-and-invoicing approach can also lead to frustrated customers and subscription terminations if multiple canceled invoices and new invoices are produced with each change. Typically, companies that transition to a recurring revenue model use their existing CRM and ERP systems. Since most ERP systems are designed for transactional businesses, it can be difficult for them to handle sales spanning multiple periods. When product sales reach $75 million to $100 million annually, the problems with old systems start becoming insurmountable. Thus, nearly two-thirds (67%) of survey respondents reported actively exploring new processes or systems to support recurring revenue products or services. The same report concludes that finance executives have high expectations. Most (57%) of the surveyed finance executives indicated that solving their "quote-to-cash" pain points (product configuration to payment) would lower finance and sales costs by at least 5 percent. A similar majority (55%) also believed it would increase enterprise revenue by at least 5 percent. And nearly three-quarters of respondents (73%) said that both sales and finance would benefit from a solution that supports dynamic and recurring contracts. In addition, more

than seven in 10 of the surveyed finance executives (71%) indicated a more efficient pricing and approval process would substantially improve their organizations' profitability (Marletta, 2019).

Trends in the B2B SaaS world

The B2B SaaS world has become highly competitive. Companies are accelerating their transition to the cloud and focusing much more on software development and/or software-firm acquisition. Industrial giants like Siemens, Sandvik, and Honeywell are investing billions in software. It's inevitable that we'll witnesses some changes in dynamics in the B2B software space. With more competition come the following trends:

1 **Commoditization.** The golden era of SaaS subscription models is ending. The low-hanging subscription fruits have been picked as software spaces transition more and more to SaaS and new vendors pop up weekly. It's estimated that there were over 100,000 SaaS vendors in 2020 and that there'll be over a million by 2025. So, many more businesses are fighting for the same customers via the same channels. It's becoming more expensive to attract and retain new subscribers. As a result, customer acquisition and retention costs are increasing. An additional challenge to this greater level of competition is accelerated commoditization leading to a potential reduction of average revenue per subscriber in comparison with the increase in customer acquisition cost.

2 **Low adoption.** A 2021 report by Productiv shows the proliferation of SaaS solutions being acquired and deployed in B2B companies with or without the oversight of IT ("The State of SaaS Sprawl," 2021). This report shows that an organization has an average of 254 SaaS solutions. They also report that the average user engagement stands at 45 percent. Some functions, such as security, IT, and sales, have the highest number of deployed SaaS solutions. So there's competition for adoption and integration in the digital stack. It's essential to keep this in mind when selling subscriptions.

3 **Pricing erosion.** To add to this situation, more companies are introducing freemium offerings or free-trial periods. This creates margin pressure, and switching costs to alternative subscription providers are lower for subscribers than for one-time customers. Incumbents have to worry about churns and be willing to offer greater levels of discount for multiyear contracts or for an expanded scope of business.

4 **Move from SaaS to PaaS.** Recognizing the fragmentation of the SaaS space and some of the pain points reported by customers, the very large cloud offerings identified an opportunity to disrupt the SaaS space by offering PaaS solutions. "In the 2020s, the headline disruption for many software companies will be the growth of PaaS. Between 2016 and 2018,

PaaS revenues grew at nearly twice the rate of SaaS—44 percent a year versus 26 percent, respectively. Much of that growth came at the bottom of the software stack. The Big Three cloud vendors, with their vast scale and resources, have developed PaaS services that now rival those of the leading software vendors" (Roche et al., 2020). Digital marketplaces also can substitute individual software offers packaged in one turnkey solution.

5   **Move to a self-service model.** Customers don't necessarily want to see salespeople in order to buy subscriptions. Most analysts in the digital space report that about 60 percent of the sales process has moved to some form of digitalization. Prospects can do their homework on their own and decide whether there's value in the subscription they need. The implications of this trend are numerous: first, there's a need for transparency and clarity in the subscription packages and pricing. The "call sales for pricing" is no longer acceptable. Second, the user experience along the customer journey must be impeccable. Third, subscribers want to be in charge of managing their subscriptions. Anything else is a good reason to cancel!

6   **Software must be ready for subscription fatigue.** "Software has been at the epicenter of innovation entrepreneurial opportunities. But industry experts caution that the world now seeks more than solutions simply offered online." "Twenty years into the SaaS/cloud era, 'it's becoming harder to find any white space building the next "Cloud for x" solution,' agrees Andy Vitus, partner with Scale Venture Partners. 'With fewer and fewer obvious opportunities, entrepreneurs are already starting to figure out what comes next: a generational shift in software itself. Software has long been a tool that people use to accomplish a task—like scissors or a calculator.' AI and machine learning, APIs, and IoT are opening up a new dimension for software-based delivery, he adds. 'Each of these technologies supercharges the others, opening the door to truly next-generation software that intuitively works for us. Software with the power to deliver a new wave of productivity and growth'" (McKendrick, 2020).

 Lightning Strike:
Love the Problem, Not Your Solution

Ash Maurya

What are the most common pitfalls that trip up digital innovators? Tops on my list is **falling in love with your solution**. I've previously labeled this predisposition toward the solution the "innovator's bias." In science, one of the ways we attempt to overcome this kind of bias is through reasoning from first principles. The same can also be applied in business.

With first principles you boil things down to the most fundamental truths... and then reason up from there.

—Elon Musk

The "innovator bias" is a sneaky troll—rearing its ugly head not just during ideation but throughout the innovation life cycle, often when you least expect it. At each step, some of the most fundamental truths come from a deep understanding of problems before solutions.

The big idea

When we first get hit by an idea, the solution is what we most clearly see and what we spend most of our energy on. But most products fail—not because we fail to build out our solution but because we fail to solve a "big enough" customer problem. All your initial energy should be channeled toward finding evidence of a *monetizable customer problem,* not toward acquiring more resources to build out your solution.

So how do you find a "big enough" problem?

Begin by recognizing that your true job is to create a customer (not your solution). Customers are results or outcome driven. Look for a job they're trying to get done (jobs-to-be-done) and study how they're getting it done (existing alternatives). If the job is adequately getting done, that's bad news for you, because it's hard to displace an existing solution with a similar-sounding value proposition. If, on the other hand, you find that the job isn't getting done "well enough," that's great news for you. The obstacles or problems preventing the customer from achieving their desired outcome is where you'll find space for innovation and for your subscription offer.

This emphasis on problem versus solution was the core mind shift I wanted to get across with the Lean Canvas and why I modified the original Business Model Canvas. When I heard entrepreneurs and digital innovators pitch their Business Model Canvases, I heard a lot about what they were going to build (value proposition / solution) and a lot about how they were going to deliver it to customers (channels, key activities, key partners, key resources, customer relationships). But I didn't hear anything about why customers would need or want their solution in the first place, or how they would get customers to switch from what they're doing today to a new solution. *So, no problems in your business model is a problem.*

The Lean Canvas isn't a better Business Model Canvas: it's a different canvas altogether. Even though I changed four boxes, it's simply the addition of the Problem box that continues to generate the biggest mind shift in the resulting business model.

The ever-growing feature backlog

Let's fast-forward to a launched product—one with lots of customers. With lots of customers come lots of new feature requests. Who do you listen to? If you listen to all your customers, pretty soon you'll have a bloated monster on your hands. Even if you listen to just your most valuable customers, you might still end up building stuff that even they don't use. The reason for this is that most feature requests are framed as solutions, not problems. And customers are often not good at devising solutions—even to their own problems.

> It's not the customer's job to know what they want.
>
> —Steve Jobs

A better way to prioritize your customer feature requests is by first understanding the root problems that triggered the request in the first place. Where were they? What were they trying to do? Why? You can answer all these questions by simply applying the same jobs-to-be-done thinking process from above.

Here's an example from our LEANSTACK software:

Feature request 1   I'd like to be able to be export my Lean Canvas as a PDF.

Feature request 2   I'd like to be able to change the colors on the Lean Canvas.

Feature request 3   I'd like to be able to change the fonts on the Lean Canvas.

Each of these was a simple-enough feature request, but rather than just implementing them, we got the requestors on the phone. We asked them what they were trying to accomplish (outcome) and explored why the current product was failing them (problem). In this case, what we learned was that these users wanted to use their Lean Canvases in investor presentations and that the default view was not visually interesting enough. Once you understand the job, the axes of "better" get clearer. Instead of implementing their feature requests verbatim, we mocked-up a "presentation mode" feature and showed it to them. That's what we ended up building.

Pitfall   Most customer feature requests are framed as solutions, but customers are often not good solution designers.

Antidote   Love the Problem, Not Your Solution.

Becoming better at understanding the customer problem

Truly uncovering and understanding the customer problem is an essential skill for anyone involved in designing innovative subscription-based digital offers. It's like developing and strengthening a muscle. It takes a fair amount of learning, practice, and repetition. You must remember that your competitors also are studying your customers' problems, possibly using the Lean Canvas. So, you must focus on using the right research and investigation tools to get to the true customer problem. By *true*, I mean the problem that's the most painful for the customer, a problem that might not be that obvious, or a problem the customer didn't even know they have. That's the core of your subscription value proposition. Not only do you have to discover the problem better than competition, you also need to respond to it better than competition in order to increase willingness to pay. That relates to another box in the Lean Canvas called the WOW differentiators.

One final takeaway

I'd like to leave you with one final takeaway. We pay a lot of lip service to perseverance and grit, but perseverance and grit will get you only so far if you're simply trying to brute-force your solution. Starting with a solution is like building a key without knowing what door it'll open. You can try testing your key on lots of doors, or you can begin with a door you want to open. When you fall in love with the problem, versus your solution, you start building keys to doors that take you places.

About Ash Maurya

Ash Maurya is the creator of the Lean Canvas and the founder of LeanStack. Ash wrote *Running Lean: Iterate from Plan A to a Plan That Works* and *Scaling Lean: Mastering the Key Metrics for Startup Growth*. @LEANSTACK —www.leanstack.com

References

Campbell, P. (2020). Subscription fatigue: What it is, and what subscription businesses can do about it. *ProfitWell*, April 1. www.profitwell.com/recur/all/subscription-fatigue

Hawkins, A. J. (2021). BMW becomes the latest automaker to shut down its subscription service. *The Verge*, January 14. www.theverge.com/2021/1/14/22231451 /bmw-access-subscription-shut-down-nashville-cancel

Kellman Baxter, R. (2021). Will subscriptions work forever? The future of a popular pricing tactic. *LinkedIn*, May 12.

www.linkedin.com/pulse/subscriptions-work-forever
-future-popular-pricing-tactic-baxter/

Marletta, G. (2019). Recurring revenue rising. *CFO,* February 27.
www.cfo.com/cash-flow/2019/02/recurring-revenue-rising/

McKendrick, J. (2020). The next boom: Every industry will have a different
digital innovation story. *Forbes,* December 30. www.forbes.com/sites
/joemckendrick/2021/12/30/the-next-boom-every-industry-will
-have-a-different-digital-innovation-story/

Most Brits cancel product subscription in first year. (2021).
Ecommerce News, August 6. https://ecommercenews.eu
/most-brits-cancel-product-subscription-in-first-year/

Roche, P., Schneider, J., & Shah, T. (2020). The next software disruption:
How vendors must adapt to a new era. *McKinsey & Company,* June 22.
www.mckinsey.com/industries/technology-media
-and-telecommunications/our-insights/the-next-software-disruption
-how-vendors-must-adapt-to-a-new-era

Spanger, T. (2019). "Subscription fatigue": Nearly half of U.S. consumers frustrated by streaming explosion, study finds. *Variety,* March 18.
https://variety.com/2019/digital/news/streaming-subscription
-fatigue-us-consumers-deloitte-study-1203166046/

The state of SaaS sprawl in 2021. (2021). *Productiv.*
https://productiv.com/resources/the-state-of-saas-sprawl-in-2021/

Westcott, K., Arbanas, J., Downs, K., Arkenberg, C., & Jarvis, D. (2021). Digital
media trends, 15th edition. *Deloitte Insights,* April 16.
www2.deloitte.com/us/en/insights/industry/technology/digital
-media-trends-consumption-habits-survey/summary.html

Williams, A. (2021). What's happening to subscription services? *Jabil.*
www.jabil.com/blog/subscription-services-for-cpg.html

5

Digitizing Your Industrial Installed Base: Have the Cake and Eat It?

Holger Pietzsch

Recent decades have given birth to an unbelievable number of business model innovations as well as countless reconfigurations of existing ones. Startups have leveraged connectivity, mobility, and data to create numerous subscription businesses. Technology companies constitute a growing share of the stock market value, and investors seem happier than ever to allow short-term losses in support of long-term goals. Amid this noise, traditional industrial B2B players seem surprisingly quiet on digital value. Are they unwilling, unable, or undecided to join the club? It could be that it isn't their strategic ambition but their preference to synergize and their inability to prioritize that's holding them back.

Manufacturers stay longer with and closer to their products

As we inspect the smorgasbord of manufacturing business models—many of which have hardly evolved since the industrial evolution—one innovation seems to stand out as an archetype. Supposedly invented by Gillette in the 1920s, the razor/blade revenue model has worked its way into the printers/cartridges, café machines/pods, and consoles/video games markets. As a strategy, it's meant to generate reliable, recurring income by locking a customer into a platform that then requires proprietary complements for ongoing usage. For B2C markets, it basically converts one-time-only transactions into a life-cycle investment. As such, it resembles the typical B2B model for industrial equipment, which has always represented a life-cycle investment for customers.

Historically, life-cycle equipment costs of a given asset were spread over many players transaction by transaction. Customers paid an initial price when they purchased the core product, another price (interest) to the bank for financing the transaction, another price for spare parts to a possible third party, and yet another price (wages) to their own workforce for repair work. Each deal was individually valued and negotiated. Smart customers began to aggregate these costs by piece of equipment, then by hour of usage, and finally by unit of output. Lifetime owning and operating cost became the standard way of evaluating various supplier options.

Manufacturers quickly learned that they were being held accountable for any and all costs after the initial purchase of their equipment. They also understood that controlling those subsequent costs was not only a necessarily evil but an actual opportunity to capture customer value over the life cycle of their products. By the 1990s most manufacturers had begun adding aftermarket options to their portfolios. These services now include financing, leasing, repair and maintenance contracts, extended warranties, or residual value guarantees, to name just a handful. Simultaneously, they redesigned when and where they wanted to capture customer value. Varying the annual mileage limits on a car lease, for example, allowed manufacturers to either charge more per month or trigger the overage penalty at the end of the contract. Under the big life-cycle umbrella, internal business units have created sophisticated cross-subsidy practices. The manufacturing entity, for example, can subsidize the leasing entity in support of lower interest rates, trading margins for quantity. Tomorrow's parts margins (the blades) can subsidize today's core product prices (the razors) to create a larger installed base. Extended warranties can translate the costs of future repairs into up-front expenses. If successful, these structures reduce customers' owning and operating costs while increasing manufacturers' share of wallet.

Averages are yesterday's news:
The money is in the outliers and the data to find them

Extended warranties and repair contracts have taught manufacturers to accurately calculate the average cost of owning and running their products under average conditions and normal usage. In an early episode of the TV series *Elementary,* Sherlock Holmes says, "A famous statistician once stated that while the individual man is an insoluble puzzle, in the aggregate he becomes a mathematical certainty. You can, for example, never foretell what any one man will do, but you can, with precision, say what an average man will do." Within a 90 percent confidence interval, most manufacturers can predict the average costs of 1,000 miles flown, tons moved, hours driven, or pages printed. Average, however, isn't a winning business strategy.

Increasingly, the smart money will be made or saved on the extremes of the bell curve: the not-so-average day or the above-average utilization. Actors in this space, requiring very high utilization rates, for example, are eager to mitigate the risks of downtime, to keep the world within the bands of certainty, and to eliminate outliers. Selling, managing, and delivering these levels of predictability can be very lucrative. The ability to succeed lies within a provider's access to the right accuracy, frequency, and latency of data. While surprisingly small sample sizes can yield 90 percent confidence, data volumes beyond this zone can grow exponentially—especially in time-sensitive applications. This need for data has driven many manufacturers to connect their products, often reaching far into the installed base. That same data processing adds further momentum to the recent wave of IoT and AI platforms. Interestingly, the deployment of these data-capturing technologies and data-driven solutions seems to have taken manufacturers back to the beginning of defining their business strategies. With so many options for when and how value can be created, captured, or delivered, which area should be given digital priority?

Digital capabilities require companies to recalibrate their business and operating models

A business model is defined as a company's approach to creating and capturing value; the operating model defines its value delivery. A traditional lemonade stand's business model is to sell refreshments in exchange for cash; its operating model relies on productive resources to build the stand, make lemonade, and run a salesforce. The B2B business model described earlier consists in providing initial products at time zero of the relationship, followed by further value-added services along the life cycle. Value can be captured anywhere along this continuum in the form of individual transactions, service contracts, or subscriptions. The operating model needs to deliver not only the right product but all customer interactions from cradle to crave. It keeps the promise on the total cost of ownership for the customer without bankrupting the company. It does that for generations of previously sold products, comprising an installed base that can span countries and continents. Generally, great business models focus on customer needs, while great operating models excel in standardizing and scaling processes. With IoT solutions becoming more accessible, many organizations have begun to connect the assets in their installed base in order to collect usage data on its operations. The value of these data has been identified by managers on both the business model and the operating model side of the organization.

The business model school generally sees the potential to translate the data into innovative customer insights in order to generate new or redesigned revenue streams. These valuable innovations enable customers to improve their operational processes. Standard use cases include the identification of over-capacity, safety risks, bottlenecks, equipment abuse, the avoidance of unpredicted downtime, or the optimization of planning, execution, or checking processes. Frequently these solutions require customers to reengineer processes within their existing operations. However, many customer organizations are more excited about the prospects of change than they are about writing the checks. When established players start commercializing data-enabled solutions, they soon realize that most of their customers are reluctant to buy. They either expect the new service to be included in the price of the core product they already purchased, or they simply prefer to wait and see. Only a minority of the existing customer base is willing to adopt and pay for the company's innovations. Geoffrey Moore's *Crossing the Chasm* quantifies the portion of early adopters at about 16 percent. Depending on the significant up-front investments, the revenues generated from these 16 percent are often insufficient to break even, while the ability to find more customers willing to pay is equally challenging.

Managers in the operational model realize the value of the data to improving the company's internal capabilities. A better understanding of how, when, and where customers use a product provides better forecasting and supply chain management. It allows for allocating sales, marketing, and service resources to where equipment is being used. Better understanding of the customer's equipment condition drives smarter management of parts inventories and better design of the next generation of products. Most organizations can easily identify several processes-improvement opportunities if they have more, faster, and better data about the location, condition, and usage of their installed base. However, for a process change to sustain itself and to become economically viable, it needs critical mass, a tipping point of some kind. Where is this critical point? If you managed most of your work using process A, how many of your inputs would need to change for you to decisively adopt process B *and* to abandon process A? Most people prefer that to be in the +60 percent range.

> Ever feel like an enigma, wrapped in a dilemma, surrounded by a conundrum? Yeah, so do I.
>
> —Nanette Mathews

Leaders now face two stakeholder groups willing to leverage data from the increasingly connected base. One side of the house feels comfortable charging innovations for about one-sixth of the installed base, offering a mixed outlook on long-term profitability. The other side of the house assures that operational improvements would be self-sustainable if they were fueled by most of the installed base. The dilemma is that while both groups drink from the same source, their goals are generally not compatible. Worse, the middle ground (connectivity chasm) can be the worst situation to be in (Figure 5.1). My experience has been that many organizations end up in the connectivity chasm, but

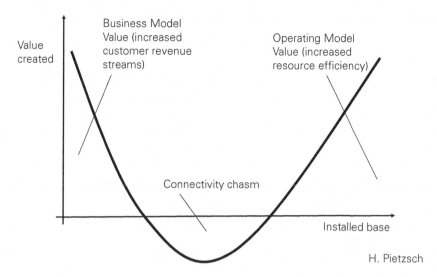

Figure 5.1. The connectivity chasm.

not because they've consciously decided to compromise. They unconsciously enter the valley because the existing and traditionally successful practice of cross-subsidizing is applied to a different game. Resulting scenarios are often similar:

- Innovation and customer demand result in a desirable offering. Pilots and experiences sufficiently justify further product development and go-to-market strategies for stand-alone commercialization.
- Customer willingness to pay paints a profitable picture in some niches but generally not for the core market, which stalls at about 16 percent adoption.
- Managers of the traditional business model realize that bundling the stand-alone innovation with the existing core product makes that product more attractive. Internal cross-subsidizing occurs, and the innovation is no longer explicitly priced or sold.
- Some pockets have reached critical mass and operating model improvements emerge. Operational managers now push for rapid acceleration but lack budgets to carry the weight on their own.
- Traditional competitors catch up, also packaging their core products with "free" innovations.
- Commoditization is taking place, and most customers now expect the solution to be "part of the deal."
- The data-generating technology stack is now large, cross-subsidized, and complex. Everybody wants more data that nobody is willing to pay for. The organization is stuck in the connectivity chasm.

Pitfalls, milestones, and other decision points

Much has been written about the early stages of business model innovation. It's Startup Land. Many industrial B2B players have emulated the playbook. Generally, much thought is given to the location, talent, and culture of the team and undertaking. Often less thought is given to defining and applying the exit criteria. With careers and egos at stake, many endeavors limp along much longer than their viability or synergies might justify. The most obvious advice is for organizations to avoid the edge of the chasm. Few companies can afford to scale solutions that customers aren't willing to pay for. Large industrial players, however, have a long history of running life-cycle solution portfolios that include underperforming elements. Even investors have begun to accept longer cash burn periods in return for network effects or winner-takes-all ecosystems. Nevertheless, exploring the chasm must be a careful and conscious decision. The emergence of cross-subsiding schemes is the most visible sign of being on the edge.

Once in the chasm, organizations often face conditions where competitive pressure and growing commoditization result in an inability to capture the value they created. This can be particularly difficult if the initial platform is neither sticky nor proprietary. Growing an installed base to capture more data that can neither be monetized nor operationally leveraged needs to be a temporary phase.

Few companies seem to have made it into the operating model zone, but the gains can be tremendous. In this scenario, organizations capture enough data across their installed base to sustainably transform their operating model. At this stage, operational gains "pay for" the cost of capturing the information. Customers might no longer pay for explicitly experience value in this scenario. The best-known example is probably the barcode that one can find on any product these days (Figure 5.2). While extremely low tech, with only one data point of information, it has transformed retail supply chains since the 1970s. More recently, a variety of low-cost players in retail, transport, health care, and other areas have mastered data to relentlessly reduce the operating costs of their business.

The innovators' dilemma in action

It took decades for industrial manufacturers to build their current set of capabilities. Sophisticated structures of nested capabilities and offers have allowed them to grow their share of wallet while reducing the owning and operating costs of their equipment. It's a successful model for most customers, delivering predictability in most situations most of the time. Business model innovations are typically rejected by most of the customer base, and revamping an operating model requires a long and expensive march through the chasm. Any choice

Figure 5.2. Product barcode.

requires trade-offs, customer focus, and long-term thinking. These are charac-ter traits that many large industrials have lost in their winning game of synergy, equipment focus, and the pressure of quarterly result.

About Holger Pietzsch

Holger (HoPi) focuses on profitably servitizing and digitizing business mod-els in the capital equipment industry including technologies, aftermarket solu-tions, financial services, rental businesses, performance contracts, and smart goods and services. During his leadership of organizations, teams, and projects around the globe, he has worked with dozens of leading industrial sales and ser-vices businesses. As a cosmopolitan, multilingual professional with fluency in German, English, French, and Spanish, he often acts as a keynote speaker and holds certifications and degrees from universities in the US and in Europe. He can be reached at www.linkedin.com/in/holgerpietzsch/.

SECTION 2

GETTING STARTED AND DESIGNING A SUBSCRIPTION BUSINESS MODEL

Why and How Manufacturers Should Get Started

O VER THE PAST FEW years, subscription business models have penetrated the B2B and industrial worlds. It began with software-as-a-service (SaaS) transitions moving from perpetual software licenses to cloud-based software solutions in the form of a monthly or annual subscription. From there, it moved to product-as-a-service (PaaS) and equipment-as-a-service (EaaS) offers.

It's undeniable that the industrial world will embrace this new type of business and revenue models over time. The trend has already begun, and I've already found over a hundred case studies of industrial subscriptions—and there are many more examples out there.

And yet, many manufacturers have not begun their subscription journey. Although they're late to the game, there's still time to get started and to do this right. Often the resistance to getting started comes from top management who consider subscriptions to be a fad or from the sales teams who resist forcefully in order to avoid cannibalization.

10 reasons why manufacturers should get started with subscriptions today

Here are 10 reasons why industrial companies should get started as soon as possible and include this program in the list of future business priorities:

1 **First-mover advantage does matter.** Many industrial verticals have already begun with subscription business models. Caterpillar and John Deere got first-mover advantage in the large equipment space. PTC established leadership in the industrial IoT area, while Honeywell, Garmin, and Boeing were early adopters in the aerospace business. Being the first manufacturer to launch subscription in a space has its advantages. First, you get to

work with the early adopters among your customers and partners. Second, you experiment before anyone else and forge critical partnerships with the best of the best. Third, and assuming you have some success, you become the reference in your sector. From there, your competitors play catch-up or take a more niche and focused approach in the same vertical. There's room for more than one digital player. But leadership matters in digital, and getting started as soon as possible gives you an edge.

2   **If you don't lead your industry, someone else might.** Your company might not be in a leadership position or willing to be first to market. That's perfectly acceptable. Not leading, however, opens the door to the unknown about who might lead the way. An empty space might become an attractive one for a company with big ambitions, especially if the sector you're in offers access to an attractive profit pool. Jeff Bezos says it best: "Your margin is my opportunity." This is *why* I often advise industrial firms to get started and launch digital innovations without having all their ducks in a row. Don't let someone do it instead of you. Experiment and get better over time.

3   **Large industrial distributors are investing massively.** In electronics and in industrial parts, some large distributors like Avnet, Grainger, MSC, and Fastenal have already made billions in investments in digital transformation. While this is good for industrial sectors, it isn't good for manufacturers who rely on industrial distribution networks to access end users. Trade channels exist for a reason, and they bring value in many ways. Seeing the threat of manufacturers' going direct and selling subscriptions to thousands of end customers, they've acted fast and demonstrated tremendous agility to move into digital areas such as IoT, IT infrastructure and services, digital services, and digital twins. They became the digital connector between manufacturers and the end users with access to tremendous level of data. Amazon Business, Alibaba, and Google Business are also not sitting on their thumbs!

4   **Customers are asking for an OpEx model because of cash constraints.** The impact of the COVID-19 crisis on business will be felt for years to come. The level of commercial debt is at a record high, whereas demand and profit levels are slowly recovering. That puts a cash strain on many businesses and many sectors. The result is a greater focus on cash conservation and optimization. Management consultants report a much greater focus on OpEx business models. They recommend that manufacturers develop a balanced portfolio of business consisting of products, services, software, and data-driven solutions offered in both one-time purchase and recurring forms. As manufacturing firms maintain compliance with the bank covenants, they must become strict about how much CapEx they can spend. They must transfer a portion of their purchases to consumption-based models. On the list of potential candidates are software

purchases and large-ticket items. Therefore, EaaS is a booming area right now. Your firm must be ready to respond with prepackaged subscription offers. You must be ready to respond to RFPs demanding both CapEx and OpEx propositions.

5 **Address segments of customers you never focused on.** That move to a blend of one-time offers and subscription offers can also boost revenue generation. Many manufacturing companies have moved away from fighting on price against low-price players mostly producing in low-cost countries. The race to the bottom can't be won simply by competing on price. The customer segment most likely called "price buyers" or "cost-conscious customers" is given low priority because of low margins, high levels of competitive intensity, and a lack of willingness to pay. Subscriptions can help tailor specific offers to these price-conscious customers, especially considering the trends toward reshoring and local production. Designing a good/better/best subscription offer can certainly provide your sellers an opportunity to sell right-engineered and predictable solutions to these buyers. Well-designed subscriptions can help grow your business by accessing these accounts and responding to their needs for low-cost, low-touch, convenience, and low thrill.

6 **Leverage your installed based today.** One of the strengths of being in manufacturing is knowing products, equipment, and hardware inside and out. You design, produce, sell, and maintain these assets. This is your bread and butter. When did you last count the number of assets in operation around the world? What if you connected these installed assets and the next wave of assets to be installed? Imagine the power of this installed base in terms of spare parts, services, connected services, predictive maintenance, and so forth. This is the first area to pay attention to. You know where the assets are, and you're an expert in your area. Therefore, Schindler, Otis, Caterpillar, and others have spent quite a bit time connecting their installed base. They have data coming in, and they can turn the data into digital innovations.

7 **Escape the price-erosion spiral.** One way to escape the spiral of price erosion or to get out of a price war is to transform your business and revenue models. This strategic move allows you to change the conversation and to focus on other topics: business predictability, CapEx savings, ongoing innovation, the benefits of servitization. This play might not work for all customers, but it's one strategic option you might add to your scenario planning. For large contracts with complex technology requiring software and services, packaging the offer in the form of subscription and an outcome-based component shows that you're confident in your offer and willing to have skin in the game. Performance-based and outcome-based contracts are a good solution to move away from product- and equipment-centric solutions.

8 **Diversify your go-to-market approach.** Traditional manufacturing supply chains include wholesalers, resellers, dealers, and potential sub-dealers. They're a long way from the end user and the consumer. The digital revolution requires deep interactions with them to benefit from the information and data they provide through product usage. It's time for manufacturers to diversify their route to market and to be able to interact freely in their ecosystems, with or without their distribution partners.

9 **Develop greater customer intimacy.** Most industrial companies lack customer intimacy. Unlike in the B2C world, having deep customer knowledge is not in manufacturing companies' DNA. Technology, engineering, and products are more common foundations of the manufacturing mindset. This is a classic case of the chicken and the egg. You need customer intimacy to design your subscription. And your subscription gives you more customer intimacy. The key is to get started even if you don't have the best customer insights. Begin with your internal knowledge and some basic expert interviews/focus groups. Then, over time, accumulate more customer data to refine and grow your subscription offer portfolio.

10 **Develop your customer-driven innovations.** Bottom line: having both a direct relationship with end users and greater customer intimacy feeds your organization's innovation engine. The more you know about usage, misusage, customer pains, customer unmet needs, the more you can provide better and more customer-centric innovations. This is the main benefit of launching and selling subscription models. The subscriber is at the heart of your value proposition and business model. It's a win-win for everyone, including the distribution partners you decide to bring along with you.

So, it's not a matter of whether but when you'll launch a subscription-based offer. It's inevitable. The question now is when you'll do this and how you'll differentiate yourself from your industry peers. It's never too late to innovate. The space might be crowded when you get there—but the essence of a good subscription innovation is the same as every other innovation you've done in the past: customer-centricity, responding to a customer's problem, doing it better than competition, and capturing your share of value. It's been done hundreds of times during past industrial revolutions. Roll up your sleeves, bring the right experts to help you, and get it done now.

10 considerations for successful budgeting and planning of your subscription programs

If you work in sales, marketing, and finance, you spend your time in planning mode. That includes preparing budgets, forecasts, and contingency plans. I've spent countless hours planning and budgeting. We all know that when plans are set, it's hard to change them. We're in tracking mode, spending time calculating variances and explaining gaps. This is a busy time for everyone. So, when's the best time to plan for the launch of a subscription program? I posit that it will be hard to do this in the middle of a planning cycle. Once SG&A plans and cost budgets are set for the fiscal year, it's hard to ask for extra spending and to deviate from agreed-upon plans. It's therefore essential to make sure that we match our subscription launch to the planning and budgeting season. Many things need to be done before you can launch a new subscription offer. Remember that this is somewhat disruptive in many ways for many functions. Selecting the right timing and the right approach for launch is critical to the success of the program. I propose 10 considerations to include in your budget preparation:

1   **Socialize your innovation right now.** If you haven't done so, ensure that everyone's aware of and on board with your recurring revenue innovation plans. That includes sales, marketing, finance, IT, legal, and accounting. They can't discover this at the last minute or in the middle of the fiscal year. You must contact them and explain to them the ins and outs of your innovation. Frankly, you should have done this last summer. But if you haven't done so, schedule some calls ASAP to get in front of the right audience. There's a lot to discuss and refine before you can enter data into your budget. Because recurring opportunities can be disruptive, you must make sure everyone is on board.

2   **Prepare a list of top-priority accounts to target in the first quarter.** Part of the process will be having your total addressable market (TAM) calculated and your sales plan contextualized for the first year within the TAM. Your sales target in volume and value needs to be defined as well as a market-share number. Many executives in the manufacturing world still swear by market-share numbers. So, be ready to have your TAM and your annual sales number ready to calculate that. Next, you need to prepare the pipeline of target accounts to hit the ground running. Depending on the number of salespeople engaged in your innovation go-to-market, you need enough target accounts. The definition of target accounts cannot be left to the salesforce. It needs to come from business development and marketing after a process of account prioritization based on rational criteria and not on gut and intuition.

3   **Calculate the required incentives to compensate trade channels.** If you're working with trade channels today, your sales plan needs to account for them. Do you go direct to end users, or do you go through distributors or resellers? Who owns the transactional relationship for this new recurring revenue offer? This is a sensitive subject that requires lots of discussion with your sales and channel team. Your budget needs to account for distribution incentives or commissions depending on how you're setting the go-to-market strategy. You also need to include a marketing support

budget for them to sell if you go through partners. There's no room for improvisation in this area. This is a ticking time bomb that requires planning, preparation, and candid discussions with existing channel networks.

4 **Get your sales plan, pricing, and margins validated by the right authorities.** For your first budget, all numbers and forecast assumptions need to be validated by the proper authorities. There's a lot of work to do since, generally, this is a new area for most manufacturers. Discussions for traditional offers should go smoothly, although the level of uncertainty is high. For subscriptions, for example, you'll have to get buy-in for all your numbers and calculate new numbers such as annual recurring revenues (ARR), MRR, churn, and LTV. Ask for help from the internal and external experts: pricing, digital services, some of your subscription vendors!

5 **Refine your cost estimates with finance and include standards in the budget.** Because new revenue models are new, this is a challenging task. Defining costs and bills of materials for subscriptions of pay-per-use offers can be tricky. On top of this, because we're potentially discussing digital innovations, calculating standard costs might be difficult for your finance and cost accounting teams. Your offer might not be fully ready or fully scalable yet. You may be unsure about how this new offer might be integrated into your existing IT ecosystem. So, there's a lot of uncertainty, but you must get this done to enter the innovation into your ERP. There's no other choice. Schedule meetings with your development, engineering, and finance teams to review all costs. Anticipate some pushback, but don't take "no" for an answer. You need to know your costs in order to know your margin!

6 **Sit down with finance and IT to make sure your ERP is ready.** The next tough discussion to have with IT and finance is to make sure your ERP system is ready to sell, invoice, and collect. Your innovation might require customized configurations in your ERP. You might have to set up credit card payment capabilities, for instance. There are many things to prepare for. Keep in mind, again, that your finance and IT colleagues may be unfamiliar with recurring revenue offers. They might be surprised by the number of invoices versus the small sales value of each invoice. It's vital for them to understand the intensity required to manage and maintain the back office for subscription innovations. Depending on your annual sales target and number of new accounts, it might be a good idea to begin considering a subscription management platform from the start.

7 **Meet with the accounting team to discuss billing and collecting challenges.** Your current ERP solution might be able to handle a few hundred new customers but not tens of thousands. Your accounting and A/R teams might be able to handle hundreds of new invoices but not tens of thousands. The billing and collecting side of a recurring business is a serious matter for discussion. Not invoicing is not an option. That would essentially

be a freemium model. My recommendation is to delay the launch and make sure you can invoice from day one. Salespeople won't sell your innovation if they're not compensated on it. The implications for budgeting and planning might include adding temporary staff to the accounting and A/R teams to support the launch and bump of new customer setups, additional credit checks, and invoices to create manually or through the ERP.

8   **Make sure you have clear agreement on who should be selling your new offer.** Not every salesperson is cut out to sell digital innovations and recurring business offers. Some might have previous experience in selling services and software. In manufacturing, most will have the mindset of selling equipment or one-time transactions. There are several options to consider for your 2021 budget when it comes to selling models: (1) all salespeople sell everything including your innovation, (2) some salespeople are dedicated to selling innovation in digital and recurring business, or (3) your distributors and resellers do the selling for you. It's essential to pick the right option for your launch and to consider all relevant sales costs in the budget. There's no right answer to this question. I've seen companies go different ways with different levels of success. It depends on the sales maturity of your sales team and the degree of digital maturity of your end customers. Pick the best model for your organization and launch.

9   **Allocate budget for sales training and the development of a playbook.** Depending on the sales model you select, as mentioned in the previous point, you need to have ready all the sales support documents. I call this the sales playbook, which includes value propositions, marketing brochures, value and customer case studies, data sheets, price lists, and so forth. The playbook should be ready to support your launch in year one. Keep in mind that digital and recurring business offers require different marketing tools and messages. Make sure you've allocated a sufficient marketing and promotional budget to support the launch and to reach the proper audience. Having a dedicated and allocated budget for this makes sense.

10 **Consider adding a sales performance incentive fund and special promotional budget.** Finally, allocate some budget for salesforce special incentives, awards, and promotions. Selling new things within a manufacturing traditional organization is hard work. Create special awards for the digital seller of the year, focusing exclusively on achievement for your innovation. It doesn't have to be a large budget. The payback in terms of internal adoption and recognition is high. Remember that your goal is to show success in your first year and to bring the "late majority" on board the digital and recurring business journey.

You understand from these preparation steps that it's best to get started while you're in budgeting mode for the following year. It's essential to have all the parties on board, your systems in place, and your decisions properly supported by funds and resources. Don't improvise or launch your subscription or pay-per-use innovation without the proper preparations. I've seen this time and time again. Your first launch needs to be successful so that you can prepare the next one and then the next one. Failure can't be an option: first impressions matter. There's no ideal time to get started, but there is an optimized timing. Doing this midyear as the business is in full operational mode creates disruption. Doing it when people are discussing plans for the following year is more ideal.

7

Practical Guide to Getting Started with Your Subscription Business Model

U NLESS YOU LIVE IN a cave or under a rock, you know about subscriptions and have subscribed to a few services online. Consider that 126 million Americans are Amazon Prime subscribers. So, for industrial companies and their leaders, the questions become: How do I leverage this new business and revenue model for my manufacturing business? How do I get started?

What do you do first? What's the first move internally and externally? If you haven't begun yet, there's still time to play in the digital space. If you've barely started or only scratched the surface for the past two or three years, it's the right time to accelerate. Consider the following statistics:

- 80 percent of large companies reported piloting significant 4.0 initiatives; only 40 to 50 percent of SMEs (less than 250 employees) said the same (Siemens, 2019).
- More than 50 percent of executives say that when it comes to IoT deployment, they're in the middle of the pack or on par with most of their peers in IoT development (Columbus, 2018).
- From 2018 to 2022, IDC projects that over $6 trillion will be invested in digital transformations (*BusinessWire*, 2019). At the same time, Accenture (2019) reports that only 6 percent of companies have managed to create financial impact from their digital investments.
- Finally, Deloitte (2021) reports that only 14 percent of surveyed C-suite executives declare that they're not confident that their organization is ready to fully harness the changes associated with Industry 4.0.

The heart of getting started: The top executive mandate

Here's a bold statement. Nothing will happen or accelerate until top executives draw a line on the ground and state that this is the goal for the organization. I call this the top executive mandate. It gives direction to the digital teams but also to the support function. For example, on April 28 during a second-quarter fiscal year 2021 conference call with financial analysts, the CEO of Rockwell Automation announced the goal of reaching 10 percent of total sales in the form of annual recurring revenues by 2025. That goal did not go unnoticed by the organization. It put the teams in execution mode and generated a lot of buzz. Putting such goals in place is the best way to stimulate thinking and action when things are stuck in perpetual pilot or conversation mode. Here are other examples and nuggets worth noting.

- **"Vizio Holding Corp.** is ramping up investment in its software business amid growing consumer demand for streaming content. Vizio, which was founded in 2002, earns the bulk of its revenue—about 90%—from selling hardware such as internet-connected TV sets and sound bars, but its software business promises fatter margins. The software unit's profit margin was 73.7% for the quarter ended March 31, substantially higher than Vizio's hardware business, at 10.6%" (Maurer, 2021).
- **"Volkswagen** will ramp up its software, mobility as a service and battery tech to stay competitive in the coming decades, as it and other automakers prepare for the largest transition in personal mobility since the invention of the car. Laying out the company strategy Tuesday, Chief Executive Officer Herbert Diess emphasized a top-to-bottom transformation in everything from manufacturing to revenue streams. If revenue was historically driven by sales of internal combustion engine vehicles, Volkswagen CFO Arno Antlitz said the rest of the decade bring income derived not only from electric vehicle sales, but also software, autonomous driving and even ridesharing. To that end, the company has been busy, planning six battery Gigafactories in Europe and an €800 million ($944 million) hardware platform research and development facility in West Berlin. The company's also beefing up its in-house automotive software arm Cariad, which VW said could generate as much as €1.2 trillion ($1.4 trillion) in revenue by 2030, via subscriptions and other sales" (Alamalhodaei, 2021).
- **Cisco's** "shift to cloud and subscriptions really took off in 2016, when Chuck Robbins took over as CEO. Robbins was an early and vocal evangelist for Cisco becoming a software and subscriptions company, and though the transition had a flattening impact on short-term revenues at first (because they were no longer getting that big up-front hardware cash), it was clear from the get-go that Robbins was committed to taking Cisco on the Subscription Economy

journey. 'We believe we will transition more of our revenues to a software- and subscription-based model and accelerate our shift across our portfolio,' Robbins said in earnings call at the time." "The numbers prove his point. Software subscriptions now make up 78% of Cisco's software revenue, and the company is on track to meet its pledge to have software and services account for 30 percent of its total revenue over the next three years" (Scholes, 2021).

- "Digitization means that experiences and knowledge from manufacturing are shared in real time, both internally and externally and between people and machines. The growth ambitions in the digital area are high, within both Sandvik Manufacturing Solutions and Sandvik Machining Solutions. The 2025 target for the business area segments is to have total sales of SEK 5 billion connected to digital solutions and services. 'It is not a big number for Sandvik as a group, but it is an important area for the future and partly a new position for us,' [Sandvik CEO] Widing says. 'We have a history of innovation, so this is a natural extension of our heritage in engineering'" (Sandvik, 2020).

- Responding to the changing buyer, as well as pressure from their stakeholders, several large vendors announced significant changes to the way they go to market. In the late summer of 2020, Chuck Robbins announced that Cisco would pursue a 100% subscription/consumption business—accelerated due to COVID-19. A few weeks later, Michael Dell announced the same thing for Dell Technologies—and all seven companies within its family of businesses—pushing $92 billion into a recurring business. Later in the year, IBM jettisoned its storied services business to focus on multi cloud, hybrid cloud, AI, and, yes, becoming 100% subscription/consumption. HPE, which has been on the journey for three years with Green Lake, announced that it will be fully there by 2022. (McBain, 2021)

It's not too late to get started. It is, in fact, the right time to do so or to do a major reset. The years 2020 and 2021 were a wakeup call for many large industrial groups. We moved from an era of "digital fad" to one of "digital impact." The COVID-19 crisis has changed the game. The need for short-term impact and for sales growth in the context of depressed demand levels is now greater than ever. If you're behind in your digital journey, the bad news is that you won't be first to market. The good news is that you can learn from others and benefit from the numerous insights publicly available.

The cons of not having started

- You'll face industry leaders and competitors with established commercial offers, an established pilot customer base, and potentially a fully scaled digital business.

- You might face end-use applications that are highly commoditized, with revenue models based on freemium pricing plus revenue sharing based on outcome and performance.
- You must design offers that are more differentiated, and you might face pricing pressure from the get-go.
- You still must do the groundwork and go through the process. Although you might go faster, being a newcomer in a crowded place might make it difficult to rise above the noise and be heard.
- You might not be able to avoid the internal barriers that might delay your readiness. There are still strong internal forces of resistance whether you go slow or fast.

The pros of not having started

- There are insights, benchmarks, and metrics available to help you. I find nuggets and best practices every day.
- You can learn from the successes, mistakes, and failures of others. You're not starting from scratch. In fact, you might be able to hire great talent who've experienced the growing pains.
- You can choose from hundreds of commercially available platforms and software that can accelerate your technological development (IoT, marketplaces, customer success platforms).
- You can select battle-tested consulting offers, whether in digital stack and solutions or in go-to-market strategies.
- You'll benefit for a great adoption and support level from C-suite executives and board members who now have decided to get started and accelerate.

At this stage of advancement of the digital transformation business, I doubt that you've fully gotten started. Most analysts report that anywhere from 85 to 90 percent of firms are conducting some type of digital program. For the sake of this chapter, let's assume you've gotten started but haven't accomplished much in the past two years, and that you're stuck in the zone of good intentions. It's now of question of really getting started! No more promises, theoretical discussions, or boil-the-ocean presentations to upper management. The pressure is real, and you have 45 to 60 days to make a major push to get on the right track. In that context, I propose a series of 10 things or activities to do both internally and externally in the next 45 days.

Five things to do internally (45 days)

You now have your marching orders, your management is pushing for impact, and you have the proper mandate. Before going outside and generating interest from customer and trade partners, there are a few things to focus on inside to get your ducks in a row and prepare your game plan.

Assess what's already being done internally
with your digital or IT teams
and list all digital projects and innovations being worked on today
Depending on the size and nature of your industrial organization, you might have digital activities already launched and ready to be launched. First, create an inventory of all these activities using a series of well-established criteria (internal/external project, funding, business unit, type of innovation, etc.). This list becomes your new best friend in the very short term, as it allows you to evaluate your current digital innovation pipeline. There are other things to do:

- Evaluate the size and nature of your installed based, as we discussed in section 1. That will help with the calculation of your total addressable market. It will also tell you the level of knowledge you have about your end customers. Chances are you're ready to use this list in some divisions, but you'll have to run a mini project to get this program going. Most manufacturing companies tend to ignore the potential of their installed base.
- Quantify the current proportion of your business coming from recurring services, spare parts, and software to establish a base: you need to know where you're starting from. Do you have 5 percent of sales already coming from recurring business models, 10 percent, or more? Study your aftermarket business, your service portfolio, and your software revenues.
- Tie your digital playbook to the low-hanging fruit in digital recurring offerings: digital services (training, maintenance, design, engineering, etc.) and SaaS transition. It's essential to show success and impact in the next 45 to 60 days. By doing so, you gain more time from top management and energize the digital teams to keep going based on initial successes. Your future digital playbook and opportunity pipeline will consist of four classifications, borrowed from Deloitte:

  - The no-brainer zone: easy to implement and high relative business value.
  - The low-hanging-fruit zone: easy to implement and low relative business value.
  - The big-strategic-bets zone: hard to implement and high relative business value
  - The pipeline zone: hard to implement and low relative business value.

- Your digital playbook for the next few months will prioritize these digital initiatives and allocate funds and resources accordingly. For more information about the model, see Deloitte's 2021 report *Designing the Modern Digital Function.*

Create a sense of urgency internally
to accelerate the digital transformation

Your C-suite and other top management might be aware of the need to diversify your business model portfolio and accelerate your digital transformation. Middle management might be aware if the cascading is done according to plan. The sense of urgency loses strength as the messages get distributed in the organization. So you must create a communication campaign to make everyone on the marketing, sales, finance, IT, and customer support teams aware of the need to bring to life subscription business models.

- Bring the outside in with key statistics and reports: there are plenty of well-written reports on digital transformation and how to do it better. Zuora recently published an excellent e-book, *Reaping the Benefit of Industry 4.0.* It's a must-read. If you want some of the best reports, contact me through LinkedIn. You can also search the websites of the largest digital consulting groups.
- Benchmark competitors in your space and assess what they're doing: conduct a quick search of your direct competitors on what their digital transformation looks like and what recent subscription innovations they've launched. The first place to visit is their website and their latest annual report. Next, you can ask your vendors for case studies in your ecosystem.
- Invite experts and thought leaders to internal events and into the C-suite: there's no shortage of thought leaders in the digital space.

Socialize recurring business models and subscriptions
with internal stakeholders

- Meet with your internal leaders to gather all internal nuggets: begin with the service leaders, the software business owners, and the innovation group. Gather all the evidence of recurring business models, previous stories of innovation of subscriptions, and anything they can share on the state of the union. These leaders will be your support system in your quest, as they have a strong interest in growing recurring revenue streams.
- Engage the finance and IT teams: schedule face-to-face time with the financial leaders to help them understand the need to beef up recurring revenues and the implications of doing so. Ask finance representatives to be involved in defining the digital playbook, the long-range digital plans, and the calculation of future cash flow. The role of finance in the subscription world is essential. They need to become allies as soon as possible. The same goes for IT. You might face two situations with the IT group: (1) they reject digital and claim that IT should be in charge, or (2) they embrace digital and want to partner and potentially drive the transformation. I've seen and experienced both sides. It's make-or-break for your digital transformation.

- Schedule one-on-one meetings with business leaders to discuss the state of the business, the strategic priorities, and the appetite for digital diversification: here, too, it might be hit or miss. Some leaders are fully on board and driving their diversification to new business models. These are the early adopters of subscription business models. They're interested in impact and success. Focus on that. Don't bore them with the details, but ask them for help.

Conduct a digital maturity assessment to evaluate your go-to-market process

You can do this on your own or use the consulting company already working with you. They might have their own digital maturity model. If you go on your own, assemble a team to review the assessment and select the right assessment instrument. I can recommend the Zuora Subscription Maturity model or the Simon-Kucher & Partners Digital Monetization Model. Both will serve you well. If you've already begun and are ready to launch your first subscription, I recommend that you do a last check of your subscription pricing strategies by running the Subscription Pricing Readiness Assessment I designed and use with most manufacturing companies.

Conduct an organizational readiness assessment to evaluate your strengths and weaknesses

Most consulting reports published in the last couple of years on the topic of digital transformation focus on cultural readiness. They offer step-by-step processes for evaluating the readiness of your people and processes for a profound digital transformation program. Zuora's Subscribe Strategy Group can also work with you to perform this assessment in preparation for a 90-day push. It's worth the investment early in the process.

Working on these internal activities helps you get ready for market-facing priorities. You might realize that there are serious gaps to address prior to engaging with customers and partners. Many things can be done in parallel. But if your maturity assessment reveals a serious lack of digital capabilities, you'll have to think hard about how to upskill and reskill your team to be credible when interacting with your ecosystem. Many manufacturing firms began too fast and forgot about the cultural dimensions of the transformation. The result is delays, false starts, tensions, and eventually stagnation. The former CDO of Michelin, Eric Chaniot, stated on LinkedIn that "a digital transformation is 95% about humans and 5% about technology." I strongly agree.

Looking ahead to 2021 and beyond, it's not necessarily the technology itself that will make the biggest impact on manufacturers, but rather how well organizations deploy and manage their digital assets. In short, the success of a manufacturer's digital investments hinges on the organization's larger people strategy: recruiting, retaining and reinventing talent as Industry 4.0 unfolds.

—Rocky Subramanian,
SAP North American managing director, Midwest region

Five things to do externally (90 days)

Getting started with your subscription business requires some fundamental changes in go-to-market strategies and how you position your business in your ecosystem. Products are no longer at the heart of your business model. The subscribers are. Your value propositions are based not on ownership models but on usership and consumptions models. This implies that you need to maintain the interest of subscribers over long periods. This is new for most manufacturing companies unless they have a robust source of recurring business coming from services, spare parts, and cloud-base software. There are many aspects to consider. I propose five critical things to do in the first 90 days.

Build your value constellation
and understand the power holders

In the digital world, you must expand your traditional ecosystems. You might have to interact with brand-new players in what is now called a value constellation. Practically stated, a value constellation could draw from multiple ecosystems.

- List all the relevant players in your value constellation: start mapping all relevant players that are critical to your recurring digital innovation. You might have to speak with total strangers and get to know them fast. Why? Because they hold the value and/or have the data you need. Study your value chains and identify the power holders. They might be instrumental in enabling your revenue streams. For example, a provider of security solutions wanted to get into terminal traffic management and leverage the value of dynamic advertising when large numbers of passengers arrive from known destinations. For that, they had to interact with ad agencies, duty-free stores, and digital-billboard providers. They had no knowledge about these companies, and it took a while to establish first contact.
- Identify and prioritize the power holders and their current partnership arrangements.
- Many of these players have already begun their own digital transformations and have forged relationships with your competitors or other digital consultants. If you're just getting started, you're late to the partnership game.
- Assess dominant players and gather all competitive information relevant to your space: you can still make strategic plays in the value constellation, but you'll have to provide great levels of differentiation and uniqueness to show

how different and valuable you are. Maybe you have valuable data or relationships that might make a partnership attractive.

Develop a strategy for existing distribution and channel partners

- Distributors and channel partners play a big role in the manufacturing world. There are many discussions about bypassing distributors and launching subscription offers directly to the end-user base. I consider this a strategic mistake. Your existing distributors can be a powerful force in scaling your subscription business and in reaching the entire marketplace. Subscription "as-a-service" business models also require boots in the field to manage repairs and other service offers. Finally, your back office isn't equipped to manage very large numbers of small transactions dynamically. Bypassing channel partners means a certain level of verticalization and investment in servicing the market. In the context of COVID-19, this may not happen any time soon. The question is, therefore, how to use channel partners to support your subscription push and not whether you go direct or indirect.
- Conduct a distribution-partner segmentation process. Not every distributor will qualify to become a partner for your digital innovations. Some don't see the value or aren't interested because the money isn't there compared with the required investments. Others might be so far behind in technology that it would take them a decade to get there. So, it's essential to segment your distribution base and identify the 10 to 20 percent who might be better suited to getting you started.
- Create a multiyear diffusion and partnership plan. Start with the digitally mature and service-oriented distributors who are value buyers. These are the first in line to test the market and get you started. Then accelerate the diffusion of your subscription offers to other channel partners. Focus on the simple and easy-to-sell subscriptions that don't require high intensity of services and technology enablement. The goal is to reach a good level of market coverage with 40 to 50 percent distribution adoption.
- Develop a strategic toolbox to bring distribution on board (value propositions, TAM analysis, incentives, technology, supply chain): you must develop a subscription playbook and toolbox to make it easy for them to sign up for the program. The toolbox must include technology enablement, incentives, marketing programs, certification and education, and a sales playbook.

Acid test the robustness of your existing digital portfolio and the 12-month pipeline

The first step in your internal assessment is to internally evaluate the quality of the digital innovation pipeline. The second step is to test the quality and attractiveness of your innovations with customers and trade partners. The acid test consists in assessing the degree of customer-problem centricity, the degree of differentiation value, and the level of customer willingness to pay. Ask the digital product owners or marketing/product managers for a quick assessment of each subscription and/or innovation. You could consider doing this in the form of a value blitz or an innovation sprint. In my experience, most innovations will lack this knowledge and might be me-too innovations.

Evaluate the digital pricing strategies for your first subscriptions

Although you're getting started or figuring out how to do so, you might already have subscriptions in place across your business units (SaaS, for example). Some subscriptions might be ready for launch in the next few months. Have a dedicated process for reviewing the pricing strategies and tactics for these subscriptions. If nothing's available, hold preliminary discussions about what needs to be done in subscription pricing, how pricing will be set, and by whom. There are many examples of manufacturers that launched subscription opportunities with pricing as an afterthought. Most of these subscriptions were priced based on cost only and/or on being given away for free until pricing was ready. This isn't a good way to begin. There are enough sources of knowledge about subscription pricing that can help you have intelligent discussions on what needs to be done. Spend the time to find them by visiting the Zuora website, the Profit-Well website, Kyle Poyar's blog, or by doing a Google doc search.

Design a first digital roadmap based on your initial 45-day analysis

These 90 days are essential in gathering all the appropriate input to get you started. Of course, you must show short-term impact, so you need to do things in parallel. The first four external things to do focus on gathering customer needs and validating attractiveness and willingness to pay. You're gathering information through assessment of your go-to-market maturity, your subscription-pricing readiness, and the robustness of your pipeline. Now, you're ready to prioritize and select what to do first and what to invest on.

- Prioritize the launch sequence for the next six months, focusing on impact: the digital team is ready to place initiative on a roadmap based on maturity, attractiveness, and readiness. You can also allocate short-term resources to invest to ensure that the pipeline of launches can be executed from both a technology and a business perspective.
- Revisit pricing of these opportunities by conducting value-based and digital pricing blitzes: invest in additional value-based pricing and subscription pricing activities to ensure that the pricing is well positioned to compete in the market while capturing a fair share of customer value.
- Develop a pilot-project strategy to avoid pilot purgatory: a critical part of your six-month plan is to get ready to go through the pilot process. Most

customers will ask for a pilot that can take from six to 18 months. Select a portfolio of subscription innovations with some that can be launched quickly and others that might need to go through a pilot. Be ready with a pilot-management process to accelerate the transition from pilot to scaling.

You now have 10 things to do to get started. Managing the internal and external in parallel with the support from a digital team builds a strong foundation for the future of your digital transformation and your subcription plans. It might sound like a lot of work. It is a lot of work. But this is what you need to get started on the right foot.

The six categories of digital innovations to get started

Many manufacturing executives ask me what innovation to start with and what subscription offer to start with. There's no easy answer to this question. I often answer by telling them to look at their competitors and what they're doing. I encourage them to study the needs of their customers. Finally, I offer a list of standard digital innovations that can take the form of a subscription or usage-based business model. This is very much in line with Mohan Subramanian's (2021) thoughts, recently published in the *Harvard Business Review*. He proposes four tiers of digital transformation innovation: operational efficiencies, advanced operational efficiencies, data-driven services from the value chains, and, finally, data-driven innovations from digital platforms. This approach implies a sequential and maturity-based innovation development process. From my perspective, there are six categories, which I rank in order of priority and difficulty, that I recommend considering when thinking of subscription business models.

1   **Internal efficiency opportunities.** Many manufacturing companies start inside before going outside. They test and experiment with digital solutions in their own asset base. For example, Caterpillar and Scania equipped over 500,000 pieces of equipment with sensors and learned how to leverage the data internally before offering connected products and services to dealers. Schindler also installed their predictive maintenance solutions in 100,000 elevators to optimize their services solutions before packaging subscriptions for installers and repair companies. The goal of starting internally is to learn, to test, and to design the best possible digital innovation for the market. But it's also to gain in efficiencies internally and prepare a strong business case. Remember that if you're a manufacturer and operate assets, your customer might ask you: "Have you tried your solution internally, and, if yes, what were the savings?" You need to have this answer ready!

For many companies, digital transformation has been accelerated due to a response to the global pandemic. Companies are also keenly aware of the need to reduce waste, focus on process improvement, and increase operating rigor. Solutions that safely connect workers to the enterprise are powerful drivers to enable business continuity and growth in 2021.

—Pat Byrne, GE Digital CEO

2 **Digital and connected services.** A second route to subscriptions is to focus on those that support the digital business. These can be existing services sold up front in a contract and repackaged in the form of monthly or annual subscriptions. They include maintenance, warranties, online condition-based monitoring, remote customer support, training, engineering services, and design services. They can be sold via subscriptions or integrated as part of a good/better/best PaaS packaging strategy. During the COVD-19 crisis, we've seen an explosion of subscription services sold in augmented reality (AR) solutions for remote support/guidance and for remote augmented training. The easiest way to begin is by focusing on services and getting internal teams ready to understand customer and subscribers much better. I believe this is a prerequisite to the next steps of the subscription maturity journey.

We needed to move from transactional to recurring for many parts of our digital portfolio. For an expanding range of digital offerings, more and more customers are buying into the idea of continually experiencing new functionalities, new features, new capabilities, and specifically, enhanced added value over time.

—Rahma Samow,
Head of Siemens Healthineers Digital Health Global Sales,
Marketing and Digital Go-to-Market

3 **Software-as-a-service (SaaS).** Many manufacturers already offer cloud-based software in the form of SaaS subscriptions. The trend toward subscription is evident in the forecast, as IDC expects that, in 2024, 66 percent of all software revenue will be purchased with a subscription business model, and this trend is seeing a CAGR of 14.4% (Thomason, 2020). There are two types of SaaS players. The first relates to pure SaaS players, where software solutions are created in the cloud, for the cloud, and priced in the form of a subscription. The second type are traditional companies transitioning their on-premises, perpetual software licenses to the SaaS model. This is where traditionally we find the manufacturing business. Today, industrial players can be in both categories at the same time. In fact, many still operate in the on-premises world while also developing SaaS offers.

Bottom line: the portion of software sales in the sales portfolio of manufacturing is bound to increase significantly over the next decades. Siemens Digital Factory generates over 15 billion euros in software sales per year.

> Honeywell wants software to be a bigger portion of its business and says about 10% of total sales are derived from software. That isn't a small amount of money; the company generated nearly $37 billion in sales last year. For investors interested in the potential of Forge, Honeywell says software sales are growing faster and earning higher profit margins than the rest of Honeywell's business. (Root, 2020)

4   Connected products and services (PaaS, EaaS, HaaS, DaaS).

Over the past decade, manufacturers have made significant investments in digitally equipping and instrumenting their products and the plants that produced them. The goal is to search for the most promising IoT-powered use cases that would create value and return on investment for themselves, their partners, and their customers. Despite years of work and large investments, manufacturers have yet to supercharge margins by meeting the mandate to add value for customers who expect connected products, equipment, and devices to be more than a gadget. The technology side is taking care of itself. For many industrial companies, with billions of installed sensors, the issue is that they're drowning in volumes of connected-product data that sit in cloud repositories and data lakes, without generating meaningful insights and action and without being monetized into recurring revenue streams. Many manufactures have spent their initial efforts, and the best part of the last five years, investing in data collection, in real-time monitoring, data analytics, and massive aftersales operations. This is a very solid basis for the next step to get started with monetization and value capture. Manufacturers must now focus on delivering advanced connected outcomes. It's time for them to transform their investments into true "as-a-service" providers with actions that improve business outcomes such as higher product uptime, increased ancillary service opportunities, exceptional experiences, and greater customer satisfaction. They can do this by pairing connected products, services, and information with enterprise capabilities that digitally engage and execute work—actions and interactions—across any operational, technical, or even mobile boundaries at industrial scale.

This category is the heart of manufacturing digital transformation. Over the past 10 years, massive investments were made in IoT and IIoT to capture the benefits of predictive maintenance and asset optimization. New business models have been invented: product-as-a-service, equipment-as-a-service, device-as-a-service, and other X-as-a-service opportunities. Some experts refer to this as anything-as-a-service, where customers buy a subscription for a product, a piece of equipment, a building, or an entire plant.

The benefits of this model are clear: no CapEx requirement, longer product life cycles, all-inclusive subscriptions, and outcome guarantees.

> As IIoT sensors produce 1.44 billion data points per plant per day, IT/OT integration is critical to improving operational efficiency while accelerating success through digital-transformation initiatives.
>
> —Keith Higgins,
> Rockwell Automation, vice president of digital transformation

5 **APIs and data.** Cloud APIs have transformed the technology industry and, with it, our digital economy. By enabling SaaS and other cloud-based applications to talk to each other easily and securely, cloud APIs have vastly expanded the value of these applications to users. Using new edge-to-cloud solutions with built-in IIoT APIs, these companies will be able to connect these assets to the cloud almost as easily as if this equipment were a cloud-based application. In fact, by plugging a low-cost IoT gateway with these Industrial IoT APIs in to their industrial equipment, they'll be able to deploy industrial IoT applications that allow them to remotely monitor, maintain, and control this equipment. Then, using these industrial IoT applications, they can lower equipment downtime, reduce maintenance costs, launch new equipment-as-a-service business models, and innovate faster. Industrial companies have been trying to connect their assets to the cloud for years, but they've been stymied by the complexity, time, and expense involved in doing so. By giving a voice to billions of pieces of industrial equipment, these industrial IoT APIs will help bring about the productivity, sustainability, and other benefits that Industry 4.0 has long promised.

> 2021 will be the year industrial companies begin seeing their markets transformed by APIs, as more of these companies begin using Industrial IoT APIs to enable industrial air compressors, water heaters, storage tanks and other industrial assets to talk to the cloud.
>
> —Olivier Pauzet,
> SVP of IoT products and solutions at Sierra Wireless

6 **Platform and marketplaces.** The last area of potential subscription innovations for manufacturers is that of digital platform and marketplaces. In the B2C world, we've witnessed the exploding number of digital platforms and e-commerce platforms, including the birth of some of the largest digital unicorns in the world. Industrial companies also can have the ambition to create similar vertical-based digital platforms to connect entire ecosystems. This is the most advanced digital business model there is. Platform pricing can take many forms. Marketplaces are also designed to be

self-sustaining ecosystems offering buyers and sellers an opportunity to transact with and learn from each other.

Companies getting started do not start right off the bat with the most advanced and difficult digital opportunity: platform and marketplaces. They begin with SaaS and connected services to gain the necessary customer intimacy and the experience needed to execute well. They also need to make sure that they bring distribution partners on board by focusing on simple subscription offers. At the same time, they develop their PaaS or EaaS offers. It's not unusual to open multiple fronts when getting started or when accelerating your subscription journey.

The prerequisites to a successful subscription business strategy

When getting started, you must reinforce some of the prerequisites of a successful transition to the subscription world. I list five, but there might be more.

1   **Monetization mindset.** Getting started or accelerating cannot happen without a strong monetization mindset. This means focusing on how to extract revenue streams from digital innovations and on how to invoice from day one when you launch your subscription. Monetization also means paying attention to pricing

2   **Service orientation.** The foundation of a digital transformation is the ability to move from a product-centric to a service-centric business model. Moving to the "as-a-service" world means having a service culture and a dedicated service organization. Look at your manufacturing business today and gauge your current level of service orientation. Who'll maintain and service the assets that belong to you and that are in place in your customer process? You and your service technicians? Your distributors? Maybe a third party?

3   **Customer experience.** In the subscription business, the subscriber is king. We acquire them at a cost and then retain them to capture a maximum of their expected lifetime value. Success in the subscription business means focusing on the ability to renew subscribers, to upsell them, and to empower them to manage their destiny. We all know that manufacturers are just getting started with marketing programs focused on experience. They have a long way to go.

4   **The right technology engine.** You might be able to do things manually for a while. But your back office needs automation as soon as possible to avoid manual activities and monitor and track customer usage. For that, your legacy IT infrastructure needs to be complemented with licensing and entitlement software to meter and track usage. You also need a comprehensive subscription engine to invoice your customers and collect payments. A

subscription engine removes all manual processes and connects seamlessly with your CRM and ERP systems. It simplifies the internal experience for finance, accounting, and sales operations while empowering subscribers to freely manage their subscriptions.

5 **Speed and agility.** Finally, the subscription world is not the traditional manufacturing world. Things move fast in the digital world. You might face new competitors that were born in the digital world. You also need to iterate and experiment quickly. This means that your digital incubators, digital factories, and other startup studios must learn to be agile and fast. It also means that your go-to-market speed needs to improve.

This chapter focused on what to do first in the first 45 days, what to get started with, and what muscles to build to be successful. Getting started is all about putting the organization in action mode and beginning to plug away. I hope you've learned a few things to add to your short-term roadmap. Remember that building a subscription business is a team sport. You'll need to pull from many sides of the organization to be successful.

References

Accenture. (2019). *Your business as-a-service: Putting the right pieces in place.* www.accenture.com/_acnmedia/PDF-119/Accenture-As-a-Service-Business-Acceleration.pdf

Alamalhodaei, A. (2021). Volkswagen's new business strategy puts software and autonomous driving front and center. *TechCrunch,* July 13. https://techcrunch.com/2021/07/13/volkswagens-new-business-strategy-puts-software-and-autonomous-driving-front-and-center/

BusinessWire. (2019, April 24). Businesses will spend nearly $1.2 trillion on digital transformation this year as they seek an edge in the digital economy, according to a new IDC spending guide. www.businesswire.com/news/home/20190424005113/en/Businesses-Spend-1.2-Trillion

Columbus, L. (2018). The state of IoT intelligence, 2018. *Forbes,* November 4. www.forbes.com/sites/louiscolumbus/2018/11/04/the-state-of-iot-intelligence-2018/

Deloitte Development LLC. (2021). *Designing the modern digital function.* www2.deloitte.com/content/dam/insights/us/articles/6810_TMT-Digital-transformation-series-no-15/DI_TMT-digital-transformation-series-no.15.pdf

Maurer, M. (2021). Vizio looks to boost software business with IPO cash. *Wall Street Journal,* June 23. www.wsj.com/articles/vizio-looks-to-boost-software-business-with-ipo-cash-11624440601

McBain, J. (2021). *What I see coming for the channel: 2021.* Forrester, January 21. www.forrester.com/blogs/what-i-see-coming
-for-the-channel-2021/

Rockwell Automation, Inc. (ROK) CEO Blake Moret on Q2 2021 results: Earnings call transcript. (2021, April 28). *Seeking Alpha,*
https://seekingalpha.com/article/4422123-rockwell-automation
-inc-rok-ceo-blake-moret-on-q2-2021-results-earnings-call-transcript

Root, A. (2020). Honeywell Forge to sell A.I. solutions to building operators. *Barron's,* February 26. www.barrons.com/articles/honeywell
-forge-to-sell-a-i-solutions-to-building-operators-51582726851

Sandvik. (2020, November). Increased focus on digital solutions.
www.home.sandvik/se/stories/articles/2020/11
/stefan-widing-on-industry-4.0/

Scholes, L. (2021). The cloudification of Cisco. *Subscribed,* May 13.
www.subscribed.com/read/news-and-editorial
/the-cloudification-of-cisco

Siemens. (2019). *Countdown to the tipping point for Industry 4.0: Practical steps for manufacturers to gain competitive advantage from Industry 4.0 investment.* https://assets.new.siemens.com/siemens/assets/api
/uuid:fb9d1e59-4d83-41ab-af28-3ef298710d43/countdown-to
-the-tipping-point-for-industry-4-sfs-whitepaper-en.pdf

Subramanian, M. (2021). The 4 tiers of digital transformation. *Harvard Business Review,* September 21. https://hbr.org/amp/2021/09
/the-4-tiers-of-digital-transformation

Thomason, M. (2020). *Worldwide software license, maintenance, and subscription forecast, 2020–2024.* IDC, July.
www.idc.com/getdoc.jsp?containerId=US46248121

Eight Considerations for Managing a Subscription Business Model in an Industrial Business

GARTNER AND ZUORA REPORT that 70 percent of companies have deployed, or are considering deploying, a subscription business model. The subscription economy is taking the business world by storm. But designing and launching a subscription business model doesn't mean automatic success. You can have the best design phase, but you still have to make sure that an innovative business model succeeds in traditional ownership-centric cultures. Even in B2C and the pure SaaS (software-as-a-service) world, many subscription-centric startups fail or don't scale well. There's no guarantee of success for anyone. In the industrial world, I propose that the key to success is designing your subscription business model with scaling and managing in mind within your traditional business model. I also encourage you to learn from the best practices in B2C and the SaaS world. Below are eight key considerations that can help you manage and scale your subscription model.

1   **Engage your support functions as soon as possible.** Some internal functions are critical for the integrating and scaling of your subscription business model. First, finance needs to be trained on the open/CapEx trade-offs and the implications for revenue recognition and cash flow. Finance also needs to embrace new financial KPIs. IT needs to understand the need to manage a subscription management engine that's fully integrated into existing ERP and CRM platforms. IT also needs to be able to handle a greater volume of customers and transactions. Legal teams need to focus on new general sales conditions and service contracts related to a recurring business model. Finally, and maybe most challenging, sales needs to

grasp the challenge of selling recurring offers instead of or in complement to industrial products. There's a need for alignment and proper preparation.

2 **Think location, location, location.** By location I mean position in the organization during the design, scaling, and post-scaling efforts. Some industrial companies manage subscription-focused innovations in incubators as part of digital transformations. Others incubate new business models within the core business as part of the innovation pipeline. Finally, I've found many cases where industrial companies acquire or launch subscription-rich startups and keep them totally separate from the core business. There's no right or wrong. All options have implications based on your culture.

3 **Focus on experience and simplicity.** Recurring and subscription business models focus heavily on the user. The subscriber is at the center of the business model. Therefore, we need to keep things simple for the user across the board. Simplicity means ease of use, transparent prices, simple choices in solution sets, ease of making changes to your subscriptions structure and model, and so forth. Users expect progressive disclosure; they can't be guessing or jumping through multiple screens to find basic information.

4 **Leverage the value of the system and innovate.** Industrial companies have two advantages versus digital natives: they have a large installed based, and they truly understand the hardware/software interface. That's gold! With access to product data and subscription behaviors, industrial natives are powerfully positioned to innovate and create the next generation of digital services and products. It's amazing what can be learned from managing hundreds of users and how they consume your offer.

5 **Communicate early on the different KPIs and what defines success.** Managing a subscription business model means educating your internal stakeholders on the critical KPIs (key performance indicators). At a recent Zuora Institute event, I discovered many new acronyms:
   - CAC—Customer acquisition cost
   - ARR—Annual recurring revenue
   - MRR—Monthly recurring revenue
   - ACV—Annual contract value
   - ARPU—Average revenue per user
   - CLV—Customer lifetime value

6 **Educate your team early on about which KPIs are important and which make a subscription business successful.**

7 **Anticipate channel conflicts and synergies.** The richness of a subscription business model lies in the ability to have a direct relationship with customers and end users. If your business relies on channel partners, make sure to manage potential objections and conflicts carefully. Easier said than done. Some companies (e.g., Caterpillar and Schneider Electric) have found ways to segment their channel partners and jointly go to market with those

who are most progressive. Other partners might simply get compensated as part of the existing relationship. With the emergence of the D2C (direct-to-consumer model), the position of traditional channel partners is potentially sensitive as you engage directly with their customers. Prepare well during the design phase.

8   **Embrace go-to-market best practices from the SaaS world and B2C.** Don't reinvent the wheel when it comes to pricing and packaging your subscriptions. There are best practices and knowledge nuggets you can use from the B2C SaaS world. There are also pitfalls to avoid (Liozu, 2019). For example, the good/better/best subscription package is by far the most frequently adopted. Many industrial companies lack the budgets and capabilities required to conduct deep customer research to inform their subscription model. Learn from the success and failure of others!

Think about your subscription business model in the context of the maturity model: from Zuora's The Subscribe Institute Event, I learned that there's also a subscription maturity model (Zuora, 2021). Most companies go through the process of learning and becoming more mature. When designing your subscription business model, keep this in mind and adopt the crawl-walk-run methodology. The key is to avoid what Zuora calls the Wild West of subscription, where "the focus is on signing up new subscribers above all else, not on retention. Metrics are backward looking and rooted in traditional focus of shipping products. Where systems exist, they are disparate and support only a reactive management of the business. Pricing and packaging is haphazard (Konary, n.d.)." By injecting design thinking and best practices early in the process, you might be able to leapfrog to more advanced stages.

The subscription tsunami is real. This book offers a number of case studies of subscription models in industrial companies and good examples of subscription-based innovations. Remember that industrial companies will not transition to 100 percent subscription! It'll be a blend of transactional and recurring sales. Any industrial company that can profitably reach 20 to 30 percent of their total sales in a recurring format is a true champion! The challenge is managing multiple business models at once and the ability to adapt for each model. Subscription business models don't scale well without applying the key considerations listed; nor can they be managed by dozens of individuals who manually process thousands of billing and collection transactions. Consider investing in subscription management software and pick the right one for your business. Welcome to the subscription economy!

The three pillars of industrial subscription

Over the next five years, consultants and experts alike project that trillions of dollars will be generated from digital innovations in the industrial space.

Innovations in SaaS, PaaS, IIoT, predictive maintenance, automation, smart assets, and AR/VR will lead to the development of new subscription models and to an increase in manufacturers' recurring revenue levels. There are three pillars for gauging the attractiveness of a subscription offer: the subscription differentiation versus traditional on-time purchase offers, the subscription pricing strategy, and the subscription experience. In the B2C world, providers of subscription offers are experiencing tremendous levels of competition leading to accelerated commoditization and price wars. For them, the source of critical differentiation mostly comes from the subscription experience. To a certain extent, this level of competitiveness has entered the IoT space in recent years. But manufacturers still benefit from product and pricing differentiation. They can design, develop, and execute subscriber-centric offers focused on true differentiation. Let's review how these pillars come in to play for manufacturers willing to accelerate their transition to recurring business models.

Product differentiation

The product is the subscription, which might contain hardware, software, services, and a great overall experience. When designing and testing their subscription offer, manufacturers must collect basic customer insights as they would do for any innovation program. A subscription offer is truly differentiated when it focuses on the following:

- **Solving customer problems and addressing user pains: that's essential.** What's happening with the customer that they might need to consider a new business model? Is it purely a need for more OpEx-based procurement to protect cash? Are they struggling with the integration of product and software? Are they stuck in the perpetual software license world? A good value proposition for a subscription focuses on three customer pains or problems. These must be burning platforms for change.
- **Creating value for all users.** When solving these burning problems or pains, it's essential to quantify the value of what manufacturers can do for their customers. What does it mean to move to a recurring business model in terms of dollars and cents? Remember that a subscription isn't a leasing plan! There are, of course, financial savings but also considerations around unlimited upgrades, maintenance, training, software, and so on.
- **A win-win with distributors and partners.** In the manufacturing world, designing a subscription offer without considering partners is a strategic mistake. Subscription business models need to consider strategic partners and existing distribution. Anything other than a win-win will lead to conflicts and potential failure.
- **Energizing digital monetization and boost sales.** Finally, a differentiated subscription offer must stimulate sales and energize sales teams. With proper segmentation up front, cannibalization can be minimized, and

the sales team can focus on customer segments that truly need and value a consumption-based purchase.

Because manufacturers can still differentiate themselves, they must spend enough time designing and testing their recurring business model, value proposition, and revenue model. The adage of "garbage in, garbage out" still holds true here.

Pricing strategy

This is the second pillar of a subscription offer, and a critical one. Manufacturers often lack skills in monetizing their digital innovations and in pricing them based on value, not cost. Many lack a pricing team, and the result is either a freemium model or a cost-based subscription offer. Pricing is an essential part of your subscription business model. There are four considerations to integrate in your subscription pricing development:

- **Design and package your pricing based on your users' needs and preferences.** Selecting the right pricing package based on your customer segmentation is key. Some of your customers want an all-inclusive subscription package; others might prefer a stripped-down version of the offer. Select the good/better/best packaging option. If you have very different buying personas, select a functional packaging option. One size does not fit all!
- **Build the right pricing model drawing from best-in-class digital champions.** Once your package is defined and armed with the right value metric for each segment, you can think about a fully variable pricing model, a fully fixed model, or a hybrid. Here, as well, there are many options. Pricing packaging and pricing models must be aligned and simple for the customer to grasp.
- **Focus pricing on customer lifetime value.** In the subscription world, the concept of lifetime value (LTV) is very important. Make sure to design your pricing with both customer acquisition and renewal in mind. The longer customers stay with you, the better for your future cash-flow plans.
- **Reward partners and evangelists with proper and transparent incentives.** Subscriptions are designed with the ecosystem in mind. Partners and distributors play a key role in execution success. Therefore, subscriptions must be differentiated and create incremental financial value. That value can then be shared with critical partners.

Pricing is generally an area where manufacturers lack maturity. Concepts of value-based pricing, willingness to pay, and value pool sharing are rarely discussed or integrated in the design of their recurring business models. Pricing is important to the subscriber experience. It needs to be simple to find and understand, transparent and complete, and predictable over time. Section 3 of this book focuses on subscription-based pricing. Be ready for much more content.

Subscription experience

The third pillar of a great subscription is the overall experience for both the manufacturers' internal stakeholders and for distributors and customers. In the B2C world, experience has become a number-one focus. This is now the battle-ground in the media, entertainment, and music worlds, for example. Because competition is fierce and pricing is eroding over time, it's the last area of true differentiation. In manufacturing, the experience is equally important, especially when combined with product differentiation and solid pricing strategies. Manufacturers are paying more and more attention to experience in customer and technical support. They must allocate the same attention and energy in designing a great subscription experience. One way to do this is to partner with the best subscription platform solution. In the subscription world, the subscriber is at the center of the business model. Because manufacturers are not born in the digital world where experience is part of the DNA, the internal experience is as important.

A superior experience …

- **empowers manufacturers to experiment and launch quick customer pilots.** It's the classic case of the chicken and the egg. Without a subscription engine, manufacturers can't launch and experiment with their customers. But without a subscription ready to launch, they can't justify the implementation of a subscription engine! I recommend focusing on having the right engine in place to avoid bad internal experiences, delays in launching digital innovations, and too much manual work. Remember that subscriptions are part of the new normal! They'll happen one way or another. Select the right technology partner, deploy the subscription engine focus on superior subscription, and get to work!
- **enables scaling with an automated back office.** Part of the execution plan for your digital innovations is to scale fast and begin invoicing from day one. Manufacturers struggle with the scaling process for many reasons. One is the lack of automation in their back office because they lack the proper tool. They need to select a subscription engine that connects with other IT components as well as one that can handle the diversity in pricing models and distributor relationships. Remember that it takes money to make money!
- **allows subscribers to make as many changes as possible.** From the subscriber's perspective, manufacturers must remember that B2B users are also B2C consumers! They understand what a subscription is, and they want to benefit from the same agility and flexibility they do in their personal

lives. They want to be empowered to manage their subscriptions as they see fit. That includes upgrading, downgrading, growing, suspending, and so forth. They don't want to call your sales reps each time they want to make a change. A bad subscription experience leads to higher customer churn.

- **displays subscription pricing with a simple and transparent enrollment process.** Finally, manufacturers need to embrace the best practices in pricing from the B2C world. They need to make their pricing easy to find with a simple landing page and without having to jump through hoops to subscribe. Too often, we see subscription offers on manufacturing companies' website that state "contact your sales rep to buy." This isn't acceptable in a world where the customer wants to be free and empowered.

The combination of product differentiation, value-based pricing strategies, and superior subscription experience is powerful. All three are needed to succeed in the recurring business world. Some manufacturers have hired experts from the B2C and SaaS worlds to help get all three pillars right. Others rely on marketing and pricing consultants—a good way to begin. The urgency is to develop internal capabilities to be able to do this on their own and systematically. One critical piece of the puzzle is to select a subscription management platform that can manage all three pillars when you reach the scaling phase of your growth plan. The right platform will manage and deliver superior performance on three pillars. You'll need to fight the not-invented-here (NIH) syndrome, which is quite prevalent in large industrial and engineering firms: "We have engineers and developers. We can our own platform." No comment!

References

Konary, A. (n.d.). 5 stages of the subscription business model. Zuora. www.zuora.com/guides/5-stages-subscription-business-model/

Liozu, S. (2019). Considering a subscription model? Avoid these rookie mistakes. *Industry Week,* June 18. www.industryweek.com/leadership/article/22027763 /considering-a-subscription-model-avoid-these-rookie-mistakes

Zuora. (2021). Subscription Business Maturity Model. www.zuora.com/get/subscription-business-maturity-model/

9

Top 10 Tips for a Successful Equipment-as-a-Service Business Model

Guneet Singh Bedi

T HE "AS-A-SERVICE" BUSINESS MODEL is pioneered and well adopted by the software industry, dubbed software-as-a-service (SaaS). Examples of industrial and hardware subscriptions are emerging daily. Instead of buying assets outright, end customers of equipment get the right to use and pay on some metric of outcome or usage. In the context of equipment, this is usually not a pure lease or rental model and nearly always includes elements of servicing, repair, consumables, and in some cases even outcome (service level agreement [SLA]/uptime/performance) guarantees. This model, commonly known as equipment-as-a-service (EaaS), provides higher and predictable revenues. It's no surprise that operations and maintenance (O&M) of an asset, even more in industrial environments, is 80 percent or more of the total cost of ownership. This model also allows strengthening customer intimacy, as it leads to an ongoing relationship with multiple touchpoints between end customers, servicers, and manufacturers with often shared business outcomes. EaaS is a new concept that requires a lot of change management and a particular attention to up-front offer design. This can disrupt the "way of working" with your market and within your organization while defending against a range of nontraditional competitors drawn in by the democratization of the marketplace.

Working with numerous industrial companies in EaaS, I've developed a list of key learnings for use in the design of EaaS business and revenue models. Remember that this is a journey and that, depending on your industry and organizational culture, there might be other lessons you'll learn along the way.

Here are **10 of my learnings** as "Tips" from organizations that have gone through this journey.

1. Find out what your market and customers need

Let me begin with the journey my company took; and before anything else, came a "voice of the customer" study. Often, we build a hammer and then everything looks like a nail. EaaS wasn't launched until qualitative and quantitative research was complete. More than 200 senior executives from US and German industrial organizations were highlighted: 63 percent wanted to offer enhanced products/services, 48 percent wanted to explore different payment terms, and 50 percent of German companies wanted to change their business models. So, we knew that EaaS had a market.

It's essential to listen and understand whether a "pay-per-use" model and OpEx is relevant for your market. EaaS isn't just for businesses in distress, or for small companies. You might be successful and growing, but are your customers' needs fundamentally changing? Do you understand the "voice of the customer" and fully understand their reasoning?

While EaaS may mean less revenue up front, it can offer more stability and predictability in the long term. You open more revenue opportunities throughout the product life cycle. For example, you could adopt a schedule so that you can plan any downtime for when it's least disruptive, or proactively stay in touch with customers to predict maintenance needs or faults. Further, you can work to create additional equipment performance enhancements or improved equipment designs based on data you obtain from customers. All this information comes from the "voice" of your customer.

2. Value discovery is key to identifying and quantifying the right value pools

It's imperative to agree with customers on the value created besides a pure CapEx to OpEx focus. EaaS isn't just leasing, and operators of the equipment will adopt pay-per-use usually if it includes all O&M costs, and in some cases also the costs of consumables and associated SLA warrantability. The first step is to identify value pools associated with better equipment use. Common value pools include unplanned downtime reduction, lower cost of repair, new recurring revenues, outcome-based gain-share, longer asset life cycle, reduce planned downtime, and so on.

The second step is to quantify the economic value associated with these value pools and perform professional pricing analysis on value-based calculation of commercials. This isn't always easy, since customers may not want to share sensitive operational data. A provider of manufacturing automation solutions solved this problem by working through a series of studies with potential customers to build a value-calculation tool that pooled data from those studies, without disclosing individual company data. Another way to derive value is through a detailed total cost analysis, comparing the costs of purchase and ownership with those of a subscription. A total cost analysis should identify the financial breakeven time for a traditional purchase agreement, which is important for setting EaaS contract terms. It also uncovers the lifetime ownership costs a supplier would pay if they moved to a service model.

Calculate customer-specific price points based on a realistic analysis of the life-cycle costs. These include the direct and indirect costs of the infrastructure over its life cycle. This takes CapEx and OpEx into account, as well as management, administration, and overhead. This allows a business to estimate the cost for subscription-based models.

3. Get intimate knowledge of the "equipment" operations and maintenance

EaaS promises for end customers the replacing of significant up-front costs with ongoing costs on equipment usage, which are backed by progressive approaches that warrant particular outcomes. Consequently, manufacturers will have to move away from a "make, sell, ship, forget" mindset to a much more flexible "make, sell, own, operate, and remember" and function-on-demand. For distributors and service providers, EaaS allows offering vendor-agnostic and brownfield (including legacy equipment not with the latest instrumentation) as-a-service offers that allow higher equipment performance, fixed maintenance budget guarantees, and higher uptime.

So, staying relevant with EaaS requires a shift to a "service first" mentality, encapsulated in intimate knowledge of the operations and usage of your equipment. EaaS should not only leverage digital services to make assets work harder and smarter but also offer the cost certainty that chief financial officers dream about. Remember to investigate specialty insurance and guarantees with EaaS and financing models that cater to "as-a-service" models.

A simple example: if, as a coffee machine manufacturer, you want to enable cafés with a coffee-as-a-service model, you need to cover all repairs and maintenance, take responsibility for the machine's running without interruption, and maybe include coffee beans in the price per cup. This setup unlocks various value pools: new and predictable recurring revenues, lower cost of repair for manufacturer while reducing unplanned downtime (even with possible uptime guarantees), fixed maintenance costs, and aligning cost of goods sold (COGS) with revenues without up-front CapEx for customers (the café). Intangibles of peace of mind for a café and a focus on winning customers with world-class coffee are a bonus. However, all of this requires you to have intimate knowledge of how your equipment is used and includes world-class predictive services.

4. What's the right economic model?
Choosing between different XaaS models

Once you have a solid foundation on the value approach, you can determine the type of XaaS model you want to offer. Further, you can work to create additional usage options, new markets, or improved designs based on data you obtain from customers. Engage in profession pricing studies and evaluate the right economic model. Here are some common models to think about:

- **Unlimited subscription.** A subscription plan that allows for an unlimited number of services for a defined period.
- **Predefined subscription.** A plan with access to a set number of services for a defined period.
- **Subscription plus overages.** A subscription plan for a predefined amount and a specified period. Overages are billed based on actual usage.
- **Freemium.** Access to basic services for free, and you charge a premium for advanced or full features.
- **Consumption-based.** Plan is true pay-per-use basis. This model typically includes a minimum commitment.
- **Outcome-based.** In this model, you charge based on the value you deliver to the customer.

5. Perform a risk assessment:
Right value-sharing model and possibly insurance can help

The goal of "as-a-service" is to both increase revenues and make revenues more predictable. However, new areas of risks are created. There are four broad areas of risk for which you need to conduct a risk assessment (Figure 9.1).

Besides analyzing the risk for your organization, decide how to share risk and which risks you can live with and which risks you'd like to partner on. There are many specialty insurance and underwriting services that can help. Also, some technology and consulting firms will be willing to share risk and do risk-reward partnerships.

Since EaaS requires manufacturers to bear much more risk than when simply providing equipment, managing those risks becomes a critical business discipline. If business outcomes are being guaranteed, or if the SLA carries onerous penalties, the financial exposure could quickly become a problem if several

Technology & Cyber Risks	EaaS needs new technologies such as IoT and AI. Systems and processes will change, and you'll acquire new data from your customers' environment. The ever-present specter of unauthorized intrusion is a key concern. Identify all associated risks and mitigation plans, including a cyber risk insurance policy.
Strategic Risks	Strategic risks are intricately linked to brand, reputation, and customer experience. The deployment of new technologies could impact the perception of a company.
Organizational Risks	Can your organization deal with the changes of moving from a one-time sale to an ongoing revenue and customer relationship model? Is your leadership willing to change? Is your CFO on board, as there will be major changes in your financial and contracting systems? Don't underestimate the cultural risk.
Financial Risks	It can be a large financial risk to invest in new technologies and unfamiliar business models. Who you partner with and how you maintain liquidity can greatly influence your level of risk.

Figure 9.1. Risk-assessment areas.

contracts go wrong. Risks assessments must be done when writing a contract and maintained throughout its life, and the need for risk mitigation should be drummed into service delivery staff.

6. Don't underestimate the cultural shift in moving to subscription revenues

A new model and any business transformation need alignment across your organization. EaaS is no different, and without a plan to manage the cultural transformation, you're trying to cook without the right spices and will never create a delicious meal.

Each department will play a role in the process, not just sales, marketing, and IT. Cohesive planning and goal setting that include common key performance indicator (KPIs) across all departmental leaders is a best practice that should be the rule and not the exception. This can include identifying organizational gaps and agreeing on areas where third-party vendors or new hires might be needed.

Introducing EaaS in most industries today means being disruptive and embracing innovation. The cultural shift, especially in old-school businesses, then becomes about being a bold company versus an overcautious, conservative one. You could be a true pioneer and need to get comfortable with not knowing everything before jumping in. For example, we focused on competency-based hiring, as opposed to role-based hiring, in every department. This ensured an innovative, fast-fail mindset with an entrepreneurial culture. We got away from traditional departmental KPIs or goals, instead using common goals for each department, focused on the success of our partnerships.

7. Micro goals are key to the success of EaaS

- Before you launch anything, consider breaking those objectives down into micro goals. Setting micro goals can help in a variety of ways, from enabling you to satiate the internal need to see progress to creating flexibility to adapt your efforts as more of your business transforms into a subscription mindset.
- Think about your EaaS journey in terms of a road trip. According to Google Maps, it takes 41 hours to drive from New York City to Los Angeles, but most people won't drive straight through. They'll set up stops along the way where they can sleep or see landmarks and monuments. These destinations are akin to your micro goals, where you can stop, assess your progress, and make any updates or pivots as needed. Also, this allows for celebrations and for the skeptics to join the EaaS journey. Time is also an important element here. There is an adage, "slow down to speed up," and EaaS won't generate millions of billions in year one; so, focus on the immediate wins.
- The key to creating effective micro goals is to begin by building a vision of final success. As part of the vision-building process, you can determine the critical elements needed to meet your desired business outcomes and then map out the smaller steps along the way. These steps are your micro goals. And to determine realistic but aggressive micro goals, you can align them with the overall vision, as well as with the horizon of meeting them. You don't need an automated billing or technology ready for thousands of devices from day one.

8. Get your friendly CFO to embrace the right revenue forecasting and contracting processes

EaaS may mean less revenue up front in order to open more revenue-generation opportunities throughout a product's life cycle. No CFO would hate a fivefold increase in new revenues and more predictability in revenues, but this won't happen overnight. Practical changes to contracts and financing processes are necessary, and you need to work with your finance (and/or legal) department to draw these up. Establish the criteria that would result in a withdrawal from service (e.g., if the new model would benefit neither you nor the customer). In the early years, evaluate each customer systematically before extending contracts; to start, contracts will not be "one-size-fits-all."

In the short term, the lower revenues up front combined with higher costs and investments with partnerships outside the company cause a unique challenge called "swallowing this fish." Especially for industrial customers, it is far more complex than SaaS, where primarily it's the cost of cloud services; there's millions in equipment costs. Investments are needed to build new capabilities—technology, skills, communications, operational functions, sales teams, and so on. In many cases there's cannibalization of existing revenue streams. Bain & Company summarizes this well (Burton, Burns, & Kermisch, 2019).

9. Create a strategy for distribution and channel partners

Successful EaaS considers distribution and channel partners. First-movers are likely to capture higher value from the shift while developing closer relationships with their customers. One strategy is to have the channel participate and benefit from the value. Another strategy could be to forward-integrate and be the distribution channel and transition further into the services of your equipment. I encourage you to begin with the first win-win model I explained. However, a second strategy is absolutely a possibility and could be the more lucrative for manufacturers. An ongoing service relationship can reduce the operating expenses for end customers, and as a manufacturer you might want to increase revenues and not share these with your channel. This strategy of forward integration can alienate your channel, so evaluate this carefully.

If you opt to share the value with your channel, then incentivize your partners to position and sell EaaS and with similar or better margins/commission versus traditional equipment sales. You can set up your channel to realize this margin up front by working with specialty leasing or EaaS funds (yes, they exist) or have them participate in the EaaS subscription for these higher margins over the subscription period.

Remember that EaaS includes maintenance and, more importantly, could have SLAs/warrantability for operating equipment at high performance levels without breaking them. This cannot happen without "boots on the ground." All your channel partners that help in servicing and repairing your equipment can benefit from labor savings and lower cost of repair, maintenance, and spare parts. You can enable them to get new revenue streams and make existing revenue streams more predictable, recurring. Various studies showcase that 15 to 25 percent additional value is created with EaaS versus traditional sales, while end users save 12 to 15 percent on the total cost of operation. So, over the equipment life cycle, you can easily make up to five times the revenue. I recommend sharing this with your channel—whether distributors or service companies.

10. Just do it! Getting the ball rolling

One of my favorite business frameworks is Amazon CEO Jeff Bezos's famous 70 percent rule. For EaaS you need to make decisions with 70 percent of the information you wish you had. You can build trusted partnerships with your customers through EaaS and generally aligning the interests of manufacturers, asset operators, and servicers. Yes, you don't have everything figured out—but if you don't do it, someone else will. Do you want to be the one eating other people's lunch, or do you want have your lunch eaten? Your first business strategy or technical release for EaaS won't be perfect or even be the solution your market needs. So what? It's a step in the right direction. The focus should be on learning and improving the journey toward your BHAG (big hairy audacious goal) with EaaS and digital technologies. Pinpoint a handful of customers primed for a pay-per-use arrangement. Use those customers as a baseline to calculate price points, contract terms, and establish criteria that would result in a withdrawal from the contract.

In conclusion

There's no silver bullet for the success of an EaaS program. It all depends on the clear vision and roadmap in the early stages of the undertaking. Adopting a holistic approach that encompasses business strategy, leadership commitment, talent, and strong partnerships paves the way for a successful transformation to a subscription business model. Beginning with the business outcome in mind and mobilizing the whole organization have never been so critical to success.

Remember, revenue from services becomes more profitable than the manufactured product itself.

Don't wait for disruption—be it!

About Guneet Singh Bedi

Guneet Singh Bedi currently serves in Relayr's management team as CRO & SVP/GM. Relayr (https://relayr.io) is Munich Re's Industrial IoT and Equipment-as-a-Service division and has taken dozens of companies through this journey. Guneet is a seasoned technology executive with experience and demonstrated successes in global technology companies across enterprise software, IoT applications, and the computer networking industry. He has held various roles at Cisco Systems, Symantec Corporation, Oracle Corporation, and Telelogic AB (acquired by IBM). Guneet has lived in various cities in the US, India, and Europe, and in his spare time is passionate about mentoring CXO's of early-stage startups. Guneet received a BE in Computer Engineering from National Institute of Technology, India, and an MBA from the Kellogg School of Management, Evanston, Illinois.

References

Burton, M., Burns, D., & Kermisch, R. (2019). Choosing the right pricing model for equipment as a service. *Bain & Company,* November 22. www.bain.com/insights/choosing-the-right-pricing-model-for -equipment-as-a-service/

10

Executive Checklist: Tips for Industrial Software and Hardware Vendors Migrating to a Software-as-a-Service Business Model

Scott Miller

DIGITAL TRANSFORMATION HAS LAUNCHED the industrial sector into a new era of innovation where software-as-a-service (SaaS) cloud solutions are leading the charge. From a client end-user perspective, this innovation helps drive new efficiencies and better productivity that improves their own market competitiveness and bottom-line results. From a vendor perspective, "as-a-service" innovation provides an opportunity to add even more value to their clients—value that ultimately drives additional growth and new monetization opportunities.

With the SaaS market expansion expected to grow to $140 billion by 2022 (Gartner, 2020), cloud-enabled solutions now dominate what used to be an on-premise enterprise landscape. But while other sectors lead the charge in digital maturity, the industrial sector is somewhat playing catch-up in this digital transformation space (Kane et al., 2017). As more industrial vendors enter into this transition period from on-premise to SaaS offerings, executive teams will need to be more laser-focused than ever to drive company-wide success.

And with new opportunities and change inevitably come challenges and obstacles. Make no mistake: in particular for more market-mature industrial vendors, migrating a solution portfolio from on-premise to software-as-a-service (SaaS) will most certainly impact every aspect of one's organization—not only for product, business, operations, and revenue models, but also for clients and employees. Enter the need for sound planning and effective SaaS transition leadership.

Based on observations of the best, the bad, and the downright ugly when it comes to SaaS migrations, executive teams will need to be mindful of the following tips to ensure success as their company embarks on their journey as a SaaS vendor. These include best practices, lessons learned from other organizations, and early-stage leadership team planning activities that should be top of mind to navigate the complexities and nuances of migrating to SaaS.

1. Develop a detailed change management and communications plan that captures key messages around the SaaS vision...and what's in it for your team

Strong leadership that shows a passionate belief in the benefits of moving to a SaaS model is the price of market entry for a successful transition. Beyond an executive commitment to the change, a well-articulated vision can play a major role in gaining employee buy-in and motivating successful change. Your employees' day-to-day world is about to change, which is why having a detailed plan for communicating and helping navigate through this transition could be the difference between success and failure. This plan will also help achieve alignment on expectations, which will be critical, as teams will be reprioritizing activities and resources and launching their own departmental projects to ensure that their people, processes, and systems are SaaS-ready.

2. Create an effective SaaS transition and implementation committee

This project team will be your eyes and ears as well your internal SaaS champions and problem-solvers. Consisting of both management leaders and key representatives across departments, this team will drive a laser-focused coordination of efforts. The future success of the company needs your brightest minds and most skilled implementation experts. Team members should plan for dedicated offsite workshops and allocate a fixed percentage of their time to this initiative.

Typically, a SaaS transition committee is governed by the VP of product with additional champions from sales, finance, operations, and marketing. Each department head should also include a high-performer (i.e., a doer) within the committee to drive the necessary planning and execution of activities across their department to ensure a successful SaaS transition.

3. Be involved with the SaaS roadmap from day one

Many executives and management teams can be left disappointed with a SaaS transition because they don't fully understand the nuances early in the process. Educate yourself and be involved from the onset for some major decisions. For example, ground-up rebuilds for SaaS might be required in cases where on-premise software code cannot be leveraged (impacting time-to-market and business case), or perhaps dedicated cloud servers will be required for your top clients (potentially negating expected SaaS cost efficiencies). Being involved in the early stages of SaaS planning will address all aspects of the process and ensure that there's no confusion or surprises prior to SaaS transition.

4. Be realistic about the short- and long-term financial implications of SaaS

In 2012 Adobe announced a widespread migration from legacy on-premise perpetual licenses to cloud subscriptions. Revenues declined the following two years by as much as 8 percent because of a drop in larger one-time lump-sum perpetual licenses in exchange for subscriptions (Figure 10.1). Disappointment? Hardly.

Overall revenue growth from subscriptions began to materialize in 2015—Adobe has tripled in revenue since 2012 with a company stock valuation that has exploded almost 20-fold, going from a share price of $33 in March 2021 to $610 as of October 2021 (Nasdaq: ADBE). Their five-year plan on subscriptions has paid off, and recurring revenues far outweigh the work effort required to acquire one-time perpetual license fees. Many board members (and CEOs,

Figure 10.1. Adobe's successful transition to software-as-a-service (SaaS).

for that matter) can fear the possibility of an initial drop in revenues (as well as impact to revenue recognition) because of migrating to subscriptions. It's important to be realistic about the short-term and long-term implications of SaaS subscription pricing and to educate all stakeholders around the financial forecast and underlying SaaS pricing assumptions.

(It's also important to note that although B2C software may typically see an initial revenue decline migrating to subscriptions in the initial years, B2B enterprise software, on the other hand, may actually see an increase; subscription pricing in some cases could be significantly higher than on-premise perpetual license if hosting, integrations, and application management are extremely complex—which is often the case for large enterprise deployments).

5. If you lack pricing maturity and have no internal pricing expertise, you're most likely leaving money on the table

Companies that lack pricing maturity often resort to erroneous SaaS pricing rules-of-thumb, guesswork, or even cost-plus pricing (which is especially difficult where software costs can change from one year to the next depending on the level of development efforts). In these cases, the outcome is often suboptimal and such companies fail to achieve their desired objectives with little or no ROI on their SaaS investment.

Alternatively, mature pricing organizations treat pricing as a process and ensure that a rigorous value-based pricing approach is adopted not only to maximize their revenue and value potential but also drive to excellence in sales enablement, change management, and deal execution. This end-to-end process is more clearly defined within the Digital Pricing Framework™ (Figure 10.2).

Adopting a value-based pricing process and company-wide implementation requires the right capabilities on both the technical side and the change management side. *We have one chance to get this right* was a mantra from one software executive transitioning their company to SaaS. Make sure your company adequately invests in both time and know-how pricing expertise to drive the most optimal go-to-market pricing strategy for your SaaS offering.

6. Develop a pricing strategy for new clients and another for migrating clients

A one-size-fits-all SaaS pricing strategy catering to both new and on-premise migrating clients drives suboptimal pricing and profitability outcomes. On-premise clients have already made investments with your software and respective purchases of supporting hardware and third-party software. The total cost of ownership (TCO) SaaS benefits conversation in their case will be different from that with a new client—this is a significant consideration when

Figure 10.2. The Digital Pricing Framework™.

designing a SaaS pricing strategy. Your on-premise clients will also potentially require incentives to upgrade from both a value-add and pricing perspective. Separately targeting new versus migration clients with two different strategies ensures that your sales plan drives a more favorable financial outcome.

7. Prepare for new performance metrics and incentive plans

SaaS companies apply different performance metrics than traditional on-premise perpetual license companies do. These new metrics will translate to new benchmarks, targets, and incentives for yourself and your management teams: annualized recurring revenue (ARR), number of connected devices, earned versus deferred revenue, customer lifetime value (CLV), and churn rates (CR), for example, will become your go-forward key performance indicators. Sales teams will also be quick to request an outline of new incentive plans under a SaaS subscription model; many companies will switch from one-time bonus payouts for perpetual licenses to ongoing annual incentive payouts with subscriptions. The key will be getting your management teams quickly accustomed to new metrics and tackling the sales incentive question sooner rather than later.

8. With SaaS comes new services: This value-add needs to be a part of all future sales conversations

From hosting to application management to cybersecurity and data protection—these new services represent new value-add offerings to your clients. Unfortunately, many sales and product teams are ill equipped to message these benefits beyond a "we're on the cloud" conversation. It's not uncommon, for example, for ill-prepared sales teams to migrate on-premise clients to SaaS by merely converting dollar-for-dollar the client's original on-premise maintenance and support (M&S) fees to a respective SaaS subscription fee; this practice negates any part of monetizing the SaaS value story and is a quick way to erode margins, as your company bears the burden of the underlying hosting and application management costs. It will be critical to arm sales with the necessary SaaS price–value story, marketing collateral, and SaaS objection-handling skill sets in order to drive the most successful conversation with both new and migrating clients.

9. Consider adopting multiple license models in those cases where the market has not yet embraced cloud or subscription pricing models

For many enterprise B2B vendors transitioning to a SaaS business model, there's potential to apply multiple revenue models. For example, an opening sales offer position could include a new SaaS subscription model while adopting a fall-back term-based license offer where demanded by the client—this is particularly common with vendors selling to government agencies, who may neither be ready to implement SaaS solutions nor have the operational budget (OpEx) to support annual subscriptions. Although managing two revenue models (and possibly delivery platforms) can be much more costly, it may help to risk mitigate against a market that has not yet fully adopted one particular revenue model or delivery platform of choice. It has also been argued that launching a new cloud-enabled software product with both SaaS subscription and term-based licensing models is seen as more favorable by investors than launching a new product with a SaaS model alone (Nurkka et al., 2017).

In some instances, clients may still want to own the software outright via a perpetual license model. In these cases, be sure to optimally price your perpetual license alongside a respective annual M&S that's a fair representation of your annual support services (e.g., out-of-the-box enterprise software annual

M&S is typically 22 to 25% of the one-time license fee, whereby customized and highly integrated solutions can be as high as 25 to 50%). Be sure to also monetize future major upgrades under perpetual license models.

10. Adopt a recurring client solution mindset to better align with recurring revenue models

SaaS subscription models can provide an opportunity to rethink how your company engages with their clients. From a client perspective, they're now paying an annual subscription and expect equal value from a solution from one year to the next—this can be tricky for traditional hardware vendors that sell on a per-order basis; the SaaS story, however, provides an excellent way to integrate an improved ongoing solution mindset with an opportunity for subscription bundles that include hardware, software, and services.

For example, a video-capture camera company shifted from a hardware and video management software line-level invoice sales approach (i.e., a one-time sale) to a bundled subscription offer that encompassed hardware, software, and services. Imagine in this case a five-year term, annual subscription offer, that includes free installation, unlimited cloud video storage, cybersecurity and backup services, hardware refreshes every 2.5 years, and on-site annual service checkups for their transit-installed cameras that includes replacement of any worn units. These clients now receive recurring annual value beyond a one-time-sale mentality that is strongly linked to the recurring subscription models.

11. Set your sales team up for success: Train, incentivize, track, and reward success

Transitioning from selling one-time perpetual licenses to SaaS subscriptions requires a new level of sales expertise. Training, change management, and new incentives are key considerations when leading a salesforce through this transition. Where budgets allow, consider planning for a SaaS sales summit combined with announcements and sales workshops around new SaaS pricing strategies. Selling the SaaS value story, overcoming objections, and introducing incentives will solidify the transition. This will be a significant change for sales teams, and a degree of hand-holding is required. Top sales leaders who are onboard and who "get it" can quickly become your company's go-to SaaS evangelists.

12. Take this as an opportunity to improve your solution offer

Migrating to SaaS is an opportunity to make major enhancements compared with your original on-premise offering. There is an expectation among users that SaaS equates to leading-edge user interfaces (UI) and user experiences (UX), as well as ease of accessibility (*anywhere, anytime, from any device*). Workflow and improved analytic dashboards are also typical upgrades in the case of industrial SaaS offerings. With new and improved value-add and features also come opportunities to improve how you monetize your software offering and convert your on-premise clients.

Conclusion

Transitioning to SaaS is an exciting journey for your organization and establishes the groundwork for future successes. SaaS also brings a renewed opportunity to innovate and establish market differentiation, delivering continuous value-add improvements to your clients and tapping new market segments. In addition, with a renewed discipline around software product development, your teams will be better prepared to meet the speed-to-market demands of a fast-paced digital transformation era.

As a final tip, be sure to take in those moments of success, celebrate, and reward those who helped make the company's journey to SaaS possible.

References

Gartner. (2020, October 20). *Gartner says worldwide IT spending to grow 4% in 2021.* www.gartner.com/en/newsroom/press-releases/2020-10-20 -gartner-says-worldwide-it-spending-to-grow-4-percent-in-2021

Kane, G. C., Phillips, A. N., & Palmer, D. (2017). *Achieving digital maturity: Adopting your company to a changing world.* Deloitte University Press, July 13. www2.deloitte.com/us/en/insights/focus/digital-maturity /digital-mindset-mit-smr-report.html

Nurkka, J., Waltl, J., & Alexy, O. (2017). How investors react when companies announce they're moving to a SaaS business model. *Harvard Business Review,* January 12. https://hbr.org/2017/01/how-investors-react -when-companies-announce-theyre-moving-to-a-saas-business-model

About Scott Miller

Scott Miller is the president of Miller Advisors, a boutique product strategy and pricing consultancy firm with a specialty in B2B digital solutions (www .b2bsoftwarepricing.com). He is also a speaker and instructor on best pricing practices with the Professional Pricing Society (PPS) and the International Software Product Management Association (ISPMA), bringing over 20 years of experience from a variety of senior consulting and global corporate pricing roles.

SECTION 3

SUBSCRIPTION-BASED PRICING

11

Twelve Data-Driven Pricing and Monetization Strategies for Business-to-Business

Michael Mansard

As people consume more and more subscription services in their daily lives, they are more open to (if not expecting) similar models from their business partners. When a product or technology gains transaction in the home, it's a sure bet that sooner or later it will expand its reach. In other words, the subscription economy is everywhere from B2C to B2B. And the numbers prove the point: according to the 2021 Subscription Economy Index (SEI), in the past eight years, subscription businesses have grown 400 percent. Though not every B2B company is ripe for a transition to subscriptions, there are more that are than aren't. Making the shift to services requires you to look at your B2B business with fresh eyes. To help, we take a deep dive into 12 data-driven practices you'll want to keep in mind as you assess your company's viability in the subscription economy. Six practices can be adapted from the B2C world ("borrowed" from those companies whose DNA is in selling direct to consumers), and six practices pose new opportunities specifically for B2B companies.

Six B2C monetization strategies to adapt for B2B

1. Create a digital acquisition strategy—
from test to launch to land to expand
As a consumer, you're likely quite familiar with freemium offers, free trials, and test drives. But as a quick level-set, here's the difference. With the freemium

model, you're able to access just a subset of features for a product or service for free. Free trials give you access to everything on offer, but in a time-bound manner (e.g., a 30-day free trial). Test drives are like a free trial, except with stronger "hand-holding" from the vendor to make sure you're getting the most from the product or service.

As an example, Spotify offers a one-month free trial, as well as a freemium version that comes with ads and lower audio quality. In both cases, Spotify leverages those acquisition strategies to convert as many free users as possible to their paid tiers. Here's how that's working out for them: in Q4 2020, Spotify had 345 million total monthly active users, 44.9 percent of which were paid users (Sawers, 2020). Yet paid subscribers drive a staggering 87 percent of its revenue. And although its 155 million freemium users generate a lot less revenue, they help generate valuable behavioral data and remain a relevant pool to be converted into paid users (Shareholder letter, 2021).

Regardless of the use case, digitization makes customer acquisition models much more scalable and easier to operationalize. And these acquisition models are especially good at addressing the long tail of customer acquisition. Yet they're often not well known or leveraged by B2B companies except within the software-as-a-service (SaaS) space.

Why is it so critical for B2B companies to leverage these strategies? Zuora's Subscribed Institute analysis shows that the fastest-growing companies use these models more—and do a better job of it. For high-growth companies, almost 25.8 percent of their invoiced volume contributions are, or were, linked to a free trial, 70 percent of which are converted to paid (compared, respectively, with 22.6% and 52% for lower-growth companies).

Zoom's web conferencing platform provides a great example of a company optimizing free-to-paid conversion. Its "basic" offering is a freemium model that gives hosts access to Zoom Meetings with core features, but with a 40-minute meeting limit.

At the time of its IPO, almost 55 percent of its 100,000+ customers used Zoom's basic offering before moving to a paid tier. The company's 344 larger customers contributed 30 percent of revenue for the fiscal year ending January 31, 2019, according to Zoom's S-1 (US Securities and Exchange Commission, 2019). With the COVID-19 videoconferencing surge, Zoom has surpassed 300 million daily meeting participants, with obviously a lot of additional conversions to paid.

When looking at the traditional B2B space, there are several good examples of companies employing freemium or free trials as a path to paid conversion. Airbus's Push-to-Talk platform Agnet has a free trial. So does Honeywell, with its process simulation and modeling platform called Forge UniSim. Alcatel-Lucent Enterprise's communication-platform-as-a-service platform, Rainbow, leverages both freemium and free-trial models. In a nutshell, our research with

Stephan Liozu found that at least 100 large traditional B2B companies are offering digital subscription models today.

So, what are the right application cases for these models at a high level? Free trial is almost always a good choice; its time-bound nature limits the risk. And research shows that the right level of generosity with the trial duration matters, usually 30 days, but that shorter is often better.

Test drives increase the cost of sales, as they are more high-touch than a free trial, but they can be worth it for higher-value and more complex solutions. You can also expect test drives to come with a higher conversion rate.

Freemium typically has the lowest conversion rate, and this model is too often chosen by default without enough due diligence. It can be a viable option for free-to-paid conversion, as long as it's properly investigated and designed. This includes taking into consideration

- the cost of running a freemium model
- the right balance between included features and limitations so as not to impede future growth
- the "genuine" potentiality of revenue models for free users

Freemium usually makes sense for markets with a very high number of users—100,000+—because of its lower conversion rate.

It's critical for B2B companies to get very familiar with these new acquisition strategies as soon as possible—freemium, free trial, test drives—and then to put them in play, keeping in mind their applicability for different offerings, different segments, and different use cases. Finally, when relevant, you can combine these strategies to tap into different segments.

2. Give subscribers control (don't worry; it's good for your growth)

As consumers, we've come to expect ease in starting and managing our subscriptions—from changing frequency to adding services to pausing or cancelling. In fact, when it feels too hard to do one of these things or to find the unsubscribe button, we start wondering "is this company trying to force me to stay?" A recent illustration of this point: Amazon, often seen as a powerhouse of customer-centricity, is paradoxically under the scrutiny of several consumer organizations for the complex cancellation process for Amazon Prime subscriptions. The Norwegian Consumer Council (NCC) found that it required scrolling through six pages and making several choices just to unsubscribe.

On the other hand, Netflix is a great example of putting subscribers in control: it's easy to subscribe, it's evergreen, you can move from one plan to another easily and at any time, and you can update any of your details or payment methods. In 2020 Netflix took subscriber-centricity to a whole new level when it announced that it would proactively pause subscriptions (i.e., stop billing) for subscribers who hadn't streamed anything for the 12-month period after signing up or if they hadn't streamed at all in the previous two years.

Several SaaS companies are (again) leading the pack in terms of offering this same kind of B2C freedom and flexibility: HubSpot, Zoom, Box, and Atlassian are all known for making subscription management as easy as what customers are getting at home.

It's critical for B2B companies to understand how important freedom, choice, and flexibility are for subscribers. Enabling subscription flexibility helps drive conversion, adoption, expansion, and retention—or what we call the land-and-expand model.

Atlassian, for example, had until recently a particularly impressive self-service/self-care model—with no direct sales team at all. While most B2B companies may not go to this extreme, it's critical for B2B companies to understand the importance of giving subscribers the freedom to purchase according to their preferences and the flexibility to ensure the right land-and-expand strategy. Offering this subscription flexibility helps drive conversion, adoption, expansion, and retention.

The Subscribed Institute's research shows how critical it is to empower subscribers, especially given that 70 percent of your revenue comes from existing customers. Companies that let their customers make changes to their subscriptions after the initial sign-up grow three times faster than peers that don't. Even more compelling (and sometimes counterintuitive): the companies that let subscribers suspend their subscription when needed reduced their churn by an additional 6.3 points (vs. ones that don't); this corresponds to saving approximately one in six additional customers (Zuora, 2021b). And, as in many things, the pandemic has accelerated these trends: since the beginning of 2020, we've witnessed an exponential increase— more than 40 percent—in businesses offering the "suspend" option to their customers. Today, about 20 percent of Zuora's customer base is using it across verticals (Zuora, 2021c).

In short, empower your customers to have control over how they interact with your offerings; it'll do good for both your subscribers and your business.

3. Automate invoices and electronic payments

Compared with traditional business, with their one-off transactions, subscriptions provide potential for much greater lifetime value that can be maximized via the recurring nature of the transactions.

Two of the components of these recurring transactions are critical to get right: invoicing and payments, because subscriptions mean more invoices and payments to process per customer. And here's why it's tricky: invoicing and payments are a source of overhead costs if not properly automated, and if you don't do it right, customers will be dissatisfied. Glitches in invoicing and payment processes are one of the biggest sources of involuntary churn, which can silently, but surely, kill a subscription business.

Because of lower price points, B2C subscription businesses had to tackle invoicing and payment automation long ago (or at least the successful ones did!). Without doing so, there's no way to scale a business, as most, if not all, margins would be eaten by back-office processes.

Therefore, the best, highest-converting consumer subscription offerings have seamless digital invoicing and payment processes that let their customers select their favorite payment methods. These automated processes also have smart workflows in place to proactively manage customer events. For example, many subscription services leverage a solution called a payment-method updater, which lets merchants automatically incorporate changes made to a customer's credit or debit card, including expiration date, new card number, account closure, and brand migration.

By comparison, it's not uncommon in the B2B space for the cost of invoicing to clock in at around $10 per invoice (and it can often be a lot more). Such numbers can be tolerable for "classic" one-off invoices of amounts large enough to make $10/invoice a negligible cost, but as the volume of invoices and payments per customer grows in a recurring subscription business, this cost would be a real problem. Beyond undesired overhead costs, non-automated processes are also often linked to later payment, weaker collection, and, consequently, higher write-offs.

It's often (wrongly) said that digital invoicing and digital payments aren't mainstream in B2B. But the Subscribed Institute's data show the exact opposite: almost 90 percent of high-growth B2B companies are leveraging digital invoicing, and very close to 50 percent are doing recurring digital payments, versus respectively less than 80 percent and less than 22 percent for low-growth companies. Inspired by consumer-like practices, high-growth subscription B2B companies tend to leverage practices that make renewal a non-event as much as possible. For example, 56 percent of customer contracts are on automatic renewal, which certainly impacts churn positively with a significant 13-point positive difference versus lower-growth subscription businesses.

We highly encourage you to think about digital invoicing and payment from day one of transitioning to subscriptions; paper processes should remain the very rare exception.

4. Automate marketing tasks and customer communications

Many B2C companies have invested in marketing automation capabilities, and rightfully so. Automating marketing tasks and workflows greatly improves the subscriber experience across channels.

In the world of subscription business, subscribing is just the beginning, so it makes sense to streamline those activities beyond sign-up. Subscriber-oriented communications have a critical impact on your business and should be aligned with marketing insights and automated as much as possible to ensure consistency—for example, subscriber onboarding and new features/capabilities communications or communications in response to marketing insights like cross-/upsell potential scoring, churn risk scoring, and so on. And unlike the systems of the past, modern automation solutions let you manage these important subscriber touchpoints with the personalization needed to ensure the relevance of your messaging.

Let's look again at Netflix, which is considered best-in-class for pretty much everything, including marketing and communication. It has a smooth onboarding process. It makes sure that you're meaningfully engaged by sending you personalized communications and notifications. Those messages can be linked to the fact that you've paused and haven't finished an episode of *House of Cards* or that there's a show you may like within their huge catalog. It's said that more than 80 percent of Netflix content is watched following one of its recommendations ("How Netflix's Recommendation Engine Works?," 2019).

Netflix has created an amazing engagement loop at scale, automating millions of unique journeys thanks to the power of data. And this is a key factor of Netflix's significantly low monthly churn rate—less than 4 percent (Bowman, 2020). This automation also allows Netflix to continuously iterate on pricing, while keeping most of its existing subscribers on board de-facto, providing a high perceived value-for-money.

Of course, the Netflix example goes beyond marketing automation and includes a significant amount of data science. But it shows what the best practices can look like. Translated for the B2B space, your marketing automation investment should be leveraged to cover the end-to-end subscriber journey, from discovery to renewal.

This is important, as too often B2B companies leverage their marketing automation investment to focus just on the front end of the process, which only marks the beginning of the story in the subscription journey.

5. Build an ecosystem to capture the entire customer journey

Many companies are on a mission to build a cross-industries ecosystem to address customers' ever-changing needs, expand their footprint, and accelerate innovation. In the subscription economy, the importance of ecosystems becomes even more important. That's because companies employing subscription models develop a deeper relationship with their customers, which helps them better address their needs.

In B2C, Apple's App Store business is a great example. The App Store, which includes services like Apple Music, iCloud, TV+, and iPhone warranties, grossed around $64 billion in 2020 (Leswing, 2021). Another interesting place to look is the telecommunications space. Telecom operators have successfully expanded beyond pure phone and data plans to provide value-add and over-the-top offerings such as reselling streaming services, cloud storage, security, and connected home services. Recent research shows that 21 percent of pay-TV households subscribe to streaming video services through their cable operator. Today, these new digital services account for close to 4 percent of their revenue on average, with best-in-class examples like DoCoMo, Softbank, and China Telecom surpassing the 10 percent mark (Goldsmith, 2018).

In B2B the software industry is again leading the pack. Salesforce managed to build a very successful B2B application store with its ecosystem called AppExchange, hosting 3,400+ apps for its 150,000 customers. It generates an undisclosed amount within the $6.3 billion Salesforce Platform and other annual revenue segment, powered by a 15 percent revenue-sharing model (Salesforce, 2021). Actually, to give some perspective, the latest data disclosing the AppExchange marketplace revenue is from 2016 and states $1.5B (CodeScience, 2021), but given the massive growth of Salesforce and AppExchange since then, it's safe to assume that today's figures are significantly higher than this 2016 number.

RIO, the digital brand of the $26 billion TRATON GROUP (MAN Trucks, Scania), has been developing a cloud-based subscription logistics platform to support all parties of the delivery chain in digitizing their business. RIO includes an ecosystem marketplace where it is possible to subscribe to services from third parties such as Continental and DAKO.

Banks and insurance companies are also developing ecosystem services, leveraging their massive scale and reach to fight the heavy disruption happening in their industry. For example, DBS's SME Banking unit offers a Start Digital service, encouraging businesses to digitize through their accounting, cybersecurity, HR/payroll, digital marketing, and digital transactions solutions via ecosystem solutions.

In short, developing and monetizing an ecosystem can be a meaningful approach to generating additional recurring revenue streams across the end-to-end subscriber journey.

6. Go direct to consumers—don't let channel partners hold you back

Many businesses rely on channel partners or distributors as part of their go-to-market strategy, but this usually means lots of friction when launching a subscription offering.

Of course, subscriptions aren't incompatible with indirect selling, but very often channels can lead to a massive slowdown of efforts. To sell subscriptions through a partner requires convincing partners of this shift and managing resistance to—and fear of—the transition. Partners may be worried about losing hold of those customer relationships and losing revenue because of new business models. Even if channel partners are convinced, they need to convince and transform their own teams. In short, it can quickly become a massive change-management program (and headache) that creates a roadblock to progress.

In the B2C space, many companies have opted to launch direct-to-consumer offerings to accelerate their recurring revenue. For example, Fender, which traditionally sold its products through retail centers (like Guitar Center), has now gone direct to consumer, both with its products (traditional products offered via its website, plus new customized offerings as through its Mod Shop) and with its new services such as Fender Play, a subscription-based guitar-learning platform service. The Fender Play subscription offering can be seen as a real lever to its direct-to-consumer strategy. Prior to launching Fender Play, the company discovered that 90 percent of new guitar players quit within their first year. Meanwhile, engaged Fender customers spent, on average, more than $10K/year on additional guitars, gear, and so forth. With the launch of Fender Play, Fender managed to build more than one million direct relationships with customers in about three years. The outcomes of this D2C service offering are tangible: in addition to new subscription revenue streams, Fender gains invaluable firsthand insights on customers and their engagement, which can potentially lead to more core "product" sales (Zuora, 2021a).

Beyond B2C, some B2B companies have made bold decisions when launching a new subscription offering. Alcatel-Lucent Enterprise, a global leader in enterprise telecommunications, relies on a very effective two-tier distribution strategy for its hardware and services business. When it launched its communication-platform-as-a-service platform, Rainbow, it opted to bootstrap the new business by going direct-to-customer as a starting point. It was critical for the company to gather and analyze firsthand learnings to maximize its chance of a successful launch, and to better tailor its go-to-market strategy.

B2B companies should recognize the importance of testing their launch direct-to-customer, at least as a starting point, if they don't want to be held back by their channels.

Six monetization strategies unique to B2B

7. Business development and sales teams are still a must

Though putting the subscriber in the driver's seat and automating as much of their journey as possible via self-service is an important practice for B2B, B2B companies almost always still need a dedicated business development and sales team as well.

A great proof point? Atlassian, the poster child for the self-service model, built their enterprise sales team recently after letting their solution partners run their enterprise sales cycle. To be clear, Atlassian is not abandoning their self-serve model; instead, they're complementing it with enterprise selling. Slack also went through a comparable journey.

Another example is Honeywell Forge, the enterprise performance management SaaS platform from the $36B manufacturing giant that provides insights to operators of buildings, industrial facilities, airlines, and so forth. Today, Honeywell has 350 people focused exclusively on selling Honeywell Forge (Tzuo, 2020).

According to KeyBanc Capital Markets' SaaS Surveys data (2019), it's clear that a "traditional" sales-led approach by both field sales and inside sales remains the primary mode of distribution in B2B, contributing around 80 percent to a business's sales, depending on the company's size. To be clear, internet sales as a primary channel may represent almost 30 percent of contribution when the median initial contract size is less than $1K. But this figure quickly drops to 15 percent in the $1K–$5K tier and then to 7 percent in the $5K–$15K tier before almost disappearing in the next (and bigger) tiers.

A key recommendation for companies embracing new subscription models is to make sure you have a sales team with deep digital service sales experience focused on the new offering. This often means bringing in "new blood" from the outside for more traditional B2B companies. A second key recommendation is to make sure that your compensation model is (re)designed to fit the specificities of the subscription economy, leveraging associated metrics such as annual recurring revenue (ARR), total contract value (TCV), and churn.

Beyond traditional enterprise and account-based strategies, the sales team should be able to leverage digital acquisition strategies like we mentioned previously—free trials or freemiums—to feed the pipeline.

Key to remember here is that at some point, a B2B subscription business will most likely require a sales team, as larger deals still require high-touch sales processes. But enterprise sales and self-care/self-service are not mutually exclusive; they have to be smartly weighted to optimize cost of sales.

8. Focus on retention and up-/cross-sell

Expansion potential is usually different in B2C than in B2B. The key drivers for growth in B2C subscription businesses are acquisition of new customers and retention. In B2B subscription businesses, the key drivers for growth are acquisition and expansion (i.e., upsell and cross-sell).

In B2C, there's often an individual subscriber (or a group of subscribers, such as a household), so there are fewer potential buyers and less expansion potential. In B2B, however, there are many stakeholders, many processes, many adjacencies, and many buyers to provide a massive springboard to future growth. B2B subscription also makes metric-based pricing easier to implement, which facilitates further upsell, as we discuss in point 10.

B2B subscription businesses expand by positioning at the right time: more users (metric upsell), more modules (cross-sell), more add-ons/options (cross-sell), and so forth. Again, these are all critical to the land-and-expand strategy favored by B2B and made achievable because of the relationships you develop with your customers and the valuable data you're able to derive from those relationships.

Again, Zoom is a great example here. Pre-COVID, Zoom grew 88 percent in 2019, with a mind-blowing 140 percent net retention rate (NRR)—the rate at which recurring revenue has been retained (net of churns, contraction, and expansion) from a cohort of subscribers from one year ago. Zoom manages to handily offset their churn thanks to an incredible upsell and cross-sell model.

The Subscribed Institute's data confirm the benefits of this approach: 84 percent of the fastest-growing companies have a >100 percent NRR.

Finally, expansion is important for B2B subscription companies because it's economically efficient. According to KeyBanc Capital Markets' SaaS Surveys data, it costs on average $1.60 to acquire $1.00 of new revenue, whereas it costs $0.69 to upsell/expand $1.00 of incremental revenue. As a side note: the cost of acquisition for new businesses is increasing more rapidly than the cost of upsell/expansion.

Expansion is a mission-critical aspect of nailing revenue growth in the subscription economy. "Sell and forget" is a recipe for failure.

9. Customer success management is a must-have

It should now be evident how critical managing the subscriber journey is to your success. A key pillar supporting this is the emerging function of customer success.

The role of customer success manager first appeared in B2B and is now making its way to the B2C world. Back in the late '90s, many B2B businesses had minimal customer support. Addressing customer questions and solving customer problems after purchase was considered a resource drain. That's when, according to the CSM Association, a CRM company called Vantive decided to build the first customer success management team. Since then, this strategy has been adopted widely in the SaaS space, with companies like Salesforce, Zoom, and Zuora investing significant resources in their CSM teams.

CSM teams focus on making sure that customers realize value from the solution they subscribe to and that the solution stays relevant. The role is hugely important because existing subscribers will probably soon represent 70 percent of a business's revenue, according to Subscription Economy Index data. To capitalize on the huge expansion potential embedded in that cohort (and to minimize massive churn risk), you have to take care of customers throughout their journey—not just when they're having issues. CSM teams help optimize the customer journey in myriad ways including successfully onboarding new customers, running customer business reviews, tracking customer health metrics, getting stakeholders up to speed on new features, following up on renewals, and much more.

A recent article co-authored by INSEAD professor Wolfgang Ulaga on customer success management (Eggert et al., 2020) showed a clear acceleration of CSM adoption in B2B. Yet, the study also surprisingly showed how dramatic that acceleration was: there was an almost 24-fold increase in individuals self-defining as CSM on LinkedIn between 2015 and 2020—from fewer than 4,000 to 93,000. A second surprise was the rapid adoption outside the expected verticals where it's mainstream (i.e., software/SaaS). Actually, there are now many CSMs at large powerhouses across the globe: Honeywell, Grundfos, SKF,

ABB, Alcatel-Lucent Enterprise, and so on. This makes perfect sense, as customer success is applicable to any subscription business.

Given that CSM is a recent phenomenon, it's interesting to provide a bit of perspective on team sizing. Often heard is that each customer service manager should manage $1M to $5M of annual recurring revenue (ARR). The wide gap can be explained by many factors, including customer segmentation. Indeed, a CSM lead could manage two large enterprise accounts representing $5M of ARR, while on the other side of the spectrum another CSM lead could manage 100 customers (probably with more automation) totaling $1M of ARR in the SMB segment. It can even happen within the same company.

One last point to show how important CSM has become: many venture capital firms won't invest unless a company has an effective CSM team. So B2B companies need to invest in CSM capabilities from the get-go, and by that we mean from the very first subscriber.

10. The importance of metric-based versus flat-fee pricing

In the B2C subscription world, an easy-to-understand subscription pricing model is often critical to ensuring adoption and success. For example, subscription fashion service Rent the Runway offers three different tiers to its members following good/better/best principles, each with different amounts of rental items and shipments included.

An even more ubiquitous example is how mobile phone companies create their plans. Back in the day, they were full of metrics—minutes, number of texts, and so forth—that were designed to align with the operator's cost structures, not with customer value. While it's more complex in B2C to leverage metric-based pricing, it's actually quite straightforward in B2B, and it's more desirable because it benefits both the subscriber and your business.

First, let's define what we call metric-based pricing. It has two key elements: a pricing metric and a pricing structure. The pricing metric defines the rating measurement for customers, such as per user, per minute. It can be associated with a commitment that is a business decision: for example, a customer subscribes to 500 seats for the next nine months and then to 800 for the next three months. A pricing metric can also be metered to be rated after the fact, for example leveraging an IoT sensor, and thus opening up a usage or pay-per-use model.

Second, the pricing structure defines how the price level changes over time with usage, for example. Returning to our previous example, the price per seat could be linear ($500 per seat, regardless of the number of seats) or degressive ($500 for the first hundred seats, then $400 for the next hundred seats, and so on). Of course, a metric-based model can combine multiple pricing metrics and structures even within one plan. Rent the Runway, for example, uses the number of shipments and items to determine pricing. Zoom combines users, meeting minutes, GB of recording storage, and so on to determine pricing tiers.

Even in more advanced use cases, it's possible to combine multiple attributes to define a context-dependent pricing metric. Uber's pricing, combining distance, duration, or surge, is a good example. One last example is the high-water-mark model, where the highest aggregate quantity consumed for a given period is charged. We typically see this model used in platform-as-a-service subscriptions (cloud storage, etc.).

Of course, there are limitless nuances and variances compared with a classic "one-off" pricing model. Thus, metric-based models allow for a lot of creativity and freedom to meet a customer's needs compared with a flat-fee structure. They also offer a more natural path to expand, either by adding "more of the same" or by simplifying inter-tier upsells using metered guardrails (e.g., a company could offer a Silver edition that includes 5,000 API calls per month with $0.05 per additional call, and then offer a Gold edition that includes unlimited API calls).

Metric-based pricing simplifies further expansion negotiations with customers when the metrics are mutually accepted. Obviously, subscribers should be able not only to adjust up but also to scale down. The more choice and flexibility you're able to offer, the stronger your relationship is, allowing you to "right sell" at any time.

Subscribed Institute data confirm how effective these pricing mechanisms are. Companies that have revenues derived from a combination of usage pricing and recurring pricing grow 1.3 times faster than those that don't (Subscribed Institute, 2021). And when looking specifically at usage, it can boost year-over-year upsell by 1.5 times, while reducing churn. Yet Subscribed Institute data show that usage should be kept to a "healthy ratio" to optimize revenue growth, specifically 1 to 25 percent of the overall subscription revenue contribution. Why this sweet spot? One explanation could be that too much variability might come at the expense of necessary mutual predictability in B2B business. For example, a customer could begin with a highly variable and flexible "pay-per-use" plan as a first step, but as both customer and provider start being able to build more joint predictability, the customer is likely to upgrade to a committed tier with a potential ramp-up (in exchange for a more appealing deal).

In short, pricing metrics can be used as a vector to help convey the value of your offering to your customers. Thus, leveraging a metric-based model can be a meaningful contributor to your growth. Employ metric-based pricing whenever possible, while also including a "healthy dose" of usage-based pricing. This combination will make the revenue expansion discussion between your sales/CSM teams and your customers much smoother.

11. Beyond price points, payment flexibility and frequency are real differentiators

B2C invoicing and payment models are usually straightforward and simple. Netflix and Spotify are good examples. You pay in advance at day zero for the service, often according to an "anniversary" billing schedule (i.e., same day you initially subscribed) and with limited frequencies such as annually or monthly.

But like other "traditional" B2B practices, the possibilities are much wider when it comes to payment models and terms, and this is enriched further by the recurring nature of such a business model. There are three important things to bear in mind when it comes to B2B subscription payments.

First, high-growth companies are better at getting paid fast, despite the tighter working-capital control from buyers that the current economic environment amplifies. Indeed, payment terms have become an even more critical aspect of a B2B subscription deal.

Yet, Subscribed Institute data show that subscription companies with the fastest growth have an average payment term of 18 days versus 22 days for lower-growth companies (Konary, n.d.). We believe the root cause of shorter payment terms is associated with stronger subscription value proposals but also with more systematic sales compliance: internal policies and practices, as well as automation.

The second, and probably counterintuitive, learning is that, regarding payment terms, "less" might not necessarily be "more" in terms of growth. Indeed, companies with more payment terms grow faster than companies that have a reduced set of options. To be even more accurate, Subscribed Institute data indicate that high-growth subscription businesses offer 45 percent more payment terms (and models) than lower-growth ones. This might be because they better cater to each customer's unique requirements with their accounts payable. In short, they're using payment flexibility as a sales weapon. It's a successful sales strategy, but as you can imagine, it increases complexity in your back office, which then builds demand for automation.

Finally, despite the increased adoption of digital recurring-payments methods (similar to B2C), there's an imperative to continue to manage more "legacy" payment approaches. This is especially true for the most expensive subscriptions. Our Subscribed Institute data clearly show that the utilization rate of legacy payment models increases sharply as average revenue per account increases (Konary, n.d.). For example, wire transfer or check payments are used for almost 35 percent of customers' payments when in the revenue tier that exceeds $10K, but only about 12 percent in the $2K to $10K revenue tier.

In short, despite the increasing penetration of digital invoicing and payments showing a real "consumerization" around B2B payment practices, keep in mind the implications of properly handling your subscription payment strategy due to its direct correlation to growth.

12. Channel transformation remains a necessity (but you'll need to help partners "see the light"!)

We've discussed the importance of developing a direct-to-customer model to ensure new subscription business success; it's often an imperative to get things in motion for your business. However, being able to scale via partners and channels often remains vital, especially in B2B, so a combination or hybrid approach is often the best.

Going back to Alcatel-Lucent Enterprise's (ALE) Rainbow example: after proving the model by reaching more than 300 percent growth in 2020, ALE decided to accelerate on the partner front. They had gathered enough data points, relevant addressable use cases, new buyer personas identification, or customer success stories, so they determined that it was the right time to really begin their partner transformation. They weren't starting from scratch: they'd already begun evangelizing a handful of core early-adopting partners. More importantly, the ALE team acknowledged the importance of complementing their traditional partner footprint with new types of partners, such as digital advisory agencies and digital transformation practices of large system integrators. This has been a key success factor in supporting Rainbow's (and ALE's) move into deeper vertical and business-critical use-case awareness, but it's also been important as they look to properly address new buying personas for their digital solutions such as CDOs or CMOs.

As in a classic partner play, it's critical to craft a two-sided value proposition: one for the end customer and one for the partner. And, similar to a subscription business needing to have its own sales team, a company moving to subscriptions will also need to rethink the partner compensation scheme considering subscription economy principles. This means accepting that new metrics must be employed to measure success, metrics that impact compensation for the partner. It can also mean radically changing the way the partner is being commissioned; in many cases, moving to subscriptions also means that part, if not all, of the digital services are run centrally (instead of being fulfilled or installed at the customer).

As a result, the classic partner model in which the partner resells to the end customer with a markup and where the partners (protectively) keep the details of the end customer to themselves will no longer fly. In the subscription economy, there's a need for all parties involved to know the end customer, even just for provisioning, operationality, or billing purposes (not to mention for gaining deeper insights that can be leveraged for additional monetization opportunities). To address this, many companies are moving to one of several commissioning/sales agent models: one where they pay recurring commissions to their partners; or to a "sell via" partner model where they let the partner re-invoice the end customer; or to a "bill on behalf" model where the partner invoice is issued by the main provider.

Manufacturers can learn from the successful SaaS transitions of Microsoft and Adobe, both of which happened because of their strong partnerships with resellers and partners. Other technology companies have learned from them and embraced intentional partner management strategies supported by a robust technology backbone (e.g., partner relationship management software, market-place software, the right billing solution that includes partners).

Finally, an important point is the role played by partners. We've emphasized how critical it is to manage the subscriber's life cycle from an economic perspective. We also made clear why CSMs are key in this context. Clarifying how partners need to contribute to customer success management, even by becoming an extended customer management arm, will be of utmost importance. This also means that proactively sharing subscriber data with partners will be essential to ensuring a proper insight-to-action loop.

Channel transformation will most likely become a necessity as you scale your subscription business. It will deeply impact the entire process, from partner enablement to commissioning. Two key changes will be the need to acknowledge the potential role of partners as an extension of your customer success management and the potential need to source new types of partners beyond the "usual suspects."

B2B pricing and monetization quick guide

It's clear that moving to the subscription economy is a journey, not an overnight trip. We've only scratched the surface on pricing and monetization. To fully optimize the subscription model for your business, every single business function—from product management to finance—will need to be looked at with fresh eyes.

To get started—especially if you're budget-constrained and feeling a sense of urgency—here's a high-level summary of practical guardrails and recommendations:[1]

- Start with a **segmented offering from the get-go.** Good/better/best is a pretty safe bet. Ensure a fair balance of features between the different tiers to **make relative positioning easier to understand for future customers** (and easier to defend for a sales team).
- Remember that **features do not necessarily have to be technological.** For example, having a dedicated/named CSM and/or the flexibility to suspend at any time can both be seen as "features" you can package.
- Ideally, **use a metric-oriented pricing model**: it's even more important for more advanced offering tiers.
- **Add relevant metrics on some key features** to further simplify positioning. You can also leverage usage-based metrics to foster further expansion opportunities beyond "just" features.

---

1   Obviously, we can only recommend developing a proper ad-hoc pricing and monetization strategy very early on versus applying prebaked recommendations. Indeed, pricing and monetization are two extremely critical key growth levers that are overlooked and too often enter the mix way too late.

- Make sure to **add a handful of options/add-ons**, especially for features that only address a minority of customers that could highly value them.
- Ensure that you have **simple and outside-in-oriented qualification criteria** to nudge the customer to the right offering (via self-questionnaire and/or sales rep). For low-/no-touch sales models, you can also nudge future subscribers with a "preferred" or "recommended" icon on one of the tiers (often the "mighty middle" one).
- Anticipate **dynamic subscriber journeys** from day one by weaving links and narratives between the different tiers and options. As you go, you'll identify finer triggers; yet it's key to go into a land-and-expand motion as soon as possible.
- Remember that **"right selling" is critical in the effort to maximize lifetime value**, so allow down sells or suspensions to enable expansions.
- Invest in **CSM as soon as possible**—ideally when you sign your first customer—to maximize your chance of being a retention and expansion powerhouse.
- If you're heavily skewed to indirect sales today, **go direct-to-customer to build some success before trying to convince your channels**, but do it in order to "make the case" and convince them later on.
- If you need a **pragmatic framework to structure your pricing and monetization brainstorms**, there are some outstanding ones available, such as the Pricing Model Innovation Canvas (PMIC) from Stephan Liozu (2018).

About the Subscribed Institute

The Subscribed Institute is a dedicated think-tank focused on the challenges and opportunities of the subscription economy. With more than 1,000 executives from over 500 subscription companies, the Institute serves as a unique source of ideas, data, and connections for business leaders around the world. More at www.subscribed.com/subscribed-institute.

About Michael Mansard

Michael is a seasoned subscription-economy business strategist. During his five-year tenure at Zuora, he has been accompanying more than 200 companies globally and across industries, from startups to large enterprises. Leveraging his 11-year experience at Deloitte Consulting, at SAP, or as a startup mentor, he has developed an original multidisciplinary profile. His skills range across enterprise business processes (order-to-cash, close-to-disclose, procure-to-pay...), strategic sales, financial controlling, and digital/IT architecture. Michael holds a dual master's degree from ESIEE Paris in Business Management and Information Technologies. He currently serves as Principal, Business Transformation &

Innovation within Zuora's Strategy & Operations field group. He has recently authored several thought leadership pieces, including "Industry 4.0: An Executive Playbook for Business Model Transformation" and "Subscription Economy Maturity Model."

References

Bowman, J. (2020). Netflix is killing the competition in this one key category. *Motley Fool,* September 15. www.fool.com/investing/2020/09/15/netflix-is-killing-the-competition-in-this-one-key/

CodeScience. (2021). *A beginner's guide to the AppExchange.* https://learn.codescience.com/rs/466-LVH-765/images/A%20beginner%27s%20guide%20to%20the%20AppExchange.pdf

Eggert, A., Ulaga, W., & Gehring, A. (2020). Managing customer success in business markets: Conceptual foundation and practical application. *Journal of Service Management Research, 4*(2–3), 121–132. https://doi.org/10.15358/2511-8676-2020-2-3-121

Goldsmith, J. (2018). New research shows 21% of pay TV households subscribe to online video service through their pay TV provider. *Fierce Video,* April 2. www.fiercevideo.com/new-research-shows-21-pay-tv-households-subscribe-to-online-video-service-though-their-pay-tv

How Netflix's recommendation engine works? (2019). *Springboard India,* November 5. https://medium.com/@springboard_ind/how-netflixs-recommendation-engine-works-bd1ee381bf81#

KeyBanc Capital Markets. (2019). *SaaS survey results.* www.key.com/kco/images/2019_KBCM_saas_survey_102319.pdf

Konary, A. (n.d.). *Payment terms: Impact on B2B business growth.* The Subscribed Institute. www.zuora.com/resource/benchmark-payment-terms/

Leswing, K. (2021). Apple's App Store had gross sales around $64 billion last year and it's growing strongly again. *CNBC.com,* January 8. www.cnbc.com/2021/01/08/apples-app-store-had-gross-sales-around-64-billion-in-2020.html

Liozu, S. (2018). A canvas for pricing model innovation. *Pricing Advisor,* September, pp. 8–10. www.stephanliozu.com/wp-content/uploads/2021/02/2018-Pricing-Model-Innovation-Canvas-PA-0918.pdf

Salesforce. (2021). *Financial Update Q4 FY21.* https://s23.q4cdn.com/574569502/files/doc_financials/2021/q4/CRM-Q4-FY21-Earnings-Presentation.pdf

Sawers, P. (2020). Spotify: Users up 31% to 271 million in Q4 2019, podcasts convert free-to-paid subscribers. *Venture Beat,* February 5. https://venturebeat.com/2020/02/05

/spotify-users-up-31-to-271-million-in-q4-2019-podcasts
-convert-free-to-paid-subscribers/

Shareholder letter. (2021). *Spotify,* February 3. https://s22.q4cdn.com
/540910603/files/doc_financials/2020/q4/Shareholder-Letter
-Q4-2020_FINAL.pdf

The Subscribed Institute. (2021, March). *The Subscription Economy Index*™.
Zuora. www.zuora.com/resource/subscription-economy-index/

The Subscribed Institute. (2021). *Usage-based pricing: What is the right mix?*
Zuora. www.zuora.com/resource/subscription-economy-index/

Tzuo, T. (2020). *Getting IOT Right: A Conversation with Honeywell's
Usman Shuja.* Zuora, August 31. www.zuora.com/2020/08/31
/getting-iot-right-a-conversation-with-honeywells-usman-shuja/

US Securities and Exchange Commission. (2019). Zoom Video Communications, Inc. Form S-1 Registration Statement. www.sec.gov/Archives
/edgar/data/1585521/000119312519083351/d642624ds1.htm

Zuora. (2021a). *Fender.* www.zuora.com/our-customers/case-studies/fender/

Zuora. (2021b). *Subscription changes: What separates the fastest growing companies from the rest?* www.zuora.com/resource
/subscription-economy-benchmarks-report-1/

Zuora. (2021c). *Subscription suspend/resume: Impact on churn mitigation.*
www.zuora.com/resource/subscription-suspend-and
-resume-impact-on-churn-mitigation

12

Pricing Mistakes and Best Practices to Consider When Thinking Subscription Pricing

THERE'S NO DOUBT THAT pricing digital solutions is hard. Pricing industrial products and services is already a challenge, as many industrial companies don't have dedicated pricing teams. From Michael Mansard's excellent chapter, you can also see a number of things to consider when monetizing and pricing digital innovations. Are SaaS companies doing better than industrial ones? To find out, I recommend that you subscribe to Kyle Poyar's blog and check out the OpenView website for great content. They often conduct excellent research on pricing practices in the SaaS world. Early in 2021, Poyar posted this entry on LinkedIn:

I've now collected data on how 2,200 SaaS companies approach pricing. The stats continue to surprise me:

1 56% don't publish their pricing online. In 2021.

Quick tip: Buyers will be seeking out this information before they talk to you and companies like Capiche are bringing transparency to SaaS pricing. Take control of the pricing conversation with your prospects. This is especially important if you have transactional sales or a PLG strategy.

2 52% have NEVER tested or piloted their pricing and another 13% have only done it once.

Tip: The best companies treat pricing like they treat their product; it should be consistently getting better.

3 12% have people in their org dedicated to pricing and packaging.

Tip: Look for a full-time hire as you're approaching $50M ARR and/or as you become a multi-product company. The ROI makes it a no-brainer.

4 6% have done actual pricing research on buyer needs and willingness to pay.

Tip: Ask about willingness to pay before you even decide what to build next. (Poyar, 2021a)

Clearly, the answer is not a definitive *yes*. The reality is that everyone is struggling to price. The reasons are not too different across the B2C, B2B, and industrial worlds. Companies don't pay attention to pricing, they tend to consider pricing a secondary activity, and they don't develop pricing capabilities from the get-go. The result is a lack of pricing excellence and a lot of money left on the table. In this chapter, I propose several sections. I begin with a list of mistakes to avoid in setting your industrial subscription pricing. Then I offer 15 key pricing statistics from the B2C and B2B SaaS worlds to guide you in your pricing process. I continue with some best practices drawn from many experts and papers I've read. I finish the chapter with a Lightning Strike essay from Kyle Poyar on how to use the freemium model.

10 mistakes to avoid
when setting your subscription pricing in industrial markets

Many of these companies are just getting started with these flexible consumption business and pricing models, and they're prone to making mistakes from the very beginning. It seems like industrial companies need to pay closer attention to the successes and failures of their B2C counterparts. In case they're not able to do this, though, I describe 10 mistakes that B2B and industrial companies should avoid making in designing and packaging their digital subscription pricing.

1 Setting their subscription prices solely based on cost. In many industrial groups, cost-plus pricing is the de-facto methodology for price-setting. It's internally focused and provides a sense of control. Applying this methodology to subscription-based pricing in a world that is dematerializing and commoditizing is irresponsible. In digital, the costs of devices and accessories are plummeting, and the rate of equipment obsolescence is accelerating. Pricing solely based on cost automatically means that prices are going down cycle after cycle. It isn't sustainable. Subscription-based pricing should be based on the three C's of price-setting: customer, cost, and competition.

2 Confusing leasing and subscription. These are two different business models. Leasing has been offered for decades in industrial markets, and finance teams are proficient at designing leasing programs in partnership with financial institutions. Subscriptions are a very different business model. Not only does it imply a move from a CapEx to an OpEx model, it brings additional value to customers besides the financing benefits. It's not unusual for customers subscribing to a product-as-a-service offer to pay several times the up-front value of the product over the duration of the subscription agreement. Therefore, subscription-based models need to be differentiated and bring concrete value to customers. Don't forget to explain this to your finance organization!

3 **Pricing too low from the get-go.** When you sell a product, if your price is too low, you can always make an adjustment. In a recurring business, your pricing mistakes are also recurring! Set your subscription price too low for a two-year agreement, and your price is wrong for two years. Because many industrial companies use competition-based pricing to set their pricing levels, they focus on penetration pricing to capture market share and set prices too low. The reality of industrial markets is that prices will only go down from where they start. It's hard to move prices up when value isn't demonstrated as part of robust marketing strategy.

4 **Using the wrong value metric from the get-go.** Your pricing metric needs to match your customer value metric. If your customer thinks in terms of runtime or linear yard, then your pricing model will have to reflect that. To do this, you need to put yourself in the customer's shoes and understand how they think. The same goes for the time of analysis of your subscription. Study your customer's profit and loss statement and find out how they measure cost and income as well as what vocabulary and metrics they use.

5 **Offering one price for all customers.** Conducting customer needs-based segmentation is a real challenge for industrial companies. One-size-fits-all offers are easier to design and commercialize. In subscription pricing, one price for all is never recommended. Proposing a "1 or 0" choice to customers limits the opportunity to capture a larger portion of the total addressable market. The ideal number of offers is three or four according to subscription experts.

6 **Lack of versioning and packaging.** Similarly, within customer or market segments, subscriptions should be designed and packaged based on the most accepted options used in B2C: good/better/best, bundles, à-la-carte pricing, core package with options, and so on. Pricing is a science, and subscription-based pricing isn't new. Industrial firms should learn from the best practices used in industries where subscriptions have become second nature, such as SaaS, media, and music.

7 **Offering freemium without a clear plan to convert users to.** The freemium is a great option to get users to test drive your business models and to establish a strong user base. Freemium models are designed to eventually transition a portion of the user base into paying customers. Here, too, some B2C companies have struggled in the conversion process. That process needs to be designed up front before the launch of the freemium

offer. Having a roadmap to move from free to fee is essential to capturing value from the addressable market. Launching a subscription without this roadmap might mean freemium forever. Remember that in industrial, savvy buyers are good at keeping things for free!

8 **Offering large discounts because you offer them for your products.** It's not unusual for subscription pricing to have tiered pricing levels based on volume or usage. However, industrial marketers should avoid transferring their existing product pricing structure to their subscription offers. High discount levels for industrial products and services are not uncommon. Procurement teams expect discounts from their vendors. However, it makes no sense to offer 60 percent or 70 percent discounts in subscription pricing. It might be a good opportunity to switch to net pricing for subscriptions. It's best to keep it simple!

9 **Not matching your subscription pricing roadmap to your offer roadmap.** The business model roadmap for your subscription offers needs to include a pricing roadmap. Your technology and your value proposition will evolve. Your offer might need to pivot several times over a few years. Your pricing models might move from a hybrid pricing model with an up-front payment and a subscription to a full subscription pricing model. It's also essential to worry about the renewal of your subscription in your design roadmap. Competition might have caught up and might be offering a similar subscription.

10 **Not offering the option to change pricing during the subscription agreement.** Your customers want choice and the freedom to make changes to their subscription. This is a lesson I learned while attending the Zuora Subscribed conference. Over the duration of a subscription, customer will add users, upgrade or downgrade their subscription, or put it on hold for a while. The more you allow this to happen, the higher your growth will be, according to Zuora. Your subscription pricing needs to be packaged right but also needs to be dynamic and flexible. And for that, you need to have the right subscription ERP in place.

15 key pricing statistics from the B2C subscription pricing field

There are many reports on SaaS and digital pricing. When I work with industrial companies, I tell them to trust the experts and adopt the best practices from the others. They've gone through the growing pains and the testing of their pricing strategies. Although I don't recommend copying someone else's pricing structure, I offer these statistics to accelerate the development of their approach. These statistics serve as references and are based on professional research from reputable companies. Remember that this book is meant to be a practical cookbook for accelerating the development of industrial subscription business models without spending a fortune doing so. So, we must trust the experts and follow best practices.

1 Most SaaS companies are underpriced. By the time they enter the expansion stage, they raise their deal pricing by 50 percent compared with their seed-stage pricing (Poyar, 2021b).

2 Only 39 percent of SaaS companies base pricing on value. Best judgment is used with 27 percent of firms and 24 percent is based on competition (Poyar, 2021b).

3 Usage-based pricing is increasing to reach 39 percent of SaaS firms versus 41 percent user/seat-based pricing (Poyar, 2021b).

4 Companies that use per-unit pricing average (value-based) grow faster than those that use flat-fee pricing (30% ARR growth) (Zuora, 2021).

5 An optimal hybrid pricing model is 75 percent subscription-based and 25 percent usage-based (Zuora, 2021).

6 Seventy percent of SaaS companies use some type of good/better/best package (Poyar, 2016).

7 Faster-growing SaaS companies (30% ARR growth or more) offer 50 percent fewer products and subscription rates than others (Zuora, 2021).

8 Companies that tend to bill annually average lower churn rates and higher growth rates (24% vs. 32%) (Zuora, 2021).

9 SaaS unicorns are twice as likely as public companies to publish their pricing (Pytel, 2018).

10 On average, 70 to 80 percent of the revenue of a successful high-growth subscription business should come from existing customers (Konary & Pineda, 2021).

11 Companies that allow users to change their subscription prices grow 70 percent more than those that do not (Zuora, 2021).

12 Focus on increasing the number of potential users. The more, the better—remember, only around 5 percent of free users will eventually end up paying you (Bhatt, 2018).

13 A good/better/best set of offers outperforms the "build your own approach" by a factor of two to five (Plettenberg, 2019).

14 A minimum contract duration of two years versus no minimum duration of contract increased ARPU by 13 percent and NPV by 19 percent, without decreasing the number of subscribers! (Plettenberg, 2019).

15 Median pricing escalator of companies with multiyear contracts is 3 percent per year (SKP benchmark study post-COVID; confidential source from conference presentation: it might be close to 5 to 7% these days).

I have other statistics to offer, but doing so would be overkill. From the above, you can already make many decisions about your subscription pricing approach.

If you have time, do your own research at these websites and conduct primary research. If you have the budget, it's worth it.

Useful tips for industrial subscription pricing

Embrace best practices from the best SaaS pricing leaders who've conducted large studies many times before. If 70 percent of SaaS companies use a good/ better/best approach, this may be the preferred approach. You could begin with a simple one-offer model and eventually move to a good/better/best model.

1   **Keep it simple (KISS).** Begin with simple pricing and pivot quickly as you learn more from your early adopters. Sometimes you need to wait to introduce usage-based components or volume tiers, for example. The key is to avoid very complex pricing structures that no one understands.

2   **Embrace freemium and "cheapmium" as an acquisition strategy with a focus on conversion.** Freemium is a not a pricing strategy. These are famous words from Patrick Campbell. More companies are embracing freemium as they master the conversion of free to paid subscribers. So it's not for everyone, and maybe not from the get-go. Freemium and free trials help familiarize users with a solution before they decide to purchase. It's a point of entry to validate value.

> We saw the number of SaaS companies with a free offering continue to increase in 2021. The biggest jump was among companies selling into Midmarket and Enterprise customers. That's perhaps not surprising if you've been following the successes of Enterprise-focused public companies with new free offerings including PagerDuty, JFrog, New Relic, Appian, and Nutanix. (Poyar, 2021a)

3   **Publish your pricing to avoid guesswork.** I'm a big believer in transparency and in avoiding asking subscribers to jump through hoops to find out about pricing. That discourages people from subscribing. If you feel your pricing is too high, tie pricing to an ROI calculation or a web value simulator to make it easier to accept.

4   **Avoid the "contact sales for pricing" as much as possible.** This is the kiss of death. Our research of 100 industrial subscriptions shows that many companies use this function on their website. This is counterproductive. You can't do a digital transformation and ask customers to call sales for pricing. It shows a lack of confidence in your value and pricing. Remember that over 55 percent of the sales process is now fully digitalized. Procurement teams and potential subscribers need information to be able to do their homework. According to industry analyst firm Gartner (Adamson, 2019), customers often advance along the various steps in the buying

process in parallel. Moreover, according to Accenture (Angelos et al., 2017), most customers are 57 percent of the way through their buying process before they meet with representatives of the vendors they're considering.

> I think that radical transparency in a subscription business is super important. And being incredibly consumer-centric. It's little things like ensuring that every time you take a payment, you send your customer an email to make them aware that that payment is coming out of their account, being clear, when a customer signs up what they're signing up for. This radical transparency around the financial transactions in a subscription model goes a long way to build trust with your consumers. (Sally Higgin, senior director, brand marketing, at shaving brand Harry's, quoted in Atkins, 2021)

5   **Create a user-friendly pricing landing page.** First, make sure future subscribers can find the pricing page. Some websites are not user-friendly and are tough to navigate. Second, make sure your pricing is easy to visualize and fits on one page. Some companies give too many details up front instead of using roll-down menus or "click here for more details" buttons. A good pricing package fits on one screen.

6   **Design for good/better/best but start with the good as a single offer to test the waters.** Don't overload your first offer and immediately give away the farm. If you're still developing your solution, call it a beta and offer a pricing package and model for this beta and not for the betas of the best solution loaded with all high-value functionalities. Your packaging and modeling will evolve over time.

7   **Design a pricing roadmap that includes pricing for retention, expansion, and renewal.** As you develop a product roadmap, also develop a pricing roadmap to match the evolution of your business plan. Pricing isn't static. You'll pivot many times over the duration of your business plan. You might begin with a simple one-offer subscription. Then move to a good/better/best packaging. Next, you might introduce a freemium model as a point of entry and/or a pay-as-you-go offer for customers who want to move to pure usage-based pricing.

8   **Empower subscribers to oversee their subscription pricing.** Allow subscribers to easily connect your platform to upgrade, downgrade, suspend, or cancel their subscriptions. This is a lesson from the subscription fatigue phenomenon I wrote about earlier in this book. Of course, you need to have a subscription engine that allows them to do so. Again, asking them to connect with customer service to do so might frustrate subscribers.

> We give our customers the flexibility to make changes to their subscription, which then of course keeps us focused on what we do for

them and how to improve in our key value proposition, which is enabling AI-driven service management. (Samantha Wilmot, vice president and general manager of CareAR, a Xerox Company; link no longer available)

9 **Do enough homework with the three C's of pricing.** I have pushed the three C's of pricing for many years now. It's the best way to perform a 360-degree analysis of what's important. Before you price, you need to understand your costs, find out about competitors' pricing or pricing anchors in the same category, and evaluate the economic value you bring to your subscribers versus competition. Adopt a discipline for the three C's and have teams engaged to work on the process.

10 **Set prices high enough to share value with your partners in the ecosystem.** If you price too low, there's little room to share value with your resellers, distributors, or agents. You might have to pay a 50 percent commission or give a 25 percent margin to channel partners. If these aren't incentivized well, they won't sell your subscription in the market. It's as simple as that. The same goes for the salesforce's commissions!

11 **Find the true level of differentiation of your subscription.** Is your subscription offer truly differentiated or not? Are you a me-too subscription, or do you bring additional and unique benefits? These are key questions. If you're truly differentiated, I recommend that you slow down and conduct a deeper analysis of the three C's of pricing. Conduct customer interviews and evaluate your differentiation value. If not, benchmark other offers in the market and see how you'll position your industrial subscription versus others. You can do this within a couple of days. For example, if you're in the field of remote condition-based monitoring or vibration analysis, you'll find dozens of competitors offering these solutions. How might you justify a higher premium?

Armed with these statistics and best practices, you should be able to make progress with your subscription pricing. There's no secret formula for this. You need to gather all relevant information, understand your context, do your homework, and make the best decisions you can. I've done this for many SaaS and industrial companies. For some, it took a day and a half in a room with the top decision-makers. They needed to upgrade their pricing and were open to listening to the expert. We got it done very fast and were able to test it in a matter of two weeks. For other companies, I used a 90-day sprint approach, as the offer was a true innovation in their industrial market and the team wanted to get customer insights while calculating the value of their subscription. So, we assembled a cross-functional team to do the work. We did it in 90 days without breaking the bank while using all internal available information. Half the battle in pricing is attention and intention. Once you have the commitment of the team, it can go very fast. It would have been different 20 years ago. But, today, many companies have done it, and there are hundreds if not thousands of subscription case studies.

Lightning Strike: How Industrial Companies Can Approach Pricing to Grow the Bottom Line

Kyle Poyar

For companies like Slack, Expensify, and Dropbox, product usage serves as the primary driver of user acquisition, expansion, and retention, meaning these companies can forgo spending large sums on traditional marketing and sales activities. Instead, they rely on the products themselves to supply a pipeline of satisfied users and "hand raisers" they can turn into paying customers. This phenomenon is what OpenView calls *product-led growth (PLG)*—a capital-efficient model through which companies can scale quickly.

The goal of every product-led business should be to get the product into the hands of the user as quickly and as seamlessly as possible. By removing any barriers to initial usage, you're giving users the chance to truly experience your product free from marketing, sales, or any other disruptions. But doing so means you'll have to offer something of *initial value for free*. This could certainly come in the form of a freemium edition, as is the case with Trello, Slack, Expensify, Evernote, UberConference, Drift, and countless other products.

The freemium approach

Freemium works particularly well for companies operating in markets with millions of potential users, when there's virality and network effects built into the product, or when you have the capital to worry about monetization later. In the case of Expensify, a travel and expense app, a freemium offering enables the company to appeal to end users who are sick and tired of outdated expense reports. They want to make it as simple as possible for these users to find and use the product. Monetization happens later, with features that appeal to accounting teams who need more sophistication and customization. As Jason Mills, director of sales and success at Expensify, puts it:

> A lot of people find us organically because we're really serving a need and a pain point, they already have. We just happen to be very highly rated, easy to find and have a great business model, because it's free to sign up and [someone can] use the product without having to necessarily make a buying decision.

With Drift, a sales communication platform, they've recognized that the virality built into their free product serves essentially as free advertising for the business. As CEO David Cancel explains:

> Another reason to go free is because we want to get on as many business websites as possible. We're willing to play along. But every one of those business websites is free advertising and a referral back to Drift, so why wouldn't we?

But contrary to popular belief, a freemium model is not a necessary component of product-led growth. Conversion rates on freemium plans are notoriously low, typically hovering between 3 and 5 percent, and can attract users who are not in your target market. Moreover, if you make the free offering too good, you could end up competing against yourself in a deal. As Craig Walker, Founder and CEO at DialPad, notes:

> We made our free service almost too good so we have a lot of very dedicated, very happy free users, and sometimes we have a hard time upselling them because they're like, "Hey, why would I need anything else?" Our stiffest competition is coming from ourselves!

The free trial

An alternative to a freemium offering is a free trial that does not require the user to enter credit card information to sign up. This method is employed by companies like Datadog and Deputy. Alternatively, you might offer a free feature that ties back to the value of your core product offering, as HubSpot did with Website Grader. Yoav Shapira, who served as VP of Engineering at HubSpot during their hyper-growth years, describes how this worked and why it was a good way to quickly prove value to users:

> Trials are good to do, but trials are often too long. At HubSpot we had a tool called Website Grader... Its entire existence was about creating time to value. It's free. You put in a URL—your site or your competitor's—and we analyze the site using our marketing methodology.

Join.me, the online meeting software provider, took a different approach. Initially, new Join.me users would start with a 14-day free trial of their premium product. After the 14 days, a user could either pay up to keep using the upgraded model or let their trial lapse and be kicked down to the basic version of Join .me. This strategy enabled the company to capture individual users who had not been granted licenses to costlier products. Join.me's VP of eCommerce at the time, Eric Bisceglia, explains:

The perpetually free model in the early days actually fueled very, very massive adoption because there was nothing good in the market that was doing that… It got to the point where in a few years, we had millions of new users each week.

Over time, Join.me's rapid growth signaled to the company that a freemium product might no longer be necessary to sustain growth. Instead, they discovered a better way to monetize their users. Bisceglia notes:

The decision was made to end-of-life the free product, move solely to a 14-day free trial, and if you don't buy, you get nothing, and you have to pay to continue. It actually turned out that there was a huge opportunity to monetize that base by turning off that fully free product and going just purely to a free trial model.

Monetize your user base

Now that you've got your product into the hands of as many users as possible, and they've fallen in love, it's time to monetize that value you've created for them. Successful product-led businesses set up scalable monetization models that make it easy to land-and-expand their customer base. PLG companies land paying customers by being strategic about the features they place in paid plans and when they attempt to convert free users into paying customers. But they don't stop there. PLG companies then use value metrics and different product tiers to increase ARPU (average revenue per user). Dropbox, for instance, takes a very data-driven approach to identifying what features they can monetize to upsell existing users and strike the right balance between user happiness and monetization. They do so with in-depth user research and customer development, incorporating pricing into those conversations. As Giancarlo Lionetti, who heads up Product Marketing and Demand Generation at Dropbox for Business, shares:

We really respect the value that we give to the user with the free product, but we do a lot of aggressive testing to see like what that threshold is. What do our users really care about?… One we'll do a lot of surveying. We'll ask our users, do they value X feature enough to pay for it, right? There's a lot of interactions with our users so we really understand the value they're getting. And if it's worth actual dollars to them, or is it just amusing. We do conjoints, we do user studies.

Slack makes another great example. Their core offering is free for an unlimited period, but its message archives are capped at 10,000 messages, and file storage is limited to 5GB. Once a free user runs up against those limitations,

Slack has in-app notifications suggesting that they upgrade to a paid version. Kelly Watkins, Head of Global Marketing at Slack, explains:

> One of the differences between a free plan and our paid plans is that one could transition to a paid plan, so you have access to your entire archive of messages for all time. On the free plan, that's limited to 10,000 of your most recent messages. So generally within the product, when you get to that threshold of 10,000 messages and go over that, we have a very small notification to you that says, "Hey, you know if you would like to have access to your entire archive, that's available, and here's how you access that."

Expensify similarly tracks usage to pinpoint when a company may be ready to become a paying customer. Specifically, what they've found, according to Jason Mills, is as follows:

> If you get about three or more users in your company submitting things your way, that's a signal to us that there's a latent opportunity here. And that's an opportunity that we need to reach out and have a better conversation around.

Expensify also charges based on the number of active users, which gives them a great expansion opportunity as individuals share Expensify with their teams, and then their departments and entire companies.

Key takeaways

In summary, don't jump straight into a freemium pricing model. It's best to begin by making it incredibly easy for people to use your product. That's focus number one. The value should come before the paywall sets in. After they've fallen in love with your product, include key features in paid plans that users are willing to pay for and communicate with your customers when their usage indicates that they're ready to pay up. Finally, grow accounts over time with value metrics and packages that naturally scale as customers get increasingly hooked on the product. With these tips, you'll be able to implement a well-oiled PLG approach to pricing in no time. Check our blog for more content on PLG or subscription pricing.

Notes

This article is an excerpt of OpenView's PLG Playbook.

About Kyle Poyar

Kyle leads OpenView's Growth Team, responsible for advising portfolio executive teams on strategies to increase revenue growth and dominate their markets. The team has helped the portfolio generate over $100 million in additional enterprise value in the last three years. Kyle specializes in pricing and packaging strategy, which is the most effective yet overlooked growth lever at a SaaS company's disposal. He's an expert in product-led growth, optimizing go-to-market strategies, and SaaS benchmarks. Before joining OpenView, Kyle was a director at Simon-Kucher & Partners, the global marketing and strategy consulting firm known as the world leader in pricing. Over the course of six years, he led consulting teams on strategy engagements with market leaders in enterprise software, business information/data services, digital media, online marketplaces, and telecommunications. www.openviewpartners.com

References

Adamson, B. (2019). *CSO update: The new B2B buying journey and its implication for sales.* Gartner. https://emtemp.gcom.cloud/ngw/globalassets /en/sales-service/documents/trends/cso-update.pdf

Angelos, J., Davis, P., & Gaylard, M. (2017). *Make music, not noise.* Accenture. www.accenture.com/_acnmedia/PDF-60/Accenture -Strategy-B2B-Customer-Experience-PoV.pdf

Atkins, O. (2021). The rise of the subscription economy. *The Drum,* May 4. www.thedrum.com/news/2021/05/04 /the-rise-the-subscription-economy

Bhatt, S. (2018). *A deep look at freemium and why you're probably going to go free in the future.* ProfitWell. www.profitwell.com /freemium-acquisition-book

Konary, A., & Pineda, J. (2021). *How to nail the "land and expand" model to drive subscription growth.* Subscribed Institute and Boston Consulting Group. www.zuora.com/resource/how-to-nail-the-land -and-expand-model-to-drive-subscription-growth/

Plettenberg, P. (2019). *ATKearney: Myths of monetization, episode 1: Pre-defined bundles or "build your own" offer?* LinkedIn, July 9. www.linkedin.com/pulse/myths-monetization-episode -1-pre-defined-bundles-your-plettenberg/

Poyar, K. (2016). Insights from 100 SaaS companies: Why it's time to rethink your packaging strategy. *OpenView Blog,* July 27. No longer available.

Poyar, K. (2021a). 7 new product-led insights. *Kyle Poyar's Growth Unhinged,* July 22. https://kylepoyar.substack.com/p/7-new-product-led-insights

Poyar, K. (2021b). Pricing insights from 2,200 SaaS companies. *OpenView Blog*, January 19. https://openviewpartners.com/blog/saas-pricing-insights/#.Ya-6Z9DMKNd

Pytel, C. (2018). SaaS pricing: Strategies, frameworks & lessons learned. *Open-View Blog*, June 4. https://openviewpartners.com/blog/saas-pricing-strategies-frameworks-lessons-learned/#.Ya-8DtDMKNd

Zuora. (2021, March). *Subscription Economy Index Report*. Available at www.zuora.com/resource/subscription-economy-index/

13

The Value Metric Is Your North Star

Steven Forth

THE SIMPLEST WAY TO implement value-based pricing is to find a way to connect your value metric to your pricing metric.

Your *value metric* is the unit by which a user consumes your solution that correlates with value. In some cases, one needs multiple value metrics or different value metrics for different segments. The value metric can be a composite of several value drivers.

Your *pricing metric* is the unit by which a buyer consumes your solution that determines the price. The pricing metric can also be a composite of several variables.

The value metrics often differ by segment, which is why one frequently wants to have different pricing models for different segments. Value-based pricing is as simple as this. Let's look at a couple of examples.

The classic example, much beloved in pricing circles, is "power by the hour." Rather than buying a jet engine, airlines lease the engine and only pay for the time that it's powering a plane. This model was introduced by Rolls-Royce almost 60 years ago and redefined the jet engine industry. A more modern example is pay-per-click advertising. Introduced to the search world by GoTo .com in 1998 and made the standard by Google in 2002, pay-per-click has largely replaced payment per impression, as it's thought to be a closer approximation of value. Advertisers are paying for attention, and the act of clicking through is a strong indicator of attention. We now have enough experience with connecting value to pricing metrics to approach it in a more formal and systematic way. Begin with the simple linking of the pricing and value metrics (Figure 13.1).

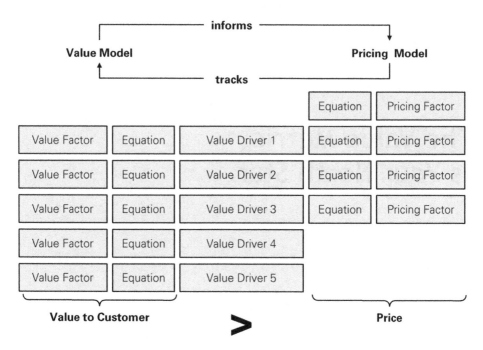

Figure 13.1. Connecting the value and pricing metrics.

For most businesses there's no single, simple value metric. There are three dimensions to value that need to be considered—economic, emotional, and community—and these interact in complex ways. Additionally, value is always relative to the alternative and depends on the current and projected business situation for the target customers. In other words, you need a value model in order to generate one or more value metrics. Because value is complex, in most cases you need a pricing model to go along with your value model. Models here are generally some form of mathematical model, a set of connected equations (sometimes referred to as algorithms in the pricing literature) that can generate a range of values for the value model and pricing model. If value and price are to be related, which is, after all, the goal of value-based pricing, then some of the variables that determine value should also be used to determine pricing. This is the second step in designing value-based pricing (Figures 13.2 and 13.3).

One simple check to see whether you're actually executing on value-based pricing is as follows:

1 List all the variables that determine whether a customer gets value from your solution (you don't need to build a model at this point).
2 List all the variables that determine your pricing.
3 See whether any of these variables are shared.

Value Metrics	Pricing Metrics
Automated Inspection (replacing physical inspection with data monitoring)	
Number of fixtures to be inspected	Number of inspections
Time saving per inspection	Alternate pricing metric
Reduction in risk from more accurate inspections	Number of fixtures inspected (monitored)
Industrial filter (that controls flow based on purity)	
Throughput and level of purity of a filtering system	An equation integrating throughput and purity
Surfacing agent (that controls flow based on purity)	
Reduction in rework	Square meters covered × labor cost weighting factor
Quality index	
Precision Agriculture System (monitoring crop health and pest load)	
Convert crops to organic	Crop type (organic and grade) × acres under cultivation
Increase crop yields	
Increase yield at higher-quality grades	
Reduce input costs	

Figure 13.2. Sample value and pricing metrics for industrial applications.

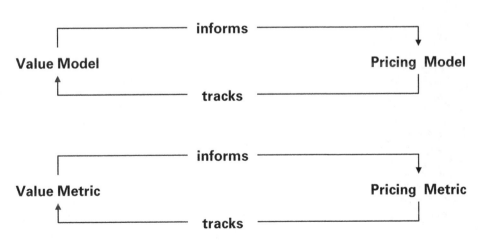

Figure 13.3. Value models and pricing models share variables.

If, at the end of this check, no variables are shared, then you're not doing value-based pricing.

If your price loosely correlates with value, perhaps because you're using your pricing software to estimate willingness to pay (WTP), or because you build economic value estimation models or EVE™ and price within the differentiation value (see Nagle & Müller, 2017; Liozu, 2016), you're engaged in something like value-correlated pricing, an important step on the way to value-based pricing.

What are these variables, and where do they come from?

They generally fall into three classes: customer properties, usage, and external. Another way of organizing them is according to those that change continuously, those that are discrete and event-driven, and those that are fixed over the period being modeled (Figure 13.4).

You'll notice that the customer and solution variables are often the same, just viewed from different perspectives, for example contract terms or usage. In a well-designed system, these are places where value and pricing connect.

There are a few things to note here. Value is determined by the interplay of customer properties, the operating environment, and how these are brought together by the solution.

Fixed variables are the easiest to handle. They're generally entered into the model by hand. Depending on your business, they could be the number of beds in a hospital, the number of steps in an automated process, the number of named users accessing a solution, and so on.

Continuously changing variables are trickier. One subset is usage data. Usage data is increasingly used in pricing, and, according to research by Zuora, inclusion of usage in a pricing model leads to better pricing outcomes (Xia,

	Fixed	Continuous	Event
Customer	Variables fixed in the contract	Usage Outcomes	Change in business model Merger or acquisition
Environment	(The background operating environment is usually assumed, though this can introduce risk)	FX rate Input cost (like energy or raw materials) Competitor prices	Competitor action Major change in economic conditions (like a global pandemic) Discontinuous change in input costs
Solution	Variables fixed in the contract	Usage Outcomes	Contingent functionality of contract changes based on customer or environment events

Figure 13.4. Organizing value and pricing variables.

2020). Variables may be tracked by other software systems, systems like CRM (customer relationship management) or ERP (enterprise resource planning). Here one wants to integrate with these systems so that their data are continually feeding the value model. Sometimes the continuous variables are external to the customer, such as exchange rates or energy prices. There are many data feeds available today that can also be used to inform the value model and keep it current.

Events are the trickiest type of data to manage. These can be unpredictable and might not even be known in advance (the experience with the COVID-19 pandemic during 2020 was an impactful external event for many organizations that had a big impact on value models). A lot of work is being done in event detection and event-driven architectures (see Bellemare, 2020, for a current perspective), and this is on the cutting edge of pricing research. The variables are important, but they need to be organized, and you need a model for that. The design of value and pricing models, and how to connect them, is beyond the scope of this chapter, but there are two general approaches: formal modeling and machine learning.

Formal modeling is the traditional approach. This is basically an application of economic value estimation, mentioned above, and related approaches. One works with customers and their customers to understand how value is created, communicated, delivered, and recognized. Once all these things are understood and the critical pieces integrated into a model, one is ready to capture value in price; Figure 13.5). It's increasingly important to include the emotional and community aspects of value in this work (Chiang, 2020).

The other approach to building value and pricing models is machine learning, especially the current approaches to deep learning. This requires large data sets that are often not available for B2B or early-stage solutions, but when the data can be gathered, machine learning is a way not only to build value and pricing models but also to keep them current. These machine-built models will need to be justified (and there may even be legal requirements to do so in certain industries such as health care). This means that machine-built models used for value and pricing will need to use the principles of explainable AI or xAI. DARPA (the people who brought us the internet) is leading much of the research in this area (Turek, 2018). Models require data, and the availability of data is one of the biggest changes over the past decade. There are four drivers for this:

- the Internet of Things
- the shift to cloud services
- the ease of integration
- the value of data

The Internet of Things is filling our world with data. This will transform how we approach building value and pricing models for many of the things in our

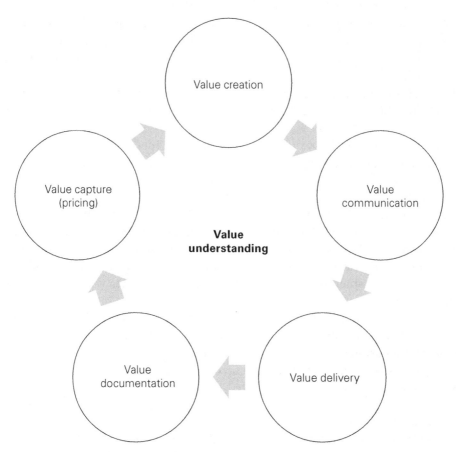

Figure 13.5. The value innovation cycle.

world and will help shift pricing of many things, from industrial devices to home appliances, to subscriptions (Davies & Fortuna, 2020). The same is true of the shift from on-premise software to services hosted in the cloud. Cloud services are easily monitored and encourage various forms of usage or consumption-based pricing. It's worth spending some time on Amazon's AWS pricing (https://aws.amazon.com/pricing/) or Microsoft Azure's pricing (https://azure .microsoft.com/en-ca/pricing/) to see what mature usage-based pricing looks like.

The integration of data across platforms is also getting easier and more common. There are many lightweight integration services available today that make it easier to connect data to value and pricing models. Is this dynamic pricing? Perhaps it's one form, but it's a form that's informed by value models that are understood by both buyer and seller.

As data becomes more available, it's also becoming more valuable, and there's a lot of work being done on how to price data (Liozu & Ulaga, 2018). This is

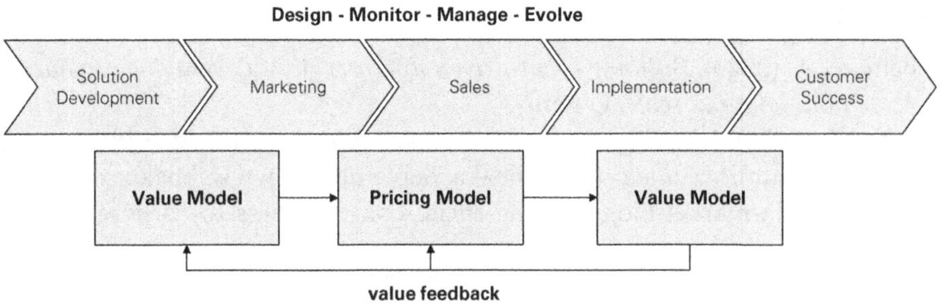

Design - Monitor - Manage - Evolve

Figure 13.6. Value and pricing models across the customer journey.

creating a positive feedback loop that's drawing more and more data out into the open, where it can be used in value and pricing models. Over time, an ecology of data feeds and services will change how we design, monitor, and manage value and pricing models.

Value and pricing models are not just for the pricing function. They connect solution development, through marketing sales to implementation and customer success (Figure 13.6). This creates a feedback loop across these functions and keeps everyone focused on the key activities of creating, communicating, delivering, documenting, and of course capturing value.

The skills needed to execute on this approach go beyond what's conventionally expected of pricing experts. Design, data modeling, customer experience, and business analysis all need to be brought to bear to design and apply value and pricing models across business processes. Developing these new skill sets and building the teams that combine these different skills will be critical to pricing teams over the coming years. This is part of the evolution of the pricing profession to the value profession and the shift from price management to value management.

Notes

Economic Value Estimation and EVE are trademarks of Monitor Deloitte.

About Steven Forth

Steven Forth is Managing Partner at Ibbaka Performance, a company bringing together value-based approaches to the market and customer with skill management to align market and capability. His own career combines deep roots in pricing with work in design thinking and performance management. He writes and speaks frequently on topics from pricing to organizational design and innovation. Living in Vancouver, he can often be found on a bicycle, in a kayak, or working in the garden. steven@ibbaka.com—ibbaka.com

References

Bellemare, A. (2020). *Building event-driven microservices: Leveraging organizational data at scale.* O'Reilly.

Chiang, K. (2020). *Weaving social consciousness into corporate identity—Community value drivers.* Ibbaka, September 3. www.ibbaka.com/ibbaka-market-blog/weaving-social-consciousness-to-corporate-outcomes-community-value-drivers

Davies, J., & Fortuna, C. (2020). *The Internet of Things: From data to insight.* Wiley.

Liozu, S. (2016). *Dollarizing differentiation value.* Value Innoruption Advisors Publishing.

Liozu, S., & Ulaga, W. (2018). *Monetizing data: A practical roadmap for framing, pricing, and selling your B2B digital offers.* Value Innoruption Advisors Publishing

Nagle, T. T., & Müller, G. (2017). *The strategy and tactics of pricing,* 6th ed. Routledge.

Turek, M. (2018). *Explainable Artificial Intelligence (XAI).* DARPA, www.darpa.mil/program/explainable-artificial-intelligence

Xia, J. J. (2020). *Drive growth with usage-based pricing.* Zuora, www.zuora.com/guides/drive-growth-usage-based-pricing/

14

Designing Your Subscription Pricing Approach

THERE'S SO MUCH TO write about subscription pricing. I recommend reading as much as you can on the topic. This space is evolving rapidly, driven by the tremendous number of subscription dollars running through the multiple commercially available subscription engines like Zuora, Gotransverse, Chargebee, Recurly, Opencell, and many more. Companies like ProfitWell and ValueShips track pricing best practices and communicate about trends and new subscription pricing models. For this chapter, I recruited two experts in subscription pricing who've worked many years to help companies design and scale their subscription offers. Both share their recommended approaches in the form of a Lightning Strike essay.

Lightning Strike: Seven Steps to Define Your Subscription Pricing Architecture

Mrinal (MG) Gurbaxani

In the last decade, the leading industrial organizations have woken up to customer-centric, subscription pricing. With many more degrees of freedom in determining pricing strategy in the subscription world, smart commercial-excellence teams are reaping the rewards of well-understood value-based pricing. How to optimally land-and-expand, bundle and unbundle SKUs and services into solutions, differentiate by delivery mechanisms, subscription term-lengths... the wide range of monetization options can seem intimidating. So, what can manufacturers learn from the darlings of subscription innovation, SaaS companies? Before getting into the seven steps, we'd like to embed an acronym, P&P, ubiquitous in Silicon Valley. Pricing is no longer simply an annual x percentage increase exercise; it's simultaneous packaging and pricing decisioning. Best-in-class SaaS companies today even have dedicated P&P functions reporting directly to the C-suite.

1. Define your P&P vision

Product, sales, marketing, finance can often have conflicting short-term monetization-related objectives. There will inherently be trade-offs, and getting aligned on the business outcomes you want your P&P to achieve in the next 12 months is the place to start. Write this down.

Depending on where you are on your market adoption journey, your monetization goals and strategies can be vastly different. For example, during the adoption phase of a new solution, it's recommended to have a simple attack pricing strategy to validate the value proposition, acquire key promoters, and grow users. Offering the right promotions and incentives is all part of your monetization toolkit at the adoption stage. Fast-forward to the growth stage, and now your monetization strategy is centered around communicating value to overcome low price anchors from adoption stage without disrupting growth. Think Netflix: they began with a simple, low price point at $4.99/month. Today, you have a menu of good/better/best options that align value with price by communicating the difference in HD versus SD, single-screen versus multiscreen, and so forth.

The key takeaway is that your P&P should not be static, it should evolve over time—but begin by writing a vision statement for what you want your P&P to achieve in the next 12 months.

2. List your customer value drivers and equations

Many evangelical SaaS companies still take an egocentric view of value estimation: return on investment (ROI). No SaaS buyer's bonus is based on achieving an ROI target from a piece of tech—it's based on hitting their org's KPIs. Even in B2B SaaS buying decisions, selling is still person-to-person, and the results need to align with the buyer's personal targets. To achieve customer-centric pricing, it's important to first articulate the customer business problem(s) you're solving, and how, by solving those problems, your solution delivers benefits to the customer. Good practice is to document the customer's business KPIs that will be directly impacted by the solution, and then define how this leads to increased revenue/margin or saved cost. Best practice is to go one step further and work out an estimated range of impact of what customers will actually achieve in terms of improved business KPIs and dollars. To provide an example from the configure-price-quote (CPQ) SaaS space, "efficiency gains of X% lead to an ROI of Y" is fuzzy at best and difficult to measure. This can be broken down into constituent value drivers. For example, they might be (1) a reduction in average cycle-time-to-quote, (2) a reduction in sales operations time spent on deal approvals, or (3) an increase in cross-sell rate. These are hard metrics that can be quantified, relate back to business performance, and can make the buyer a hero within their organization.

This value-driven pricing approach is not unique to SaaS. GE Infrastructure Water & Process Technologies has a tagline: "Proof, not promises." SKF Documented Solutions says, "Real world savings—and we can prove it!" These slogans are commitments to measure and document success at the customer level, not only hyped-up success stories during the sales process. In turn, this value measurement helps these B2B companies gain trust, understand their differential value, and craft value propositions that resonate with target customers.

In summary, if you want to achieve value-based P&P, you need to build on the right foundations. Building a common organizational understanding of how you deliver value to customers, and how much, is the cornerstone in nailing your monetization strategy.

3. Shortlist your viable pricing metric(s)

Naturally flowing from your customer value drivers, selecting your pricing metric(s) is arguably the most important monetization decision to get right (Figure 14.1). Should your pricing metric be input-based, for example based on customer size? Or usage-based, such as by number of miles traveled? Or perhaps even outcome-based, such as on a number of transactions linking directly to the value your customer is achieving? Should you have more than one pricing metric?

In 2001 Michelin launched a new tire that would last 20 percent longer than the original. However, no trucking/logistics customer was willing to pay 20 percent more per tire. Further, with the tires lasting longer, how would this potentially small increase in price justify the big drop in long-term demand?

Strategic	Customer-centric	Operational
1 Supports land-and-expand	4 Aligns to how your customer gets value and how they make money	7 Needs to be measurable, enforceable, billable and not gameable
2 Grows naturally over time resulting in ARR increase		8 Ideally stable— not impacted by seasonality, does not shrink in a recession
3 Does not discourage adoption/behaviour you want to drive	5 A known input by customer OR enables high predictability of total costs	
	6 Easy to communicate and understand why it is being used	9 Aligned with any significant cost drivers you have for providing this service

Figure 14.1. Key criteria when selecting your pricing metrics.

So, how did Michelin monetize this superior quality? By setting price by distance traveled, per ton-kilometer: that is, linking it to customer outcomes. It was a bold move, one that put its money where its mouth was. It allowed fleet managers to pay for performance, and—importantly—it gave industrial vehicle owners the flexibility to manage costs appropriately in good times and bad. If a recession hit, reducing the demand for trucking services, then fleet owners would pay less for those tires since they were being charged by the kilometer, not by the tire. Take this one step further: measure annual customer miles traveled, and you now have a robust subscription model for Michelin Fleet Solutions and a predictable line item in the trucking customer's budget. Win-win. Michelin's new monetization model resulted in their boasting the biggest profits in the industry by 2011: earnings before interest and taxes (EBIT) was three times that of Goodyear and 25 percent higher than Bridgestone.

In the subscription world, your choice of pricing metrics helps you align with and communicate the value drivers from Step 2. Practically, your feasible metric options should be viewed as a tool to differentiate yourself from the competition and to avoid the commodity trap.

4. Determine your packaging (bundling) structure

There are multiple packaging options well established in the SaaS industry today, and the customer usage and value principles apply directly to physical goods industries. No model is inherently good or bad, but it's important to recognize that there are certain situations when certain models work well, or poorly.

Before determining your packaging structure, you should have answered three questions:

1 What individual components of the solution see different levels of willingness to pay from different customers?
2 What feasible options do you have for splitting the solution into packages (today vs. short term)?
3 What makes sense strategically for your business: for example, your health check service could be split out into an add-on module, and customers would pay for it, but is there a strategic reason why you want all customers to have access to it? (Link back to Step 1).

Figure 14.2 highlights how businesses like Netflix, LinkedIn, and Slack have developed a deep understanding of all three questions and have all deployed vastly different packaging strategies to drive desired customer behavior. At an early stage of market maturity, the simplest option is often a one-size-fits-all structure, which works well when you want to drive widespread engagement. Netflix began with the simple $4.99 per month, and then segmented customers into a good/better/best (GBB) structure after deriving significant learnings. The GBB bundles force customers to trade off on value and price. This

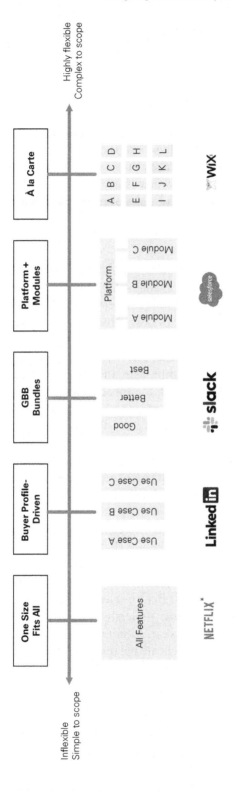

Figure 14.2. Spectrum of subscription packaging options.

*Netflix started out simple, but has progressed to GBB value-based.

is a commonly deployed structure when the solution offering can grow with customers' needs and when it's realistic for the business to differentiate packages flagging individual components. LinkedIn masters segmenting customers by persona and developing tailored packages based on typical use cases. Larger enterprise offerings such as CRM and ERP often evolve to a platform-plus-modules approach. This option works well when a specific product has universal appeal and use and, at the same time, customers need to complement that piece with highly differentiable sets of the solution. Finally, an à-la-carte model provides visibility into how each line item is valued and empowers customers to make apples-to-apples comparisons. The downside is that it fosters a cost-saving customer mindset and risks overwhelming customers with too much choice.

5. Select your pricing model

As with metrics and packaging models, there are numerous pricing model combinations that feed a subscription, available for SaaS companies, and these can creatively be applied to industrial goods and services, as Michelin did. But when is fixed pricing better than variable pricing? How about a hybrid model that has a subscription bundle plus a pay-per use (Figure 14.3)?

All pricing models have pros and cons worth considering. Fixed pricing models are usually easier to communicate and simpler to administer, which brings budgeting advantages for both the subscription company and the client. However, since a client may be using more services than paid for, these models work well when usage is predictable and consistent. On the other hand, variable pricing models are generally easier to sell to new customers because there's no starting fixed commitment, and they appreciate their flexibility. However, clients may not like it because of the cost risk of scope overruns. From the provider perspective, variable models make it harder to forecast revenue, and, in many cases, a metric can be hard to define or to measure. Finally, hybrid pricing models present the best of both worlds, guaranteeing recurring revenues plus a per-use upside, giving the perception of choice that customers sometimes demand. Nevertheless, these models require close monitoring and continuous optimization, which makes them harder to administer. For the customer, they can be more confusing to understand. Before selecting your subscription pricing model, it's imperative to have a clear understanding of the customer behavior you want to drive, now versus next year. Although businesses can switch pricing models over time, there's often a delicate balance to maintain, juggling existing customer expectations and readiness, operational complexity, and competitive positioning.

6. Price-level-setting methodology

There can be many inputs into the final piece of the P&P puzzle, not all of which are available or make sense for your business at present.

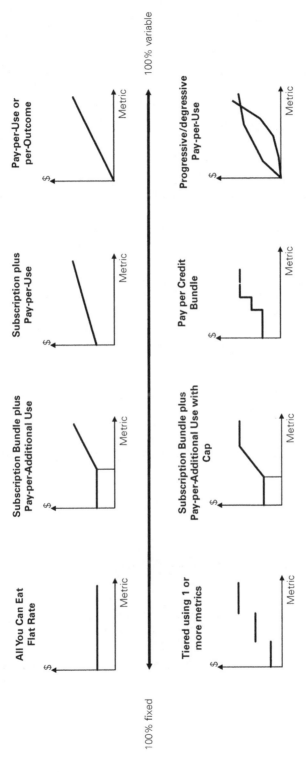

Figure 14.3. Spectrum of subscription pricing model options.

Among the topics we like to discuss in our consultancy engagements are these:

- How are you positioned in terms of price and value against competitors?
- What price have you been able to achieve in the market so far?
- What's the relative cost of "DIY" alternative solutions for your customer?
- Is there a maximum the market is willing to pay?
- How does price elasticity impact customer demand?
- What's the economic value added to a customer?
- Are there significant incremental costs that need to be covered?

A key recommendation is that steps 3, 4, and 5 be completed before attempting to set your price level. How you charge your customers comes before how much you charge.

7. Document the information gaps and an action plan to progress to an in-market P&P

Going through steps 1 through 6 will help you identify where you have information gaps. Which inputs make sense for your situation? What data could

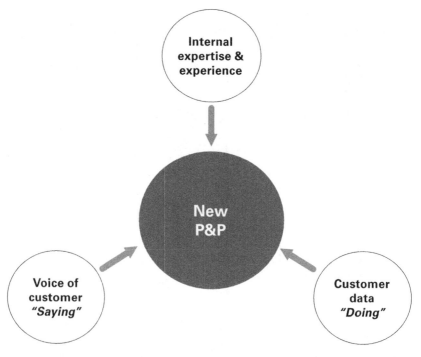

Figure 14.4. Triangulation of inputs for new P&P.

be fetched/captured to feed into price-level-setting with some additional effort? The goal is not to have perfect signals to feed your new P&P but to focus on getting a balanced view across your internal stakeholders, what your customers say they want and what they do with your solution (Figure 14.4). Finally, a brief word of caution. P&P strategy should not be viewed as static but should evolve over time. For that reason, a yearly refresh is advisable for most subscription businesses. As with product strategy, monetization strategy needs continuous improvement.

About Mrinal (MG) Gurbaxani

MG is the CEO and co-founder of cuvama. Over the last 17 years, MG has helped over 80 global B2B customers across manufacturing, distribution, high-tech, and software realize their monetization potential. As the software industry moved to SaaS, MG recognized that the shift of power to the customer was inevitable, and built a boutique consultancy, mgpricing, dedicated to this new and growing market need. After many years of solving the same problem set, the consulting know-how was codified into a tech platform, and cuvama was born. MG is passionate about game theory and is an active club chess and poker player. You're likely to find him on a tennis court or golf course on sunny afternoons. He holds a degree in Mathematics from the College of Wooster (USA) and an MBA from INSEAD (France/Singapore). He lives with his wife and two young daughters in London. Keep in touch with MG via the web www.cuvama.com and LinkedIn linkedin.com/in/mg-gurbaxani/

 Lightning Strike: Six Key Levers as You Design Your Industrial Subscription Offer

Felix Krohn

Subscriptions are catching the attention of many industrial companies, too. Manufacturing executives are examining what happened in the software world for the past eight years when most major software companies transitioned to become SaaS, that is, subscription companies, boosting their financial performance after a transition of two to three years. IoT and cloud-based services have enabled the creation of new subscription offers in the manufacturing world. Product-centric firms such as Caterpillar, John Deere, Sandvik, and Heidelberg have already begun to offer subscriptions for data and analytics around their equipment to counter the cyclicality of their revenue.

If you're exploring opportunities in the subscription age, it's crucial to, first, become familiar with a few important differences between a product-focused and a subscription business.

- The business objective shifts from the traditional creation of "hit products" to increasing customer lifetime value (CLV). Subscription businesses regard the customer relationship as a continuum where the service offering evolves throughout the customer relationship, ensuring that value is generated by consistently focusing on customer benefits and thereby driving CLV. Customer success managers help product managers develop, improve, and update subscription products based on their intimate knowledge of their customers' needs.
- Your service needs to include a positive customer experience, as it goes beyond the traditional product/brand value. Unlike licensing models that require a longer-term up-front commitment, a subscription-based model allows customers to try the service in advance—if the experience doesn't match expectations, customers will look for better alternatives.
- Your marketing and sales pitch shifts from presenting features to focus on outcomes. Customers cannot easily translate features into value by themselves, so you need to help explain the problem they set out to solve and quantify the value of their service in financial terms (ROI, EVA/EVC).
- Financial measurement needs to be reshaped. To assess a subscription business's health, backward-looking KPIs such as sales or order volumes will be replaced by portfolio value metrics: for example, annual or monthly recurring revenue (ARR, MRR), average CLV, and revenue retention rate or dollar-based net expansion rate (RRR, DBNE). These figures measure customer attrition and how effectively customers are purchasing additional services.
- The role of pricing is evolving as the focus moves from stand-alone, one-off prices to relationship-based price models. Bundling becomes more important and—together with well-designed add-on features—determines the subscription customers will eventually pay for.

Once you've engrained these important differences and your new subscription venture(s) is being equipped with the right governance models, your initial focus will be on the design of a compelling subscription offer that helps customers address and improve a relevant pain point, that is, a problem that's worth solving! Figure 14.5 lists the six key levers that industrial companies need to tackle in order to succeed in the subscription economy.

1. Segmentation is *the* name of the game. Reassess your customers, their jobs-to-be-done, pain points and resulting needs, and how they value (data-driven) services. Subscriptions require less commitment from buyers, lower up-front payments, and more flexible contracts, which can help you reach new customer segments. Further, the decision-makers and purchase influencers within your customer's business might vary when it comes to subscriptions; hence, you should carefully review your buyer persona profiles, also considering CapEx versus OpEx budgets. Segmentation must focus on how different

1 What jobs and pains do our customers have; hence what do they need?
   Segmentation (need-based)
2 What gains do our subscription services provide?
   Value proposition
3 How should we offer them?
   Offering/packaging
4 How should we charge them?
   a. Price metric
   b. Price model
5 How much should we charge them?
   Price levels
6 How should we set up day-to-day subscription management?
   Data, go-to-market, and finance capabilities

Figure 14.5. Six key levers.

groups of customers perceive value when measuring the outcomes and contribution of your subscription service to their business results (in terms of cost savings, improved cycle time, better process quality, better insights for decision-making, etc.).

2. Ensure that your value proposition is truly customer-focused and clearly articulated. Help your customer understand the gains, outcomes, and economic value added you're providing. A value proposition is about aligning your new subscription with the customer's needs: that is, the magic fit between what you offer and why people buy it. It works through the following.

- **Experience.** As said before, the product experience refers to how subscribing to your service makes the customer feel—it's the sum of the combined features and benefits and can be tracked using metrics such as net promoter score (NPS) or actual customer referrals.
- **Benefits.** A benefit is what your subscription does for the customer. The benefits are the ways that the features make your customer's life easier by increasing pleasure or decreasing pain.
- **Features.** Features are a factual description of how your service works. These are the functioning attributes of your subscription. They provide the "reasons to believe."

3. Packaging is becoming a critical discipline. Pricing professionals are becoming the product owners' best friends as they act as "choice architects," determining the right degree of customer flexibility for new XaaS offerings. Use product bundling to create suitable packages: Which features have potential to be paid for as add-ons versus which should be included in broader packages? Do we have differentiated offers for different segments? Also, consider portfolio upsell mechanics: Do we offer structured upsell paths, and, hence, are we driving demand toward higher-value packages?

4. Price model development breaks down into two questions.

- What to charge for—think long term and get away from price metrics that trend downwards or that you'll help reduce (e.g., number of users when selling efficiency tools): Which is a price metric that's meaningful to customers, accessible for the vendor (us), relates to the value provided, and is expected to grow? Should we follow market standards, or is this a way to differentiate our subscription offer from competitors? Do we want customers to understand how our pricing scales, or not? Do we want customers to compare prices with competition easily, or not?
- How to structure price tiers and price levels—watch out for a healthy risk-reward relationship: How comfortable do we feel with variable pricing elements? Do customers prefer predictability of their spend versus variable costs related to the usage or value delivered? From pure pay-per-use models to flat fees or any hybrid options—the decision has important impact on revenues. Understanding and quantifying the value and adequate price modeling are critical for pricing and revenue/profit optimization and to avoiding costly mistakes. Make sure the price model fits your strategy, reflects your cost structure, and captures the value you're delivering, according to your value proposition. The most common price model in your market might not necessarily be the right one for you, so you can be creative, but do the math!

5. Get the price level right. To decide on an introductory price, you should obtain as much data as possible from different sources: industry benchmarks, competitive analysis, economic value analysis, and market research (ideally, a mix of 10 to 15 in-depth customer interviews plus an online survey). No data point is a single source of truth; rather, you'll use the knowledge from across all four with the best judgment of your multifunctional team (product, sales, customer support, finance), also in view of your commercial goals—winning new customers, monetizing existing customers versus simply retaining them. At the same time, a test-and-measure mindset must materialize—no testing, no learning! This sounds simple, yet it's miles from a typical industrial DNA and way of working.

6. Once you've designed and priced the subscription, it's time for execution. Make sure the welcome and onboarding process is based on what subscribers need to get started and that eventually leads them to their desired outcomes. New subscribers need to take select actions upon using the new service as a key activation point. To grow your subscription business over time, you must identify the different types of revenue opportunities that are "hidden" in your customer base: customers that extract phenomenal value might be ready for an upsell. Customers that perceive good value are often excellent candidates for buying more services. At the same time, be aware of those customers who are getting low value and are most likely to churn. Customer and machine data (capacity/consumption/cost and output/OEE/productivity metrics) provide a goldmine of information for your subscription business's success. In addition, you should establish and begin tracking metrics that are focused on customer value: NPS, usage/engagement, average or total contract value (ACV, TCV), customer ROI. It goes without saying that all this requires suitable subscription billing and advanced data-analytics capabilities. Last but not least, change management is an often-undermanaged element in the subscription journey of traditional companies. Implementing a new subscription model requires significant time and effort. Finance and sales groups need to be involved early in the transformation process and sufficiently equipped with and trained around economic value-add tools and sales battle cards. In parallel, a thorough review of prevailing sales comp models is a mission-critical task to ensure alignment with the business model transformation.

About Felix Krohn

Felix Krohn is the Chief Transformation Officer at Aareon Group, the European market leader in property management software and digital solutions, a (minority-owned) portfolio company of Advent International. Until recently, Felix has worked as an independent Senior Advisor in the areas of Digital, Strategy, Innovation, Monetization, and Transformation for various private equity firms as well as corporate clients, mostly from the TMT industries. He still is a Coach for Pricing Excellence as well as a Mentor for various startups. Prior to that, Felix spent eight years at Wolters Kluwer, where he advised the CEO on business optimization and growth opportunities and where he built and led a global Pricing & BI/Analytics function. Felix had joined Wolters Kluwer from Simon-Kucher & Partners (SKP), where he was most recently a Partner and Managing Director for the firm's Spain office. Felix Krohn has an MSc degree in Business Administration from the University of Hamburg and attended Clayton Christensen's Executive Education on Disruptive Innovation at Harvard Business School.

15

Price Sensitivity Meter and Conjoint Analysis as Tools for Setting Your Industrial Subscription Pricing

THIS BOOK IS FOCUSED on quick wins and rapid go-to-market strategies and tactics. I want to make sure you learn enough to design your pricing approach using the best practices available. Remember that I assume that most industrial companies won't have the time, skills, and budgets to invest in advanced pricing research based on quantitative customer insights. I may be wrong. Some companies do invest in conjoint analysis and other research methods. Michelin, Hilti, and Stanley Black and Decker, for example, are diligently conducting customer research. My gut feeling is that they do so for disruptive digital innovations and for those having the greatest potential. Most are incremental innovations or me-too digital opportunities; they might be using best judgments or qualitative research. Nevertheless, I didn't want to write a book without mentioning two of the most advanced pricing research techniques that could be used: Van Westendorp's price sensitivity meter, and conjoint analysis. A web search for these research methods will reveal a fair amount of information about them. You'll also find critical feedback on what methods to use, why you should use them or not, and their flaws. I'm not an expert. I've used both methods keeping in mind "garbage in, garbage out." I've also used both methods with a fair amount of qualitative research to enrich the quantitative research methods with valuable insights. I've asked two experts in the pricing field to write a lightning strike each on one method. I could have researched this myself, but I defer to the experts. My objective is to show how to use these methods and what types of outcomes you can expect should you have time and resources to invest. One thing I want to mention before I let you read the expert notes is that both methods have been greatly simplified. You no longer need months and huge budgets to conduct them. I'm happy to say that digitalization has also helped simplify pricing research. That's good news!

Lightning Strike: How to Run a Price Sensitivity Meter Exercise?

By Maciej Wilczyński

Choosing the right pricing strategy

One of the key questions asked during product development efforts is *how should we price it?* Easiest is to apply a cost-based approach and add a healthy markup to the product and distribution costs—it's enough to pay the bills, but we're below the bottom line if the cost structure shifts.

Another idea is to see what the competition is doing within the pricing space. With that, it's easy to position your product as more expensive or as cheaper, depending on the overall brand strategy. However, there's a drawback here. If you're using competitor-based pricing, then it's not your pricing strategy at the end of the day, but your peers'. You probably wouldn't outsource product development efforts or sales to your competitors, so why do it with your core business model?

One strategy is simply the best but also the hardest to achieve for most companies: value-based pricing. This strategy sets the price based on how the customer perceives the value rather than on how much the product costs or the price of competitive products. To get it right, companies need to understand how much customers can pay to receive the benefits. Some try to estimate it based on previous sales, and some tend to focus on interviews, while a vast majority relies on a guess or gut feeling, as they spend too little time on that. For instance, a subscription company's average time on pricing improvements is less than 10 hours a year. In other words, we focus more on choosing the right toilet paper than on choosing the right pricing strategy.

To get it right, it's important to start from the willingness-to-pay concept. This essentially means how much your customer can pay for your product or service you offer. There are ways of doing it through interviews, as described in other sections of this book, or you can try getting it through Van Westendorp's price sensitivity meter.

Preparing the Price Sensitivity Meter survey

Van Westendorp's price sensitivity meter (PSM) has been with us since 1976, and it's one of the best techniques for determining the optimal price point. Market researchers widely use it, and it's one of the most effective tools available. It's also one of the easiest ways to discover the customer's willingness to pay.

In general, you need to ask these four survey questions to run the Van West-endorp PSM test:

- At what price would it be so low that you begin to question this product's quality?
- At what price do you think this product begins to be a bargain?
- At what price does this product begin to seem expensive?
- At what price is this product too expensive?

There are discussions around the order or exact phrasing of the questions, but "from cheapest to most expensive" tends to be prevalent in the literature. When it comes to sampling and its size, we need to focus on our goal. It's best to receive answers from the market, but current customers could also work if you don't have access to a panel or a research agency. The good thing is that ~100 survey responses are enough to drive meaningful results in B2B industries. Some research suggests it's 40 to 60, but reaching the above three-digit threshold allows for creating more segments and identifying different buyer personas. Naturally, for B2C products, we need to boost the sample size to at least 300 to 400. Keep in mind that we want to move quickly and make data-driven business decisions at the end of the day, so full statistical significance is not our goal. According to my experience, it's ~80 percent accurate, which is more than enough.

Plotting the data

Once you have all the responses, it's essential to plot them correctly. On the x-axis, you need to plot the price points, ideally in thresholds, closest to your hypothetical price. I recommend focusing on two decimal places; similarly, it's always good to round to fives and tens for more expensive products.

On the y-axis, it's critical to plot the cumulative number of responders. It's needed later, as it's essential to calculate the price elasticity and potential sales lost with the price increase.

Once done, it's possible to display it on a chart, as in Figure 15.1.

Each question asked corresponds to a line on the graph. If you follow the order proposed,

- the first question corresponds to the "too cheap" line
- the second corresponds to the "not expensive" line
- the third corresponds to the "not cheap" line, and
- the fourth corresponds to the "too expensive" line

Once it's done, you can interpret the data:

- The intersection of "too cheap" and "not cheap" is called the PMC, or the point of marginal cheapness.

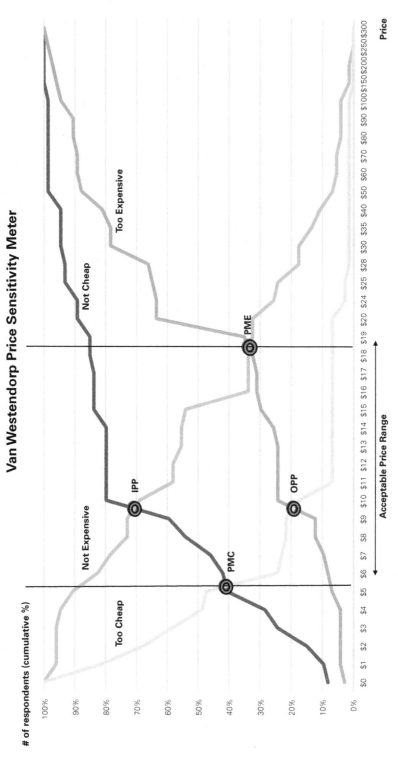

Figure 15.1. Price Sensitivity Meter interpretation.

- Its opposite, the intersection of "not expensive" and "too expensive," is the PME, or the point of marginal expensiveness.

These two are critical because this is precisely our price range. In other words, if you price the product between them, it's already good, but you can plot it further to discover the exact price point.

- The intersection of "too cheap" and "too expensive" is our OPP, or optimum price point. It's the price at which the number of respondents who consider the product too cheap equals the number who find it too expensive. You can interpret this as a market equilibrium that you've just discovered.
- Another point worth mentioning is the intersection of "not expensive" and "not cheap," called the IPP, or the indifference price point. It's the price that usually represents the median price or very often the leading brand on the market. If you combine the PSM with other survey questions, this may become useful.

This already provides a lot of knowledge, but there's more we can gain from the data set. If you take only the "too cheap" and "too expensive" lines and begin plotting them to the OPP, you can better understand the percentage of sales lost within the process.

This answers the fundamental question "what happens if I increase/lower the prices?" Also, it allows us to pick the right strategy: for example, if you want to focus on having the highest market share.

It's possible to focus on a penetration price. On the other hand, if the curve is flat, we can easily recognize how much money we're leaving on the table. It's an excellent hint to identify a customer's lifetime value-maximizing price.

Suppose you've gathered more than 100 surveys and asked other questions relevant to your business. You can now run some cross-tabs to identify different buyer personas. Doing so may lead to a complete redefinition of your current pricing scheme.

How to take your PSM even further
There are other things you can do with pricing research. One of them is the Newton-Miller-Smith extension, which adds two questions to the mix:

- At the ("not expensive" price listed by the responder), how likely are you to purchase this product in the next six months?
- At the ("not cheap" price listed by the responder), how likely are you to purchase this product in the next six months?

Both questions are rated on a 5-point likelihood scale. If you want, you can also use an NPS-like 0–10 scale, but keep in mind that it's widely known in the

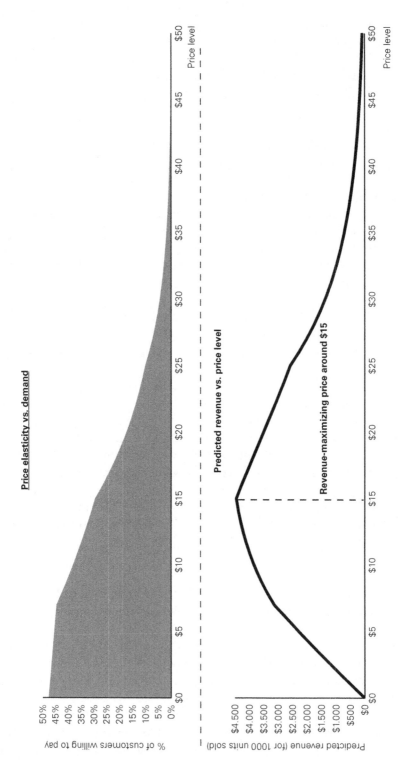

Figure 15.2. Applying the Newton-Miller-Smith PSM extension.

industry, so you don't want to bias your responders. Afterwards, apply these scores to create the two straightforward graphs illustrated in Figure 15.2.

Compared with the traditional PSM, this allows us to better understand the price elasticity of demand, which translates to "what happens if I increase my price by x percent?" You're no longer guessing; you're doing science.

On top of that, because you have the data, you can multiply the products sold by a 1,000 units to obtain the revenue curve, which shows the revenue-maximizing price. Sometimes it's different than the OPP derived using the standard approach, but that's why we're doing the extended analysis.

The biggest drawback of this analysis is that you need to use more advanced tools to run your survey. There's a need for question and answer piping, so free tools probably won't handle it. And although this isn't a substantial cost, it's always good to come prepared.

Pros and cons of PSM analyses

In general, PSM analyses are excellent for identifying your products' price points because they're relatively easy to perform, provide actionable information, and allow you to segment the data by customer. They also work great in B2B industries, as customers are more aware of their needs.

On the other hand, it doesn't take costs into consideration, so we need to cross it with internal data to see whether we retrieve a healthy profit margin. Also, it works amazingly well for new product development, but competitive pricing tends to be a challenge because the questions don't consider other products. Keep in mind that you need to put an analyst in place, so if you don't have capabilities within the organization, hiring a pricing research consultant/agency may help.

It's powerful knowledge that requires some effort and analytical data-driven thinking. Unfortunately, there are no quick growth hacks or A/B tests. The benefits of knowing your clients' willingness to pay can improve profitability by up to 12 percent, so investing in pricing provides a decent ROI.

About Maciej Wilczyński

Maciej Wilczyński is a co-founder and CEO of Valueships (https://valueships .com), a consulting boutique for subscription businesses, serving mostly SaaS/D2C. Valueships solves their clients' acquisition, retention, and monetization problems through data analytics and research. Wilczyński is an ex-McKinsey & Company marketing and sales consultant and has worked with top Fortune 500 companies in industries such as software, banking, telco, insurance, and retail/e-commerce. He is currently finishing his PhD in strategic management with a focus on pricing capabilities of SaaS companies. He is the author of multiple publications, an MBA/postgraduate lecturer, and guest speaker. He is a co-founder of Stanversity (https://industry.stanversity.com/)—a university-lecturers platform connecting the best scientists with universities in need of new study courses, mostly on the postgraduate and MBA levels. He is excited about tech, B2B pricing, monetization, digital marketing, customer insights, and quantitative and qualitative research. Connect via Facebook: http://fb.com /wilczynski24; Twitter @wilczynski24, at LinkedIn www.linkedin.com/in /wilczynskim/, and via email: maciej@valueships.com

Lightning Strike: A Practical Guide to Conjoint Analysis: Injecting More Confidence into Your Strategic Pricing Decisions

Matt Johnston

Market research and pricing are both fascinating disciplines that go, to a certain degree, hand in hand. One of the most trusted and scientifically advanced methodologies to measure willingness to pay is conjoint analysis—the holy grail of market research. In this guide I share practical knowledge and best practices to motivate companies, large and small, to benefit from the power of conjoint analysis and to boost your research success.

1. Setting the scene: Why willingness to pay matters
The goal of every business is to charge the maximum willingness to pay for each of your customer segments. Too many companies leave substantial money on the table by simply not charging what the client thinks their product or service is worth monetarily.

While company costs can help identify the minimum price floor, what's the price ceiling in each segment? In some markets, we can rely on competitive pricing data, which might be limited to substitute offers (Figure 15.3).

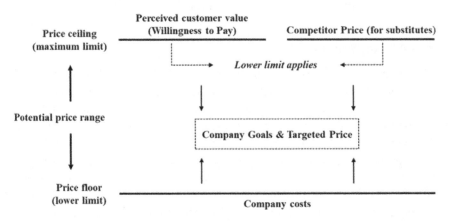

Figure 15.3. Influencing factors of a potential price range.

However, the best way to determine what your customers are willing to pay is to ask them!

How you determine willingness to pay is critical.

In my experience, companies find it difficult to appreciate that customers think in terms of value, not price. In other words, nobody cares about the costs or features of your product or service—they care solely about the value it creates for them. The upside: conjoint analysis can effectively help you here!

2. Optimizing pricing strategy: Use cases for conjoint analysis

Conjoint analysis helps you to focus on key value drivers of your offers and present them in a way that a customer can subconsciously decide which offer is most valuable. Finally, it allows you to add a price tag to this perception of value.

This is because conjoint analysis presents products in a way that simulates real-world product comparisons and asks respondents to make realistic trade-off decisions. In a decision scenario, people don't like to choose unless there's something with which to compare or contrast. By asking your customers repeatedly to choose from a variety of offers with a unique set of specifications and prices, you can gather and process information about customer preferences and price elasticity using statistical algorithms.

Eventually, conjoint analysis will help you answer your burning pricing questions:

- Determining customer willingness to pay for a product or service at an aggregate, segment, and individual level
- De-risking new pricing/charging models (servitization, monthly fee, up-front plus monthly fee, once-off fee)
- De-risking new price promotions (discounts, bundling, rebates, etc.)
- Understanding your product's price/value perception versus competing brands
- Measuring the impact of bundling versus add-on on revenue
- De-risking new price-setting
- Determining price elasticity/sensitivity at an aggregate, segment, or individual level
- Understanding customer reactions to various pricing T&Cs
- Evaluating competitive pricing threats (promotion, new low-cost challenger/entrant)

As you can see, there are a myriad of pricing use cases suitable for conjoint analysis. Most commonly brands conduct a conjoint analysis before a product launch as insurance against nasty surprises.

It's easy to reduce a price when you get it wrong, but almost impossible to increase it.

Therefore, smart brands ensure that the price they launch with is what the customer is willing to pay, and that the associated charging model/structure is how the customer is willing to pay.

3. Your research success: What's needed to conduct a conjoint analysis

As mentioned, conjoint analysis attempts to simulate a real purchase decision as closely as possible. The following best practices should always be considered:

1 Who should you target? The target audience must represent the end customer as closely as possible. Setting screen-out questions and using online respondent panel provider profiles can facilitate capturing accurate target samples.
2 What should you test? To ensure the integrity of your results, the products/services must be direct substitutes and/or competing products (apples to apples!).
3 Agree on the burning question: it can be a challenge or opportunity that needs to be addressed with all stakeholders before designing the survey.
4 Never test more than eight attributes in one study. Any more will be too much for respondents to digest and could compromise results.
5 "None of these," or a derivative of it, should feature as an option on every choice card. Because conjoint analysis tries to simulate a real purchase decision, respondents should be given the option to walk out of the store or leave the webpage if they don't like any of the product options on offer on a choice card.
6 For consumer conjoint studies, to avoid respondent fatigue and the resulting risk to result integrity, we recommend using no more than 12 choice cards in a study.
7 If you're introducing new features, products, or pricing models, we recommend that you help respondents familiarize themselves with them using text or visual explanations in the survey's introductory message.

A special challenge for industrial companies is often the available respondent pool. This can be approached in two ways. First, limit the survey's complexity—specifically the number of concepts and attributes to be tested. Second, increase the number of choice cards. The number of choice cards needed has an inverse relationship to the number of respondents. If the pool of respondents is limited, industrial conjoint studies can accommodate up to 20 choice cards.

4. A practical example from EPIC Conjoint: Testing the market acceptance of IoT smart tracker devices

A classic use case for conjoint analysis is product testing before a market launch. The leading brands invest millions of dollars to find the best combination of technical features that make a great product, which ultimately can conquer market share and increase sales numbers. Using conjoint analysis, we can understand the effect of product and pricing decisions and test thousands of different feature combinations.

In the following, we take a brief look at an IoT smart tracker device survey that was launched in July 2020 in Germany—highlighting the key survey steps.

1   **Identify your product's peer group,** against which consumers will match your offer. In this case, we test one product—an IoT Smart Tracker— that could be offered by different providers at different prices.

2   **Identify the key attributes** that matter most for your customers—and on which they base their purchasing decision. These can be technical specifications (the product itself) or softer value drivers (e.g., brand of the provider). Finally, we attach two prices: one monthly fee and one initial fee. Also, we include a free test period as a potential value driver.

3   **Ask questions** that you need to have answered in order to distinguish customer segments (segmentation questions), to have laser precision on your target audience (screen-out questions), or to ensure a specific quota in your answers (e.g., male-to-female ratio).

4   **Identify the target audience!** A crucial step in every survey is to ask the people who bought or might buy your product. Having a dedicated respondent panel provider and a wide variety of methods to distribute your survey make it significantly easier to reach the target audience.

5   **Launch the survey.** Choice cards for a choice-based conjoint analysis run by EPIC Conjoint typically look like the example in Figure 15.4. Respondents choose their favorite offer from the screen, while within the attributes (e.g., brand) the specific attribute levels (e.g., Vodafone or O2) will change—along with the two prices.

6   **Analyze the results and identify the key learnings!** At EPIC Conjoint, all the questions you add to the questionnaire can be actively used to

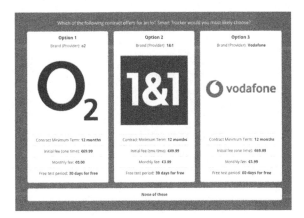

Figure 15.4. Choice cards.

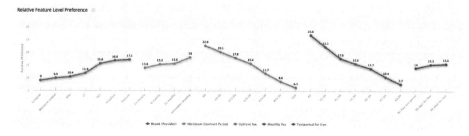

Figure 15.5. Relative preference level (whole panel, 251 respondents).

filter the results, so you can replicate your customer segment. Hence, differences in preferences and willingness to pay among different buyer groups are easily identifiable.

RELATIVE FEATURE-LEVEL PREFERENCE

Bringing all attributes and attribute levels to one linear chart makes differences in preferences to the target sample easily identifiable. For example, look at how the perception of the attribute "brand" shows two groups of preferred providers: Telekom, Vodafone, and 1&1 are generally preferred, and the other tested providers are less preferred (Figure 15.4). These findings can be identified for all other attributes, too (Figure 15.5).

RELATIVE FEATURE IMPORTANCE

Knowing what really drives your customer's purchasing decision, and what the significant value drivers are, is key for every comprehensive pricing strategy. Taking the learnings of relative feature preferences, we can calculate the importance of each attribute. In our IoT tracking device survey, we identify a clearly

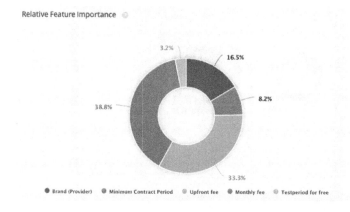

Figure 15.6. Relative feature importance (whole panel, 251 respondents).

Ideal Product

> Brand (Provider): **Telekom**
>
> Minimum Contract Period: **terminable monthly**
>
> Upfront fee: **€9.99**
>
> Monthly fee: **€0**
>
> Testperiod for free: **60 days for free**

Figure 15.7. Ideal product.

price-driven product decision: price itself drives 72.1 percent of respondents' product decisions; brand (16.5%) is only one-fourth as important (Figure 15.6).

IDEAL PRODUCT

A great starting point for every product developer is to know your target audience's most desired combination of attributes. For IoT tracker devices, the attribute combination shown in Figure 15.7 is the one most voted for.

PRICE ELASTICITY

How price sensitive are your customers—and how does price sensitivity change between different customer segments or to different product categories? Do you know the answer? Conjoint analysis can determine this by deriving a precise estimate from the trade-off decisions of your customers. In this survey, the respondent panel had a price elasticity of −0.55 to −0.57. respectively (Figure 15.8).

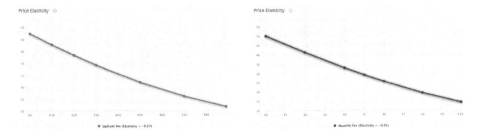

Figure 15.8. Price elasticities.

POWERFUL MARKET-SHARE AND PRICE-OPTIMIZATION SIMULATORS

The beauty of conjoint analysis is that based on what you learn about preferences and price elasticities, you can roll up your sleeves and simulate what-if decisions about optimal prices for your product or market-share changes triggered by your (or your competitors') product decisions.

Going into further detail would take an extra chapter, but look at our price optimizer (Figure 15.9). It tells you the take rate and the revenue—or profit-maximizing price—for your product, launched on a market consisting of your target audience. You can easily and precisely simulate what happens to your take rate and optimal price if you change attributes (e.g., offering a free test period). Here, conjoint analysis gives you a unique tool to identify willingness to pay—not only for your product as a whole but also for different product attributes!

5. The five things to remember for a powerful conjoint study

- **Conjoint analysis must not be rocket science.** Rely on the powerful combination of user-friendly conjoint software and professional guidance by industry experts.
- **Conjoint analysis can give businesses of any size a competitive advantage** by providing precise information on your own—and your competitors offers' market perception and willingness to pay.
- **Guarantee statistical significance of results** by asking enough survey respondents. If the number of available respondents is lower than approximately 300, try to decrease the complexity of the survey and increase the number of choice cards slightly.

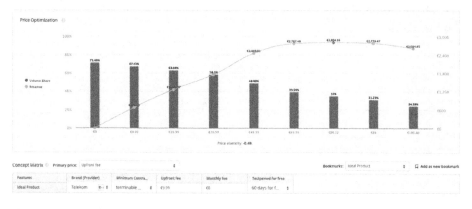

Figure 15.9. Price optimizer.

In every survey, answer the two major questions:

- **Who are you targeting?** Be clear about who your target audience is, make sure you can reach them during the survey distribution phase, and ensure that you give enough context in the survey to enable the respondent to give precise answers.
- **What are you targeting them with?** Conjoint analysis is an excellent opportunity to think about your offer not only technical feature terms—but especially regarding the value you provide. Identifying key value drivers and using them as attributes in a conjoint analysis is a perfect starting point!

About Matt Johnston

Matt is the founder and CEO of EPIC Conjoint. He is a seasoned commercial marketing professional with over 20 years of pricing, product, and segmentation experience. Matt has an extensive background in telecommunications as former Head of Pricing at Telefónica Ireland and Ooredoo Group Qatar. Visit www.epicconjoint.com for more information and to contact Matt.

16

Outcome-Based and Equipment-as-a-Service Pricing Strategies

THE FIELD OF DIGITAL pricing is changing rapidly. Just five years ago, everyone was talking about subscription pricing and SaaS pricing strategies. Today the focus has shifted to usage-based pricing and outcome-based pricing, especially in relation to PaaS and EaaS. Obviously, there are implications when choosing these progressive pricing strategies. They're not for everyone. And they remain challenging to executives in the industrial sector. Nevertheless, I've included a chapter on the topic in order to tease you and to plant the seeds for an upcoming book on advanced digital pricing strategies. I've recruited two experts to write about this forward-thinking pricing method. I hope you can relate to their content and join the conversation.

Lightning Strike: Outcome-Based Pricing in the Industrial Subscription Economy: Six Practical Steps to Share Value Successfully

Peyton Marshall

The trend toward outcome-based pricing for manufacturer services was recently highlighted by Gartner. "In 2022, more than 60% of asset manufacturers will offer outcome-based service contracts, up from less than 15% in 2018" (Robinson, 2019). Subscription pricing of packaged assets, software, and services is following rapidly. In an outcome-based subscription, the net price paid by a customer depends on the actual performance delivered by the asset/software-as-a-service. Outcome-based pricing goes beyond setting prices based on ex-ante metrics to determining prices based on realized, ex-post customer value. Outcome-based subscription prices put a vendor's money where their mouth is.

Equipment prices have had ex-post financial elements for years. Product warranties have long been offered to protect equipment purchasers from buying a lemon. Guarantees, short-term and long-term, are common in equipment sales. The shift to a subscription model, with a contractual life shorter than the life of the underlying equipment, already goes beyond outright asset purchase in shifting risk from buyer to seller. A buyer's decision about whether to renew a subscription or not usually depends on whether results have been delivered during the initial contract.

Yet potential subscribers, despite their ability to vote with their feet, are sometimes reluctant to change from traditional purchasing models, where they control the asset, to as-a-service models, where substantial ownership and control remain with the vendor. Customers changing to our solution often have to make investments in installation, integration, and training that make it expensive for them to leave after their initial subscription period. They often look to sellers to bear significant portions of the risk.

To grow rapidly, both market leaders and fast followers are increasingly making commitments in the form of rebates, credits, or other financial adjustments, based on ex-post, customer outcomes. The result is an outcome-based subscription price.

If designed right, outcome-based subscriptions can succeed for both buyer and seller. Alternatively, they can create a business disaster for vendors mismanaging their risks. The history of catastrophic "accidents" in multitrillion-dollar markets for derivatives and insurance is instructive. Let's use an illustrative example in equipment to highlight six steps to good outcome-based offer design.

Example. AirVentis is an innovative HVAC equipment manufacturer and services provider for technology facilities that include large server operations. In their subscription offerings, AirVentis

- retains ownership of the equipment
- monitors and manages the efficient installation, integration, *and* operation of the equipment and software
- provides corrective, preventive, and condition-based maintenance
- upgrades software and hardware based on the latest technology as it becomes available

AirVentis's outsourced solution is designed not just to eliminate a facility's need to invest in HVAC technology but also to reduce or eliminate a facility's need for skilled HVAC staff or consultants. AirVentis seeks to charge a higher annualized price for their solution than they would for stand-alone equipment purchase and maintenance service contracts. Their value proposition is that customer facilities deploying their solution will save on

- equipment costs
- maintenance costs
- facility staff costs
- downtime losses
- energy costs

Aiming to capture the downtime and energy value they create, AirVentis's strategy is to charge a price premium to a customer's equipment, maintenance, and staff costs. AirVentis offers an outcome-based subscription that provides customer credits based on actual downtime below a specified level and energy savings below a specified level. In what follows, we focus on the elements of outcome-based contracting related to sharing energy savings.

Designing outcome-based contracts

A good outcome-based contract should be designed based on six practical steps:

1. Quantify customer value. Go beyond conceptual messages to measure financial outcomes. What are improved outcomes worth to the customer? How much do we expect to improve these outcomes? All value-based strategies start by dollarizing differentiation.

This requires three elements for each source of shared customer value:

- a reference point (e.g., previous-year energy consumption)
- dollarization of reference-point outcomes (e.g., previous-year energy costs)
- an expectation of how much our solution is likely to improve these outcomes (percentage reduction in energy consumption using our solution)

The reference point frames the discussion. Dollarized outcomes highlight the measurable pain we reduce and/or the opportunity we address. Our expected impact on energy consumption is our central assertion of what we deliver that's different. If our evidence is strong, relevant to other customers, and persuasive, we should be able to capture value without sharing risk on ex-post outcomes. Mismatched impact expectations between buyer and seller are the central issue addressed by outcome-based pricing.

2. Communicate customer value. Value uncommunicated is value unrealized. A decision to offer outcome-based pricing should not be viewed as a substitute for effective value communication. Value communication should come first. If we can communicate and capture substantial value without sharing risk, why offer ex-post price adjustments?

By seeking to capture value without offering an outcome-based contract, we learn customer objections to the case we make for our solution's differentiated impact. Sometimes our evidence is skimpy. Often our evidence isn't perceived as relevant to the next customer, because "their operation is different." We can't test the hypothesis that we need to share risk unless we seek to sell solutions without doing so.

3. Select measurable, meaningful outcomes for ex-post price adjustments. Not all outcomes should be subject to an outcome-based contract. Outcomes must be objectively measurable in order to avoid contract disputes. There must be a confirmable, verifiable data record that both buyer and seller accept as the standard for ex-post measurement and payment. Third-party-utility meter readings usually satisfy this requirement, whereas undocumented, unconfirmable downtime reports may not. Information asymmetries between buyer and seller often create an adverse selection problem that becomes an impediment to risk sharing. An objective standard for measurement is critical.

Outcomes chosen for ex-post price adjustment should be meaningful as well. Setting up outcome-based contracts is usually complicated and expensive. If the outcome amounts subject to adjustment are small or don't resonate with customers, outcome-based contracting is unlikely to induce buyers to change their purchasing decision in our favor.

4. Consider sharing both risks and rewards. The simplest outcome-based contract is a guarantee, where the buyer's financial result net of the contract price will not fall below specific levels. This is not a risk-sharing contract. It's a one-sided, risk-transferring contract. When the buyer has extraordinary market power or when competitors are already providing guarantees, it may be reasonable or necessary to go this far.

But in most circumstances, outcome-based contracts are an opportunity for collaboration and alignment. Reconsider one-way, full guarantees to make contracts about both parties' sharing risks *and* rewards. If the seller is willing to protect the buyer against risk, then it's absolutely reasonable for the seller to ask to share in the upside. Outcome-based contract proposals should reinforce a partnership approach where both parties participate in failure and success.

5. Choose risks to be shared deliberately. AirVentis claims that it reduces customers' energy consumption. An outcome-based contract dollarizes measured energy savings. Although it might seem simplest to compare last year's actual energy costs with this year's actual energy costs, there are other approaches. Consider several important choices to make in how dollarization is calculated:

- **Should the reference standard include adjustments?** This year's targeted temperatures may differ from last year's targets. Differences in climate conditions may have an impact on the energy it takes to deliver the same temperature in the facility year over year. These are variables outside the control of the seller. Some of these exposures are risks the buyer would be taking regardless of the solution they purchase. An outcome-based price formula that adjusts the reference standard for changes in climate conditions

Energy Adjustment

60% credits to the buyer are available if adjusted energy savings are less than 30%.

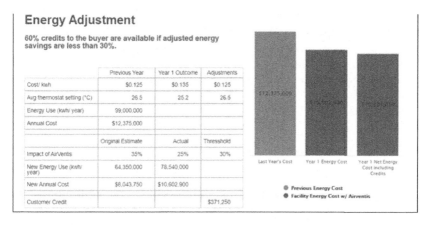

	Previous Year	Year 1 Outcome	Adjustments
Cost/ kwh	$0.125	$0.135	$0.125
Avg thermostat setting (°C)	26.5	25.2	26.5
Energy Use (kwh/ year)	99,000,000		
Annual Cost	$12,375,000		

	Original Estimate	Actual	Thresshold
Impact of AirVents	35%	25%	30%
New Energy Use (kwh/ year)	64,350,000	78,540,000	
New Annual Cost	$8,043,750	$10,602,900	
Customer Credit			$371,250

Bar chart labels: Last Year's Cost, Year 1 Energy Cost, Year 1 Net Energy Cost including Credits ($12,375,000 / $10,602,900 / ...)

● Previous Energy Cost
● Facility Energy Cost w/ Airventis

Figure 16.1. Adjustments for energy value savings.

or thermostat settings can support a fair contract grounded both in current conditions and who has control over what (Figure 16.1).

- **Who takes price risk?** The value of energy savings depends both on the energy consumed and on a variable outside the control of both parties, the price of energy. If buyer and seller share the risk that energy costs remain below a specified level, they share the risk that our solution performs but also that energy prices fluctuate. The result may be an inadvertent price hedge where the seller offers energy price protection in addition to protecting the buyer against our solution's energy performance. While the seller may have ways to hedge commodity price risks, they take on an exposure originally borne by the buyer. Pre-specifying an energy price in the adjustment formula avoids the transfer of commodity price risk to the seller.

6. Structure and monitor contracts to maintain alignment of incentives. The effective implementation of complex technology usually requires collaborative performance by both buyer and seller. Outcome-based contracts should always be structured so that both parties are incentivized to perform. When all the risks are taken by one party, the moral hazard problem becomes a barrier to good outcomes. Sharing both risks and rewards in a meaningful way aligns incentives.

Well-documented agreements related to when and how measurement will occur for contracts, along with regular contractual review, are required to maintain good communication and alignment between parties.

Value sharing as a rational response
The initial decision by a seller to share risks with a buyer is often an almost accidental response to specific deal circumstances. Value sharing should make economic sense (Figure 16.2). Invariably, outcome-based pricing requires

Value-sharing contracts are a reasonable approach when
- The purchase decision is important for both seller and buyer
- The buyer has significant market power
- Significant buyer and seller investments are required
- Post-sale outcomes are uncertain
- Outcomes require substantial performance by both seller and buyer

Figure 16.2. When value sharing makes sense.

additional investment in contracting, monitoring, and communication. A rational analysis argues that specific conditions be applicable to make the extra costs of value-based contracting worth it. Market conditions that drive sellers toward sharing risk and reward include the following:

- **The purchase decision is important for both buyer and seller.** Purchases that do not have a significant impact on both buyer and seller don't warrant the additional time and expense of investing in contracting, monitoring, and ongoing collaboration that value-sharing contracts require.
- **The buyer has significant market power.** Shifting from caveat emptor to sharing risk is often a seller's response to a buyer's market power deliberately exercised in a direct negotiation.
- **Significant buyer and seller investments are required.** Large initial investments in implementation, training, marketing, and infrastructure introduce status quo bias for the buyer once a decision is made. Sharing risk and reward establishes seller accountability for the success of the buyer's investment.
- **Post-sale outcomes are uncertain.** Sharing risk and reward is a means to align the expectations of buyer and seller and to adjust the economics of a relationship when expectations are not met.
- **Outcomes require substantial performance by both seller and buyer.** When outcomes require collaborative performance, alignment of incentives improves outcomes for everyone.

Value sharing as a disruptive market strategy
In conjunction with the rational analysis, value sharing can serve as a distinct go-to-market strategy. Thus, it can be more fundamental than a reactive seller's response to specific market conditions when it serves as a deliberate approach to disrupting a marketplace. When it's well executed, pricing based on ex-post outcomes changes the underlying price metric, deliberately aligning prices paid with customer value obtained. Value sharing becomes a uniquely differentiated part of our offering that distinguishes us from our competition, often for a considerable period.

It's one thing to sell value. Value-selling conversations demonstrate that sellers of differentiated solutions are customer-centric. Sharing value can be transformative. Outcome-based contracts are a means to change a seller's cultural approach to how they work with customers. Value-sharing contracts move beyond talking about outcomes to direct, incentivized collaboration to achieve those outcomes. They change the seller's approach to providing services. They become the central organizing theme of regular dialogue between buyer and seller. They transform transactional relationships into partnerships.

As the industrial subscription economy transforms business models with new technologies, outcome-based contracts are a means to further disrupt changing marketplaces. Value-sharing, outcome-based subscriptions will be increasingly important in driving growth in the Internet of Things. Properly designed, strategically deployed outcome-based contracts can make that growth fruitful for buyers and sellers as they align collaborative relationships to achieve mutual success.

About Peyton Marshall

Peyton Marshall is the CEO of LeveragePoint Innovations, a software company providing a cloud platform for B2B enterprises to implement value strategies and value selling. In this role, he advises commercial teams across a variety of sectors as they price for value and as they design strong value propositions for differentiated solutions. Previously, he served in product management, sales, and senior management roles in a number B2B sectors. He has been an investment banker at Goldman Sachs and other financial services firms, structuring and selling complex financial solutions to global corporate and financial institution CFOs. He has experience evaluating purchases and supporting commercial product launches from the C-suite, as CFO of three public biotech companies, CEO of one public biotech company, CFO of a private health care IT company, and COO of a private drug discovery company. He holds a PhD in Economics from MIT.

Lightning Strike: Choosing the Right Pricing Model for Equipment-as-a-Service

Mark Burton, David Burns, and Ron Kermisch

At a glance

- Makers and sellers of industrial equipment and machinery would like to capture more value from their wares by retaining ownership and charging customers for subscription rates. But the transition to this model has been slow, reflecting the difficulty in pricing accurately.

- For the model to work, sellers and buyers have to understand the value that the equipment adds to the business and agree on how to share it.
- Choosing the right pricing model depends on the seller's degree of control over how the equipment is used and what it produces for the company. Outcome-based models can deliver more value to vendors, but they also carry more risk. They set prices based on either the amount of activity performed or the financial results attributable to the equipment. Time and usage models are more common, based on the amount of time the equipment runs or how intensely it is used.
- Vendors' switching to a service model need to prepare their organizations for a transition, boosting investment in customer service and preparing investors and the organization for an interim period when costs will be higher and revenues lower.

The business model of selling equipment-as-a-service (EaaS) has been around for a while: Rolls-Royce introduced its Power by the Hour program, pricing Viper aircraft engines based on flight hours, back in 1962. More recently, the rapid rise of sensors and the advent of machines and devices connected to the Internet of Things has made it more feasible to deploy advanced pricing models based on time, usage, output, or financial results. Subscription models offer clear advantages for buyers, who can access expensive equipment without a large up-front capital outlay, while also sharing risk with the vendor. Sellers also benefit by capturing more of the total value created by the equipment.

So why hasn't the EaaS model taken off more broadly?

Our conversations with executives suggest that this pricing model is proving harder to pull off than they expected—much harder than the SaaS programs that have served as templates. In software, the unit cost is close to nil. Adobe, for example, takes some financial risk in releasing Creative Cloud for the price of a monthly payment rather than the license fee of its comparable on-site software. But it doesn't have to ship individual pieces of machinery that cost thousands, or millions, of dollars to produce—a greater risk than sharing code. Revenue disruption at this scale could lead to a more sustainable income stream, but if anything were to go wrong, the financial results could be devastating.

Still, given the potential that sellers and buyers see in this pricing model, there's a strong incentive to make it work for all parties. In our work with companies trying to get this right, three main obstacles slow their progress:

- agreeing with customers on the value created and how to share risk
- managing the internal changes required to support a service pricing model, and
- "swallowing the fish"—planning for a disruptive period of rising costs and falling revenues before the financials find their new trajectory

When executive teams understand the risks and opportunities of the EaaS pricing model, they can develop offers that work for buyers and sellers, limiting exposure and maximizing the gains for both sides.

Determining the best pricing model

Manufacturers have been trying to develop service lines that deliver more reliable streams of revenue for decades. EaaS represents the ultimate pathway to getting there: as long as the machines are running, revenue continues to flow, and suppliers share in more of the value that the equipment delivers for customers. Some of that value comes as it would with any service contract, but additional value can also come from the supplier's role as owner of the equipment (Figures 16.3 and 16.4). But to tap that value, manufacturers first have to determine the right pricing model.

Outcome-based models, in which payments are based on operational or financial achievements, can deliver more value to suppliers—provided they can assess and measure that value accurately.

- **Operational outcomes.** This model is good for solutions that perform well-defined discrete tasks, such as industrial robotics or automation equipment. One warehouse robotics provider charges per cycle, where each cycle is defined as picking a carton, bringing it to a packing area, and returning the carton to its original location.
- **Financial outcomes.** This model works well when you can establish a direct link between the equipment and measurable financial results. A

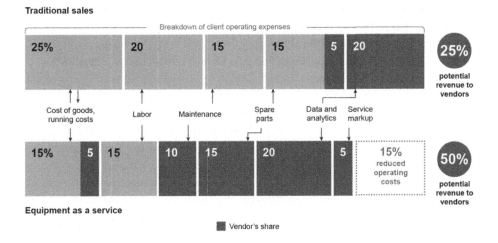

Traditional sales

Breakdown of client operating expenses

| 25% | 20 | 15 | 15 | 5 | 20 | **25%** potential revenue to vendors |

Cost of goods, running costs   Labor   Maintenance   Spare parts   Data and analytics   Service markup

| 15% | 5 | 15 | 10 | 15 | 20 | 5 | 15% reduced operating costs | **50%** potential revenue to vendors |

Equipment as a service

■ Vendor's share

Source: Bain & Company

Figure 16.3. An ongoing service relationship can reduce the operating expenses for customers while also bringing more revenue to the vendor.

Vendor revenue ($M)

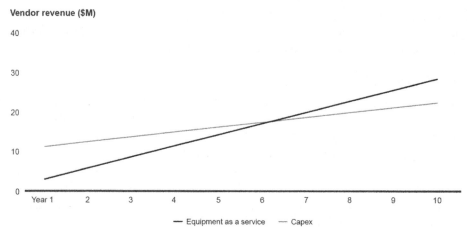

Notes: Capex costs based on first-year investment of $10 million equipment and $1 million installation, followed by maintenance costs of 5% the first year, 12.5% for years 2 through 10, and an EBITDA margin of 10%; equipment-as-a-service costs based on yearly subscription of capex revenue divided by a service life of 10 years, multiplied by 1.25, with an EBITDA margin of 10
Source: Bain & Company

Figure 16.4. Service-model revenue exceeds CapEx-model revenue over a typical 10-year life of equipment.

supplier of compressed natural gas systems for fuel stations found that station operators were put off by the high capital costs for the compressor and related hardware needed to deliver the gas to vehicles. The supplier switched to a model where stations receive the compressor and hardware and then pay fees based on the volume of gas sold. In this case, the model worked well because the fuel station operator and the supplier agreed on the revenue that resulted from the availability of the new equipment.

These outcome-based models carry more risk and are a good choice only when suppliers can be sure they can accurately measure the results—and ideally when their service support can help bolster those results. To price successfully, suppliers need to understand the value of the equipment to the customer and decide how to share risk.

• **Determine the value.** Good pricing begins with an understanding of the amount of value the customer can generate from the use of the equipment. This isn't always easy to obtain, since customers may not want to share sensitive operational data. A provider of manufacturing automation solutions solved this problem by working through a series of studies with potential customers to build a value-calculation tool that pooled data from those studies, so that no individual company's data was disclosed. Another way to get at the value is through a detailed total cost analysis, comparing the costs of purchase and ownership with those of a subscription. A total cost analysis should identify the financial breakeven time for a traditional purchase agreement, which is important for setting EaaS contract terms. It also uncovers the lifetime ownership costs that a supplier would pay if they moved to a service model.

- **Decide how to share risk.** How much control will suppliers have over outcomes? A clear view of the risks—financial, operational, and market factors—and who is accountable for them allows suppliers to work with customers to mitigate against them or to choose a different price meter that preserves the quality of the revenue stream.

Time and usage models. If suppliers determine that they can't define the value or how to measure it, they're better off choosing a model that prices based on factors that are easier to measure.

- **Time-based models** base payment on a set amount per unit for a fixed period. Even this model is being used in innovative ways. Hilti, a leading maker of portable power tools, offers a tool fleet program that gives contractors access to an assortment of tools for a fixed monthly fee. The program eliminates up-front investment and covers repairs, loaner tools, and even theft.
- **Usage-based models** tie payment to the intensity of machinery use. A supplier of mining equipment was seeing customers delay purchases because of high capital costs and uncertainty about getting a return on those costs in a reasonable time frame. The firm worked to develop an EaaS model for mining projects that allows project owners to pay per cubic meter drilled.

Preparing the organization

Selling equipment-as-a-service requires a significant overhaul of the commercial operating model. The shift from episodic sales contact to ongoing engagement has profound implications not only for a firm's financials but also for its product development, sales, and customer service. Successful sellers develop collaborative relationships with customers that allow both parties to understand ownership costs, the production process, expected profit margins, and preferred contract terms. Details about contract duration, amortization plans, and post-contract value of the equipment are essential if customers and suppliers are to make informed comparisons between buying and subscribing. Customer service will need to make big changes, shifting from mere technical support after sales to becoming an ongoing partner that helps configure and maintain equipment, as well as performing diagnostics and data analysis that help customers improve performance. Assuming responsibility for ownership of equipment throughout its service life can force suppliers to rethink product designs. When General Electric began selling its GE90 engine on a power-by-the-hour plan, it made design changes to reduce operating costs and improve serviceability. GE added sensors and intelligence that optimize performance and reduce fuel consumption. It also created digital twins that allowed for better comparisons between the performance of actual engines and models with potential design changes.

Swallowing the fish

The transition from one-time CapEx sales to a recurring revenue model can put enormous pressure on firm financials, as revenues can drop significantly in the early years. At the same time, costs will increase as companies continue to invest in equipment for customers while also investing in new capabilities required to successfully deliver services that integrate hardware, software, communications capabilities, and performance-optimizing data and analytics. When software companies made this transition from on-premise licenses to cloud-based subscription services, the financial transition came to be known as "swallowing the fish"—for the shape of the rising cost curve over the decreasing revenue curve.[2]

There is no denying that this is a challenging transition, but suppliers do have options to ease the pain.

- First, the service model can be deployed gradually, with some customers choosing service agreements and others opting for a CapEx purchase. Aircraft engine suppliers pursued this path, gradually increasing the share of revenues coming from services over time.
- Suppliers can further ease the transition by establishing separate business units or subsidiaries that purchase the equipment and are responsible for systems integration, financing and insurance, and delivery to the customer.
- Finally, first-mover advantages may allow pioneers to build up market share and increase revenues that can eclipse costs more quickly.

Before shifting to a subscription model, companies should develop a keen understanding of what drives adoption and uptake of new pricing models. They should work with customers to understand how the new pricing scheme will be received, and they need to develop clearly packaged value propositions that are easy for customers to understand and measure. And, of course, companies need to signal to their investors how the change in pricing will affect revenue and earnings.

Time to get started?

The transition from selling to service will not happen as rapidly in machinery and equipment as it has for software. Although we're already seeing movement in some categories—particularly in discrete devices such as robots—larger and

---

2   First described in J. B. Wood, T. Hewling and T. Lah, *B4B: How Technology and Big Data Are Reinventing the Customer-Supplier Relationship,* Point B Inc/TSIA, 2013.

more complex systems will take longer to shift to this model. Machinery and equipment vendors are already building high-value services around data analytics, designed to optimize system performance. These are laying the groundwork for broader service relationships. Other services are likely to be folded in, including quality control, asset tracking, and remote monitoring, eventually leading to full-service models. First-movers are likely to capture outsized rewards from the shift, developing closer relationships with their customers and transitioning revenue models early. Executives at machinery and equipment vendors' trying to determine whether it's time to move toward EaaS offers should consider several issues:

- What's the potential upside in terms of customer value, stickiness, and higher-quality revenue?
- What would it take to gain a broad consensus—among executives, board members, investors, sales teams, and customers—to embrace this shift?
- Is this team ready to make the move?

About Mark Burton, David Burns, and Ron Kermisch

Mark Burton, David Burns, and Ron Kermisch are partners with Bain & Company's Global Customer practice. Mark and Ron work in Bain's Boston office, and David is based in Chicago. Bain & Company is a global consultancy that helps the world's most ambitious change-makers define the future. Across 59 offices in 37 countries, Bain works alongside clients as one team with a shared ambition to achieve extraordinary results, outperform the competition, and redefine industries. Bain complements a tailored, integrated expertise with a vibrant ecosystem of digital innovators to deliver better, faster, and more enduring outcomes. Since its founding in 1973, it has measured success by the success of its clients. It proudly maintains the highest level of client advocacy in the industry and for its clients.

SECTION 4

SCALING & EXECUTING
YOUR SUBSCRIPTION OFFERS

17

Eight Challenges to Successful Subscription Scaling in the Industrial Space (and How to Solve Them)

Robbie Kellman Baxter

SUBSCRIPTIONS ARE EVERYWHERE. FIVE years ago, I published my first book, *The Membership Economy*, to describe the massive transformation happening in business models as organizations aligned their offerings around a long-term "forever promise" to customers. By treating customers like members, these organizations could enjoy predictable recurring revenue. These ideas were new at the time, particularly in industries outside software and digital content. Today, nearly every kind of organization is exploring the power of subscription pricing and a membership mindset, regardless of size, industry, or corporate structure, that organizations recognize. Many of these early experiments are now becoming part of the core strategy of startups and large enterprises alike.

According to an analysis for the *New York Times* by Mint, Intuit's online budgeting tool, using data from millions of its users, Americans spent an average of $640 on digital subscriptions ranging from streaming content to dating apps to productivity tools. Most consumer-products companies also offer subscriptions, including subscription boxes designed for discovery, such as Birchbox for makeup and Barkbox for pet treats. And B2B subscriptions are on the rise too. Since Salesforce first popularized the concept of software-as-a service, we've seen an explosion in the "as-a-service" space, with everything from infrastructure-as-a-service (IaaS) to communications-as-a-service (CaaS) to platform-as-a-service (PaaS) to hospitality-as-a-service (HaaS). Businesses with recurring revenue can earn valuations five to seven times those of their transactional counterparts. Investors are increasingly willing to conduct "sum of the parts" valuations, giving better multiples to the subscription revenue streams.

So, it's only a matter of time before the promise of subscription pricing transforms the industrial space as well. In my new book, *The Forever Transaction,* I outline three phases of maturity, Launch, Scale, and Lead, as businesses move to business models that focus on long-term relationships and justify subscription revenue. Phase 1, Launch, is when organizations are still evaluating and experimenting with the concept of building a "forever transaction" with their customers. In startups, this is when the organization is developing the business plan and iterating toward product market fit (PMF). But larger, more established organizations can be in the launch phase for their subscription innovations as well. In these cases, the subscription team is off in a corner, often without the same burdens as the core business units. They are mostly left alone and not yet counted on for major revenue goals. We're already seeing examples of many organizations in or who've completed this Launch stage, such as Honeywell, Caterpillar, John Deere, Airbus, Boeing, Siemens, and GE Digital. Some of these are wrapping recurring revenue services around their physical products, like consulting, support, and maintenance. Some are going a step further, for example using sensor technology to track conditions and provide guidance for optimal usage through benchmarking data. And leading-edge businesses in the industrial space are moving away from selling their physical products at all, reorienting their pricing around the value customers care about, much like Rolls-Royce did with their "power by the hour" approach to engines.

Once there is evidence that the subscription offering has found its market, and that customers are both signing up for and engaging with the subscription features, the organization needs to build infrastructure to support growth, identify the right set of metrics to evaluate the business, and evolve the corporate culture to support a more customer-centric, long-term focus. This is Phase 2, Scale.

The third phase I cover in my book is Lead. This is where organizations have a mature subscription business at scale. In many cases, they've built deep, trusted relationships with their most loyal members, most of whom have long since stopped looking for competitive alternatives. As a result of this success, these organizations often become complacent, slowing their product evolution given that customers are so loyal. In turn, they often stop focusing as carefully on acquisition of new customers. Prospects, who are still carefully considering their options, see better emerging solutions that deliver more fully on their promises. At this point, very few industrial businesses have reached Phase 3.

This chapter focuses on Phase 2, as many organizations reading this book have begun the subscription experiments and have scaling on the horizon. There are unique challenges in scaling a subscription business, even one that has found PMF. I've spent nearly 20 years in the trenches with subscription businesses of all kinds. What follows are some of the challenges that slow organizations as they scale, with a particular focus on the industrial space. These are the unexpected or unplanned-for challenges that slow or even derail the best-laid plans. In my book, I outlined six of these challenges. In this article, I add two more. I take a closer look at these setbacks, as well as a few others, particularly in the context of the industrial space. I also recommend strategies for thriving.

1 Organizational and skills gaps
2 Cannibalization concerns
3 Dealing with middlemen
4 Technology setbacks
5 Unexpected leadership priorities
6 Disappointing results
7 Tension with legacy operations
8 Innovation stall out

I provide some insight about best practices around the technology to scale, the culture for success, key metrics, and the pros and cons of transformation by acquisition.

1. Organizational and skills gaps
To succeed in the Launch phase, you need creative, nimble entrepreneurs who can work outside the constraints of the larger organization. But as you scale, that changes. To bring the membership mindset more "front and center," you need talent that has a unique set of experiences, skills, and most importantly attitude. Organizations trying to simultaneously manage their traditional processes and scale a new model may lack the people who can do both.

These challenges can be seen across the organization (Figure 17.1).

Scaling a subscription business requires dozens of little changes across the organization. Don't underestimate this component of your transformation.

2. Cannibalization concerns
The more successful your business already is, the more your team might worry about an increasing commitment to subscription negatively impacting your existing revenue and relationship. For example, let's say today you sell your system outright for $100, but you move to offer a subscription for $10 per year;

Industry	Scaling Challenges
Product	• lacks resources or skills to rebuild the product for a subscription model • unwilling to touch core "hero" products, focusing instead on changes limited to services and pricing • splits resources between both old and new product lines
Sales	• doesn't understand benefits of new model • doesn't have relationships with the right people or organizations for the new model • does not reward for new model
Operations and IT	• lacks the right technology • doesn't understand the requirements needed for new investments • ego prevents buying in favor of building • stopped cold by inability to "do it systematically"
Marketing	• overemphasizes acquisition at expense of engagement and retention metrics • defines customer journey only by product touchpoints, not customer's broader goal • silos among functional areas prevent integrated customer experience
Finance	• unable to adequately prepare shareholders for revenue impact of transformation • underestimates investment in time and money to cross the chasm to the forever model • overly complicates pricing options to meet the requests of every customer

Figure 17.1. Scaling challenges.

in that case, you need to retain a subscriber for 10 years just to match your old revenue from that customer. If only your pre-existing customers transition, and you can't deepen those relationships or attract new customers, you end up losing money as a result of your investment. Whenever an organization moves subscription business from being "off to the side" as an experiment to being part of the core business, it needs to pace its risk-taking. One approach is to list all the risks you're worried about and divide them into two groups: actions you're holding off on until you learn more, and actions you're eager to take but first need to build leverage for in order to gain permission from your organization or partners.

Once you have this list, you can design discrete experiments along the journey of scaling to neutralize risks one by one. In the case of cannibalization, you need to understand how your existing customers' behavior will change if they're offered a subscription. Will their engagement stay constant, grow deeper, or contract? You also need to understand whether your new offering will attract new customers and result in revenue you otherwise couldn't access. Another tactic is to price the initial subscription on the high side. That way, even though you might not get as much upside, your risk is also lower. Also, don't risk as much revenue. Once you know the answer to some of these things, it'll be much easier to gain support of your colleagues, partners, and investors. You'll also feel more confident yourself.

3. Dealing with middlemen
If you have dealers, resellers, or other distribution partners, you could face channel conflict by moving to a direct-to-customer subscription. You run the risk of upsetting your partners as you increase your subscription investment. If you move too quickly or too aggressively, you may lose your partners (and their trusted customer relationships) before you've even gotten your new offering off the ground.

While the benefits of a more direct and ongoing relationship with your customers are great, you might want to take your time, and keep an eye on your partner relationships as you experiment and expand.

It's also useful to get really clear, early on, about a few different paths you might take, either moving completely to a direct relationship or continuing to manage a hybrid one. Another path to consider is building your subscription offering *for* your partners, in addition to or instead of for your end customers. It's critical to anticipate the risks of an angry middleman anytime you change how you interact with your shared customers.

4. Technology setbacks
I've written a lot about technology setbacks. To thrive in the membership economy, organizations often find that they need to become "technology" companies. In many cases, along the journey, an organization either underinvests in technology or makes an investment that takes them down a wrong road. It's not uncommon for an organization to find that the technology solutions with which they launched their as-a-service offering are quickly outgrown and need to be replaced within a few years.

This happens frequently enough that I hesitate to call it an error; I instead think of it as a frequent bump in the road that an organization can expect as it scales. This means that the organization might want to put off the major investment until the requirements are clear and, at the same time, that they should also plan for significant change over time.

5. Unexpected leadership priorities
Even the best organizations face challenges or opportunities that were not on the roadmap (COVID-19, anyone?). In these cases, leadership must focus its attention in a new direction, perhaps at the expense of the well-performing and on-schedule subscription business. What's hard is that sometimes this means that the subscription scaling process is starved for resources but expected to

continue growing. And sometimes the organization will need to start over or will lose ground as a result of this midcourse halt. If you're responsible for the subscription business, you may want to assume the role of "voice of the subscription" business, advocating with focus for the required investment to continue. Or you might feel that the right decision is to take a "one firm" approach and pause your efforts.

If you take the latter road, make sure you understand that everything in subscription models is based on consistency, and that this pause in investment, continuous improvement, and relationship-building may end up destroying the model you've been building.

6. Disappointing results

A major challenge many organizations face early on as they scale is disappointing interim results.

If you've been growing steadily and seeing all your metrics continuously improving and then hit a bump, you (and your leadership) may become discouraged. Please don't overthink it. Failure is likely to happen along the way. You may make a mistake with the pricing structure or find that customers are cancelling at a certain point in their journey or based on an unexpected external influence. Or you might learn that your required investment will be higher than initially budgeted. Things like this are likely to happen. The best way to ensure that a temporary setback is, well, temporary, is to set expectations at the outset. Make a list of risks and share the risks with your stakeholders. And show them how you might respond to them. We all do better when we're not caught off guard.

You also want to be clear, ideally up front, about what results, if any, would justify shutting down the business, downsizing it, or putting it on pause. If you know what milestones you need to hit, and also what the remedies might be if you have negative but unsurprising results, you're more likely to make decisions quickly and effectively down the road.

7. Tension with legacy operations

The blessing and curse of launching a subscription alongside a successful industrial business is that there's already been a huge investment in key systems. Sometimes these systems allow the new subscription offering to scale more quickly, but most of the time, it makes things harder. Leadership wants to run the new subscription business using the legacy systems, since the organization has already invested the money and time to make them core, and since most of the central operations run through these systems. However, using the legacy footprint usually doesn't work for two key reasons.

- The legacy system was not designed for subscriptions
- The legacy system is out of date

Everything from the way you manage payments to how you handle returns will require different processes that are best served by systems optimized for this approach. You really have two options as a result. You can procure a new system that meets the specialized needs of the new subscription offering, which will operate alongside the legacy systems. Or you can invest in a system that meets the needs of the existing business, the new subscription, and the vision for "tomorrow's organization" but that will require a lot of collaboration and planning and may slow down the process of scaling the subscription.

8. Innovation stall out

The final major challenge that industrial companies face during this transformation is a loss of momentum around innovation. Scaling a nascent subscription business requires an operational orientation. Once the organization has identified a recurring revenue model that has traction, the focus shifts from optimizing PMF and developing a minimum viable product (MVP) to developing efficient, replicable, and scalable systems to support growth. In some cases, at this point, the team lead is handed over with an "innovator" passing the baton to someone who's more process driven. The energy of the team is now focused on a lot of features and systems that the customer might not see or talk about but that are considered table stakes, like uptime. Or they're trying to figure out ways to remove human cost from the system, automating what was previously done by hand now that the ideal path has been identified. Or maybe they're building out a dashboard for the internal team to track results.

This attention to efficiency, infrastructure, and operations is critical. However, it's equally important that the team continue to improve the experience for the subscriber as well. Most likely when the initial innovation team was developing the MVP, they punted on key features that would delight new subscribers or that would meet the needs of a new target segment, saying, "We'll circle back in Phase 2." But then when Phase 2 comes around, the innovation team has moved on to a new project and the MVP starts to feel, well, too Minimum and not enough Viable to be a successful Product.

Conclusion

The most important thing to remember is that the journey to a subscription model is just that: a journey. It can take years to swallow the fish, as J. B. Wood calls it. Your costs may rise and revenue decline as you transition from transactional to subscription revenue, before the two lines cross and revenue begins to increase as costs go down, making a "fish shape" in the chart. You're in it for the long term. You're investing to maximize customer lifetime value and to disruption-proof your business. Remember: you're in it for the long haul; set expectations accordingly. Expect some technology setbacks, partner conflicts, and pushback from colleagues and investors. It can be daunting, but I wouldn't encourage you to follow this path if I didn't have confidence, from working with over 100 companies, that the investment will result in a healthier and more valuable business.

About Robbie Kellman Baxter

Robbie Kellman Baxter is a consultant, author, and speaker. She wrote both *The Membership Economy* and *The Forever Transaction* and hosts the podcast *Subscription Stories*. Robbie has more than 20 years of experience providing strategic business advice to major organizations, including Netflix, Microsoft, and the *Wall Street Journal*. She has been focused on subscription and membership models for the past 20 years. She earned her MBA from the Stanford Graduate School of Business, and she graduated with honors from Harvard College. You can find more about Robbie on her website, https://robbiekellmanbaxter .com/. Additional goodies for your audience are available here: https:// robbiekellmanbaxter.com/audience.

18

Ten Recommendations for Avoiding the "Pilot Purgatory" for Your Industrial Internet of Things Project

THERE ARE SIMPLE SUBSCRIPTION offers and more complex ones. SaaS offers are more easily accepted and adopted by potential customers. PaaS, EaaS, and other IIoT solutions might take a bit longer for implementation and adoption. The situation is even more complex when selling your subscription based on usage, outcomes, or a combination of monthly payment and profit share. For these subscriptions, you must demonstrate value in the form of pilot projects or controlled deployments. In the industrial world, there's a high chance that customers will ask for a proof of concept before they deploy your solutions across their industrial installed base (especially for industrial IoT, predictive maintenance, and advanced analytics solutions). Here's the sad news, though: According to a 2017 Cisco report, 75 percent of IoT projects fail, and 60 percent are stuck at the proof-of-concept stage. A 2018 McKinsey survey (de Boer & Narayanan, 2018) found that 84 percent of companies working in IoT are stuck in pilot mode, 28 percent of them for over two years. McKinsey also reported that only 30 percent are beginning to scale. Finally, Capgemini in 2018 reported that 60 percent of IoT projects are not scaling because of a lack of analytical capabilities, and the World Economic Forum & McKinsey & Company (2018) declared that 45 percent of their respondents report lacking the right resources and knowledge to scale.

McKinsey refers to this phenomenon as being stuck in "pilot purgatory" (de Boer & Narayanan, 2018). The CEO of a manufacturing company who participated in a recent Industry 4.0 Monetization event in Milan reacted to this comment thus: "It's not purgatory, it's hell!" Most of the latest consulting and industry reports on the topic of IoT technology and pure digital innovations recognize that deploying and scaling IoT and digital opportunities in B2B and industrial markets is happening more slowly than expected. It isn't leading to the explosive growth that it did for most B2C organizations. All B2B organizations want to grow as fast as Uber, Google, and Amazon. The reality in industry is different. The slow scaling process is frustrating organizations and forcing research institutions in 2018 to cut the IoT potential forecast by half, according to *IoT World Today* (Singh & Buntz, 2018).

This situation raises the following questions: What's so different about the industrial and manufacturing sector that makes it difficult for digital IoT solutions to be scaled quickly? What leads most digital projects to become stuck in pilot mode?

Here are some leading reasons:

- Lack of willingness to conduct internal pilots on their own asset basis to validate their assumptions and business cases prior to approaching prospective customers.
- Failure to realize that industrial processes might be structurally flawed or dysfunctional and a hope that good technology can fix outdated or inadequate manufacturing processes.
- Variability in manufacturing processes and maturity levels, including diversity in machine languages, manufacturing standards, age and origins of equipment, infrastructure design, automation level, and so forth.
- Complexity of assets, which can vary from simple machines (machine tooling) to complex manufacturing lines the size of a football field (paper mills or float glass lines).
- Differences between B2B verticals and variability of end-use applications within verticals.
- Complexity of organizational structures in global manufacturing environments, where some manufacturing leaders and plant managers have more spending authority than others.
- Complexity in navigating complex buying centers and decision-making maps in matrix organizations, leading to longer project scaling (delays, missed targets, and failure to generate the desired ROI).
- Fragmentation of sources of data that might be required for digital solutions to scale.
- Failure of previous installed solutions piloted by other partners that did not deliver value. Some of these solutions have matured since then, but the damage is done.
- The thinking that industrial accounts can do this on their own. Given the level of commoditization and existing availability of commercially available solutions, manufacturers are tempted to build their own teams and go through the process on their own instead of with external partners.

The manufacturing world and industrial organizations work in different ways and at different speeds. Getting approval to deploy an IoT or predictive maintenance pilot project might take three to 12 months. Imagine the time it might take to scale this solution across multiple plants around the world! It isn't surprising to anticipate the need to work on multiple pilot projects before a customer agrees to full-scale deployment to maximize the promises of IoT for them.

The pilot purgatory is real, and it needs to be considered a rite of passage for any provider of IoT solutions targeting the manufacturing sector. It's also not a fatality. It offers a unique opportunity for differentiation and design, a powerful monetization strategy that includes a strategic and intentional pilot portfolio strategy.

Designing a pilot portfolio strategy is Step 3 of the eight-step data monetization framework I developed with Professor Wolfgang Ulaga in 2018. It's even more essential when you have pressure to accelerate deployment and deliver results. It's an essential part of anticipating the needs for pilots, selecting the right customer or prospects to conduct pilots with, and minimizing variability in your pilot portfolio to accelerate scaling.

I propose 10 specific recommendations for accelerating your exit out of pilot mode and beginning scaling as soon as possible. They're articulated around three major themes: customer segmentation, pilot portfolio strategy, and partnership approach.

Begin your scaling plan with the right segmentation process based on deep customer intimacy

1   **Add relevant classification criteria related to piloting and scaling in your digital segmentation process.** Speed of execution, digital maturity level, decision-making speed, risk aversion, and ability to mobilize funds are good examples of how you might characterize your customer base. Rerun or refresh your current segmentation process.

2   **Conduct a deep analysis of the buying center for each end use and type of customer segment.** Understand who selects and approves pilots (besides IT and manufacturing), what pilot KPIs are critical for each stakeholder (e.g., finance and operations), what each stakeholder's scaling-sequence preferences are, and the budget consideration at each stage of the scaling process. Many IoT providers focus too much on the usual suspects: IT, production, and procurement. Consider the need to talk to data teams, maintenance, facilities, and legal teams.

3   **Design a customer pilot prioritization and section process.** For each end-use application and customer segment (if available), define a formal ranking process for prioritization based on pre-established criteria:

speed, quick win, time of gestation, scalability, readiness to invest, strategic alignment, and so forth. This process can be formalized in a spreadsheet to score and rank the attractiveness of end-use applications and customer targets. The key is to select the right criteria, to use the right weighting mechanism, and to have candid scoring interactions.

Design an intentional pilot portfolio strategy to prioritize to scale faster

4 **Create a matrix crossing the most-attractive end-use applications and customer plants to map the degree of commonality.** This exercise is a good test of your degree of focus and the level of commonality in your pilot portfolio. Use color codes to create a variability heat map (red: high degree; yellow: acceptable degree; green: low degree).

5 **Validate your targeted customer pilots by designing a pilot and scaling-readiness assessment that can be discussed with customers and prospects.** This assessment can be offered as a discovery exercise with your pilot account to identify gaps to address and accelerators to stimulate. It can be adapted to the few end-use applications you're considering. It can include a value calculator for the pilot as well as for the scalable plan.

6 **Map your data requirements to focus on pilots that can complete your "data puzzle."** Remember that you're learning as much as your targeted pilot customers. While I reinforce the need to focus on a few end-use applications and customer targets, you might have to include pilots in areas where you learn from new types of data. Data connectedness might be a key criterion in the prioritization of your pilot targets. The goal is to reduce variability across pilots; completing the "data puzzle" might help you get there.

7 **Design a pilot execution playbook.** This playbook is shared with customers and prospects. It sets customer value propositions, the business case, the pilot methodology (Six Sigma, Lean SS), and expectations; defines implementation thresholds; and defines pilot success KPIs, financial and resource commitments, and scaling plans once the pilot is in control mode. Train your best application and business developers on the pilot playbook. Professionalize the pilot-management process. Don't leave anything hanging.

Complement your pilot strategy with the right partnership model

8 **Think in terms of intelligent assets.** Depending on where you stand in your digital transformation and on your industry maturity spectrum, you might be in a leadership position and convince customers and prospects to

broaden their pilot scope and to think in terms of systems and intelligent assets and not just hardware, assets, and components. The goal is to change the project scope to include connected intelligent customer assets, not just single connected products in the customer asset. This platform-thinking approach might be valuable to your customers and save them time and money. No customer will want to conduct 10 pilot projects, one for each key component of their manufacturing line. Large consulting companies and large software platform providers have understood this and have promoted intelligent assets instead of connected industrial components.

9 **Form the right partnerships with other system-component manufacturers and tech partners.** To accelerate the pilot process, you must form alliances and propose turnkey technological solutions that include hardware, software, telematics, reporting, and so forth. Thinking in terms of intelligent assets requires partnerships. Focus on successful and off-the-shelf tech providers that can quickly enable your connected solutions. Combine other manufacturers' products with yours and share the efforts and investments. Going it alone doesn't work well in digital unless you're first to market and disrupting the end-use application you're targeting. This is a rare situation today.

10 **Fight the not-invented-here syndrome and embrace the open world.** According to Capgemini (2018), more than 50 percent of organizations say that uncertain standards are a significant challenge to IoT implementation. Embracing commonly accepted standards helps translate various types of manufacturing data into common language (e.g., MT Connect). Large industrial companies tend to fight common standards and to fall into the not-invented-here trap. Competing platforms, standards, and languages confuse customers and force them to make a choice. This raises the level of uncertainty in pilot projects and reinforces the need for long pilots.

More things can be done to accelerate pilot projects and scaling plans. Without a clear, strategic, focused, and intentional pilot strategy, your organization will be stuck in pilot mode for a while. Design this strategy with exit from the pilot or POC mode in mind. It does require great focus and decisiveness, two things not commonly found in digital transformations in industrial natives. As you staff your digital teams, disrupt your approach by adding an expert in customer pilot management who can design and coordinate this pilot strategy for your digital factory or your digital transformation. That dedicated expert must have both customer application/end-use knowledge and a strong execution focus, not necessarily a strong digital expertise. A great pilot portfolio strategy must focus more on customer success and value delivery, and less on digital technology and technological purity. The combination of strategic intention, a pilot-management process, customer success, and quick execution might help you accelerate your exit from the "pilot purgatory." There's no guarantee of that, but it might help deliver your targets and managed expectations. Then, with your pilot success in place, you can think about scaling and leveraging this initial startup. The sooner you can exit pilot mode, the sooner you can learn from your customer's usage of your solutions and build better a value proposition for the rest of your total addressable market.

References

Capgemini. (2018, March 13). *Unlocking the business value of IoT in operations.* www.capgemini.com/gb-en/resources/unlocking-the-business -value-of-iot-in-operations/

Cisco. (2017, May). *The journey to IoT value.* Cisco Connected Futures Executive Business Insights. www.iotjournaal.nl/wp-content /uploads/2017/05/Cisco_IoT_2017.pdf

de Boer, E. & Narayanan, S. (2018). *Avoid pilot purgatory in 7 steps.* McKinsey & Company, April 16. www.mckinsey.com/business -functions/people-and-organizational-performance/our-insights /the-organization-blog/avoid-pilot-purgatory-in-7-steps

Liozu, S., & Ulaga, W. (2018). *Monetizing data: A practical roadmap for framing, pricing, and selling your B2B digital offers.* VIA Publishing.

Singh, P., & Buntz, B. (2018). IoT technology: A platform for innovation, but not a market. *IoT World Today,* September 28. www.iotworldtoday.com/2018/09/28 /iot-technology-a-platform-for-innovation-but-not-a-market/

World Economic Forum and McKinsey & Company. (2018). *The next economic growth engine: Scaling fourth industrial revolution technologies in production* (World Economic Forum White Paper, January). https://learninglearningarchitects.com/wp-content/uploads/2019/02 /WEF_Technology_and_Innovation_The_Next_Economic_Growth _Engine.pdf

19

Ten Considerations for Scaling Subscription Pricing: What Manufacturing Can Learn from Software

By Ajit Ghuman

THE SUBSCRIPTION ECONOMY HAS its roots in the move to cloud-based software, beginning in the early 2000s. Before this change, when software was installed on-premises, tied to physical hardware, buyers of such software would have to record this as a capital expense and only a minor maintenance operating expense. After the change, most such hardware and software moved outside the premises of a client company and was simply offered as a service, now accounted for as an operating expense. This was a major revolution in terms of both software delivery and pricing models. For software buyers, it reduced the barrier to acquiring new technologies and removed vendor lock-in because they could now discontinue services on a whim.

Today, products across many industries are sold on a subscription model, and many others will be soon. According to the Subscription Economy Index 2021, subscription companies in manufacturing have seen ~160 percent growth rate since 2018, while the S&P Industrial Sector sales growth was a negative 90 percent for the same period. This subscription versus non-subscription disparity exists across different industries. The good news is that for companies who are now thinking about making this shift, the risks and potential problems have already been identified, leading to increased probability of success with this transition.

The biggest truth of a move to a subscription model is that this change is not trivial in terms of how clients pay for a service. It's a fundamental change in business as usual that will affect nearly all functions within an organization. Successfully scaling this approach depends on having clear executive sponsorship of this change with designated authority to make cross-functional changes in order to make it work.

That said, here are 10 key considerations in making this move:

1 **Package/service bundle design.** The change to subscription pricing will now allow for a rethinking of the "bundles" that customers will buy. The move to a subscription model reduces customer barrier to entry and thereby changes the total addressable market (TAM). New customer segmentation may result in the need to design segment-specific offers/bundles that serve a segment's need well. This is usually an involved process requiring consistent feedback from both current customers and the prospective future market. The benefit on offer ranges from possible expanded market share to more revenue and/or margin. Scale is enabled via a well-fitted set of offers/bundles to the new target market that then reduce sales cycle lengths and minimize negotiations. Sometimes the introduction of new offers/bundles can also cause problems for current customers if the new offers are considered too new or too rigid for their needs; in these cases, it may be advisable to have more flexible capability-based pricing on offer for current customers rather than having them move wholesale to the new model—especially when considering scale and a need to reduce renewal, upsell, or cross-sell negotiations.

2 **Pricing metric.** The fundamental unit by which subscription pricing works is via the selection of a well-designed pricing metric. This metric can be of two types: consumption-based or capability-based. Consumption-based pricing refers to the consumption of a service as tracked by the pricing metric. Capability-based pricing pricing, on the other hand, provides selected product capabilities on a subscription basis without looking at consumption. What's most relevant is that in the case of the product/service fits, the consumption-based model, the pricing metric itself, say \$/per GB, \$/per query, \$/per item produced, and so forth, becomes a tool for alignment and scale. If the pricing metric selected aligns with how the customer evaluates ROI for the product/service and offers a predictable cost structure, it's more likely to succeed—making the transition from a monolithic, unpredictable pricing model to the promised land of "pay for what you use," making the usage of the product/service easily contextualized within the customer's business.

3 **Pricing structure.** Inherent in the subscription pricing model are some trade-offs between ease for customers and revenue predictability for a business itself. Ensuring a scalable pricing model means that these trade-offs are balanced such that the business can optimize between expanding market share and growing with predictable cash flows. The selection of an appropriate pricing structure assists with this optimization and builds on the pricing metric decision. To be simplistic, there are three options for pricing structure selection: one-part tariffs, two-part tariffs, and three-part tariffs (Tunguz, 2016). One-part tariffs are essentially a pay-as-you-go option for customers with no minimums (which customers tend to prefer because of the lower risk), and the resulting revenue varies with customer usage. Two-part tariffs provide the option for a fixed minimum payment amount with a variable component—providing a little more revenue predictability for a business. Three-part tariffs are closer to a cell phone plan model, where customers are incented to buy bundles of usage units up front. The selection of the appropriate structure can positively impact scale depending on the context in which a business operates. A young market entrant may offer the one-part tariff to maximize market share, whereas a dominant, established player may opt for the three-part tariff to maximize predictable revenue.

4 **Product instrumentation.** One of the most ignored yet fundamentally important blockers to scale in the subscription context is the instrumentation of service-usage metrics that can be continuously monitored and reliably used by internal sales and finance systems. In preparation for writing my own book on this topic, *Price to Scale,* I interviewed pricing leaders at multiple firms who made the perpetual-licensing to subscription-pricing transition, and in all cases the biggest blocker to scale was the unwillingness of the product organization to use an instrument for measuring usage of said product/service. This is generally due to a fundamental lack of understanding about what the move to subscription pricing entails—it's not a niche project being undertaken by the sales or finance teams; it's a reorientation of how the business goes to market. Often *scale* is hampered by the fact that while all sales processes and contracts have moved to the new model, there's no way to reliably measure usage or to monitor overages.

5 **Consumption-based contracts.** A restructuring of contracts when implementing a consumption-based pricing metric can yield a significant increase in scalability. In the old world, contract renewals for increased product usage were a negotiation and estimation of future required needs—this took time and often forced reevaluation of the base contract structure itself, risking customer churn. In the new model, consumption-based pricing is easily tabulated for the client with prior agreed-upon unit prices and overage costs. Overage fees are automatically billed based on these contracts, and renewal negotiations are much more easily conducted based on client usage. Well-designed contracts are a simple, yet effective means to scale in this new regime.

6 **Publishing pricing.** The publication of pricing on your website can also have a significant impact on scale. In the right setting, it can help greatly improve sales efficiency and increase deal velocity, but in the wrong setting it can lead to complaints from existing customers, requests for downgrades, or a reduction in margin. I use a 2 × 2 matrix to decide when it would make sense to publish the prices along with the packages on your website (Figure 19.1).

When you have a large market with a high degree of homogeneity, it's feasible to publish the complete pricing structure online (replete with packages and prices) to help you scale your sales engine and maximize value from the market. On the other hand, if your market size is limited (say, Fortune 100 retailers) or heterogeneous (say, across retail, pharma, airlines, etc.), the call is more subjective. I've worked in companies that have opted not to publish any pricing publicly in order to increase their sales teams' ability to sell a targeted offer to their prospects. In those cases, the packages were defined internally, but there was lower price transparency, which dissuaded package comparisons and enabled them to extract requisite value from prospects that had differing WTP. In this specific context, sales reps appreciated their ability to offer their prospects the right package without necessarily getting into the shop-a-package discussion.

Packaging - Publishing Packages Online

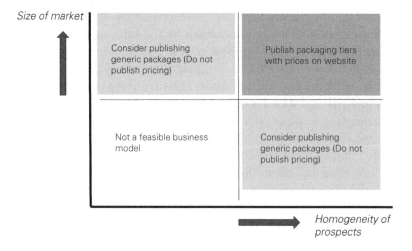

Figure 19.1. Deciding on price transparency.

7 Price-quoting process and CPQ. Once the right pricing has been set, a scalable is needed for the sales team(s) to provide price estimates to prospective clients in a friction-free process. This is easier said than done. In most larger organizations, simplicity is often traded off against implementation of complex operational systems like CPQ (configure-price-quote) that live within the CRM and provide a way for the sales team(s) to provide quotes, but the process is often complex, confusing, and slow-moving. If new pricing models are implemented poorly, sales team(s) can revolt against their adoption (and have done so), jeopardizing the entire subscription project or resulting in incorrect quotes that leave money on the table. What's important to recognize is that the implementation of such systems often takes two to three times longer than setting the right pricing strategy itself. It's highly recommended that manual, agile systems based on spreadsheets be implemented first, before the move to larger CPQ systems. CPQ systems do offer longer-term stability to these models by allowing for the capture of deal data over time that allows for pricing performance analysis, but often at the expense of sales efficiency.

The next three considerations move from operational improvements to longer-term reorientations that will be required in some of a business's key departments—changes that will need long-range strategic planning.

8 Sales reorientation. With the move to the subscription model, the everyday life of your sales reps will change. A team accustomed to sell high-value deals with little consideration to the post-sales customer journey will now have to sell lower-up-front-value deals while remaining cognizant of the customer's eventual success. This will require learning new skills or perhaps even a more fundamental change in the type of salesperson hired to sell subscription offerings. Challenger sales will make way for more consultative selling. The organizational influence that was once tightly held by sales teams will now be shared with the customer success team(s) as recurring renewal-based revenue becomes a significant percentage of the organization's revenue mix. This can play out in lose-lose battles if one does not plan ahead for this change. A relook at sales commissions to incentivize account growth is recommended to align incentives. In addition, new sales materials will have to be created alongside retraining efforts to communicate the new business model. The focus will shift more to value and ROI from capabilities—what worked in the past may not work going forward.

9 Customer success/support reorientation. Similarly, customer success and support functions will now need to rethink their approach. In traditional models, support teams served more as maintenance providers than as consultative partners. In this new, recurring-revenue world, these functions will have to become strategic partners focused on delivering value to customers—not merely customer support providers. As these teams are more responsible for the recurring revenue number, their compensation will also need to be tied to renewals, cross-sells, and upsells. Just as with the sales team(s), different skill sets will need to be developed and new talent acquired. In a sense, both the sales and customer success teams will start to look more like each other—rather than like completely disparate functions.

10 **Strategy and finance reorientation.** Finally, the move to subscription models will change how business performance is measured. Finance teams will now begin to look at metrics such as net dollar retention (NDR), a metric that measures changes in recurring revenue over time based on upgrades, downgrades, and churn. These new metrics will need to be collected and reported to the company board and will become the way the business is run. This will all require significant reorientation in finance team structures, processes, and skill sets.

In summary, the change to subscription pricing models is most definitely worth it, but it requires a significant business re-architecture that's often overlooked when businesses begin this journey. A careful examination of the changes required in the organization and the inherent trade-offs in each decision will lead to a successful and scalable implementation of this new model.

About Ajit Ghuman

Ajit Ghuman is the author of *Price to Scale* and is a SaaS Product Marketing veteran who has helped firms such as Narvar, Medallia, Helpshift, and Feedzai differentiate their products, grow revenue, and win. He likes to write on all things product marketing and is a contributor to the Forbes Communication Council and Sharebird.com. He also features in Sharebird's list of Top 50 Product Marketing Mentors for 2021. Ajit has a master's in Management Science from Stanford University and a bachelor's in Electronics and Communication Engineering from Delhi University.

References

Tunguz, T. (2016, August 1). A structural pricing competitive advantage in SaaS—The three part tariff. https://tomtunguz.com/three-part-tariffs/

20

Scaling Your Industrial Subscription with Your Trade Partners

FOR THE PAST FEW years, I've been heavily involved in digital transformations and the industrial subscription economy. Certain themes are constantly on the table. Managing trade partners is one of them. Many industrial companies express concerns about moving to the subscription economy and going direct to sell subscriptions to their end users. The subscription space is silent on the topic, although there are great case studies from the B2C and SaaS worlds (Adobe and Microsoft 365, for example). In the industrial world, things are unique, and the role of industrial distributors in many verticals is essential. The typical model is that industrial companies have direct strategic accounts and sell to the rest of the market with distribution partners. Commissioned agents can also enter the pictures in lieu of hiring full-time salespeople. In the industrial world, some giant distribution companies have disrupted industries and taken the lion's share of the value in the supply chain. Companies like Grainger, Avnet, Arrow, Fastenal, MSC, and others have morphed into a mix of industrial companies, distribution companies, and digital transformation companies. Over the past few years, they've also invested heavily in digital transformations and are selling their own digital innovations in the form of software and subscriptions. In that context, many original equipment manufacturers are playing catch-up with these industrial distributors when it comes to subscriptions.

> In a survey of corporate e-commerce channel managers, 38% said channel conflicts are their top business concern, and 44% believe that such tensions will increase in the future. (Baxter et al., 2021)

Channel conflict between distributor and manufacturer is historic. Since the beginnings of industrial channels, distributors and manufacturers have struggled to work together to grow end-user markets. The firms are fundamentally different and have different goals, which drives conflict. Manufacturers have significant fixed costs in plant, property, and equipment. They want long runs of high-contribution products. Distribution is a variable-cost or step-variable-cost enterprise. Distributors seek to drive down investments in inventory and rationalize operating expenses in short time frames. Both groups now realize that they must gain or maintain access to end users: the future of the market comes from services, software, and data. So, we see a resurgence of potential channel conflicts, as most companies have designed new digital innovations to embrace the large potential of connected objects. The driving force of conflict is digitization of the industry and the slow adaptation of both distributors and manufacturers to the digital buyer.

Two examples of channel engagement

AVEVA thinks subscriptions and distribution are not mutually exclusive. "About a third of AVEVA's business currently goes through its distribution network (100 distributors globally). However [, Kerry] Grimes[, SVP of partner sales], said he wants to get this to 50% within five years. He also laid out a three-year timeframe to get to 85% to 90% subscription revenue. 'We are helping our partners build customer success practices that gives them another revenue opportunity to sell that service. We're making all of our tools and processes available to them to do that.' As part of this, AVEVA is also renaming a portion of its customer success team 'partner success.' 'We have to change that go-to-market a bit to make sure the partners understand the whole "land adopt expand" model. It's not just getting a big deal and running off. It's about landing and continual customer support and expanding that deal,' said Grimes. 'We're giving ourselves a three-year journey to do that, as opposed to saying, "okay overnight, everyone's subscription only." I believe our model of recurring revenue is going to allow them to adopt that slowly'" (Horton, 2021).

"Volvo's online-only EV ordering. While skeptics of the agency model remain, industry leaders have taken notice, with more automakers announcing plans to pilot direct sales. This March, for example, Volvo announced plans to have EVs comprise 50 percent of its fleet by 2025 and 100 percent of its fleet by 2030, with all EVs being ordered online via volvocars.com. Dealers will continue to be an integral part of the consumer journey, providing consultation, test drives, face-to-face interaction, delivery and service. Customers will also still be able to transact in dealerships, but orders will essentially be placed online. To achieve this, Volvo plans to expand its Care by Volvo subscription platform into a simplified yet comprehensive offering. According to Lex Kerssemakers, head of Volvo's global commercial operations: 'Online and offline will be seamlessly integrated to offer a superior customer experience, whether the customer is at home, in a retailer showroom, or driving the car. This change is about how we, our retail partners and us, together make it better for the consumer.' Volvo's plans are ambitious and have the potential to put the company at the forefront of the industrywide sales transformation and help it withstand the growing competition" (Trenka et al., 2021).

So, channel conflicts have existed for centuries and are bound to continue for a long time. Although they're different this time around, they need to be resolved carefully by adopting a win-win approach to digital economics. There are sticking points about subscriptions from both the manufacturer and the channel sides. Let's look at them quickly.

Sticking points with manufacturers

1 **Lack of channel culture.** Generally speaking, manufacturers are not 100 percent proficient in understanding and managing channel needs. It's always a work in progress. Some have partner management teams; others send the salesforce to manage them.

2 **Lack of formal process to manage channel conflicts.** Managing channel conflicts is always tricky. They should be anticipated and managed through the partner-engagement model and as part of a formal process. This is rarely the case.

3 **Lack of marketing investment to support differentiated and innovated sales through channels.** I see many industrial companies with indirect sales models spending most of their marketing budgets with end users and neglecting their channel partners. In digital innovation, partners are often forgotten in the discussions. They are added at some point during the launch discussion.

4 **Lack of maturity in digital go-to-market strategies.** Industrial companies I've worked with lack the capabilities, resources, and budgets required to develop data-driven go-to-market strategies for their subscriptions (as discussed in the section 2 of this book). Teams must make sacrifices in the type of analysis they conduct. It's rare to see advanced channel strategies from the get-go.

5 **Inability to manage and fulfill both traditional offers and digital offer portfolio.** Because of resource and skill constraints, teams in industrial firms have a tough time managing the duality of subscription

business models. They must be able to manage their ecosystems well and to manage a portfolio of new and existing business models that includes a variety of channel strategies (omni-channel approach). We're far from that in practice. The combination of product, parts, services, software, and subscriptions requires deep strategic thinking and advanced channel strategies.

Sticking points with distributors and channel partners

1 **Managing the cannibalization impact.** Channel partners worry about cannibalizing their existing business and core products. Why sell something else when products and services are my bread and butter? Why rock the boat? That's a typical objection.

2 **Losing control over the accounts.** Distributors value the direct relationship with end users. It's the heart of their value proposition. They now see more and more discussions about direct-to-consumer models, omni-channel strategies, and bypassing stages in the supply chains. They don't want to relinquish control of the customer relationship.

3 **Legacy IT infrastructure and complexity to tie in distribution product-centric systems.** ERPs are designed for product-centric transactional business models and optimized with EDI, payment, warehouse management systems, and transport management systems. They aren't prepared to handle subscription and usage-based business models. This is tricky for both manufacturers and distributors. Who makes the investments? How do you connect systems? Channel partners traditionally are not keen on making IT investment for innovations. They want manufacturers to do the IT development work.

4 **Complexity of the efforts versus rewards.** Subscriptions have larger addressable markets but small transaction amounts. Partners must understand the subscription economics and compare relevant numbers. They often don't see the effort-benefit analysis working in their favor. Should I sell a one-million-dollar machine or 100 subscriptions at $1,000 per year? Who's going to sell these 100 subscriptions? They have trouble grasping the concept of recurring predictable revenues and get stuck on the small size of the transactions.

5 **Distributors don't fully understand the value of subscription innovations and might decide not to be involved in the value-capture process.** This situation is very common. Manufacturers present the value proposition of the subscription, but the overall economic value is not clear to trade partners. Where's the value for them versus the value for the manufacturer and the end user? What's in it for them? How am I being compensated for the subscription selling effort?

6 **Lack of education of the salesforce and marketing team.** In general, distribution sales and marketing teams receive a fair amount of

training on the core products and services they resell. That can already be overwhelming considering the breadth and depth of the offering. Add to this the need to train them on new subscription concepts: digital, value propositions, lifetime value, subscription metrics, interactions with customer success and other teams, and so forth. This isn't in their DNA. Who's going to train them? How do we train hundreds of distribution reps and networks of subdistributors on Subscription 101?

7 They don't need manufacturers. Some distributors are way ahead of the game when it comes to digital transformations and subscription. Avnet, for example, has an entire division focused on IoT. Grainger has developed strong capabilities in service and solution selling and has dedicated teams selling things other than products. Why should they worry about supporting the latest subscription from another OEM when they have the direct-to-customer relationship and the capability to design their own offers?

Bypassing trade channels or not: That's the question!

Often the discussion about channel partners comes down to whether to bypass them and go direct to the end users to design and scale subscriptions. Industrial companies have options to consider:

1 Fully bypass distribution all together and go at it alone.
2 Bypass channel partners for the transaction and relationship but pay commissions to the partners.
3 Partner with trade channels and get them on board your subscription journey.
4 Form a joint venture with the most progressive partners.
5 Fully delegate your digital transformation to distributors.

This is dangerous business! Of course, it depends on the amount of a manufacturer's total sales going through distribution. But the stakes couldn't be higher. Are you ready to put your core business at risk and upset your distributors? How much is your subscription business worth versus what you could risk? In the end, are you ready to fully delegate your digital transformation to your partners? From my perspective, there are so many options and ways to design a win-win partnership with trade channels that it's too risky and even borderline suicidal for a manufacturer to bypass them. So, **my answer is not to bypass but to find a way to develop a robust and integrative strategy**. My preference is for Option 3, with maybe an option to combine with Option 4. You might not be able to bring all channels on board with you, but let them make their own decision. Give them the choice of jumping into your subscription journey or not.

There are many key questions to consider when deciding how to engage channel partners:

- Who has and owns the customer data?
- Who has and owns the usage information?
- Do you give partners access to the customer data, or not?
- Who owns the transaction, and who bills?
- What are the terms and incentives for the distributor sale?
- How do you manage exclusive versus nonexclusive distributors?
- How do you introduce subscription business models, to what distribution, and how fast?
- Who's responsible for the CapEx investment for IT integrations?
- Who does the servicing for the digital innovation for PaaS or EaaS?
- Who sets distribution pricing for your subscription offers?
- Do you let distributors create their own bundles, or do you manage the subscription catalog?
- Who trains the distribution salesforce and marketing teams?
- How do we manage distribution requests, issues, support needs?
- Do I deploy a partner management technology to support the efforts?
- How do I select the right partners to start the project? Who goes next?
- Should you have a dedicated resource to manage subscriptions through partners?
- Should we create an internal advisory group to support partner development?

These are some of the many questions to answer in your partner-engagement strategy. You can see why there needs to be deep strategic thinking about this. Although I fully support bringing the channels on board, I also think there are activities that vendors and manufacturers need to do on their own during the design and development of the subscription process before engaging their partners. So, in essence, **the operating model becomes going it alone up front and then bringing in the right channel partner at some point when you're ready to show your work**. For example, industrial companies such Schindler, Caterpillar, and others work on the technology side of their digital innovation internally to develop data models that bring value to their internal operations. Then they can start bringing trade partners to the party to test and iterate.

Six pillars to consider in your channel operating model
Obviously, I could write a whole book on this topic. There's also a need for much more benchmarking and research. I've studied what's been written on the topics of digital channel conflicts, omni-channel strategies, and digital transformations. I can reduce all of this to six pillars you should focus on to get started.

1 **Perform distributor and partner segmentation.** This is a must-do activity. Marketers often focus on segmenting verticals and end-use applications for their industrial subscription offers. They need to also segment their distribution ecosystem based on digital maturity and partnership mindset. These are two critical segmentation criteria to consider. Others are service orientation, end-customer intimacy, brand loyalty, exclusive/nonexclusive preference, and technology footprint. As discussed, some distributors have already begun and are more mature than others. Some are also willing to partner with manufacturers to tap the potential of digital innovation. Pilot without your channels to perform all the validation you need to do, but scale with your best channel partners. Start direct iterations and experimentations with your exclusive digital champions and brand-lovers. Next, develop a subscription diffusion model. Bring in 10 to 15 percent of your distribution base to accelerate, expand, and hopefully create a lot of buzz. By then, you'll have demonstrated the value and attractiveness of your subscription business models. Finally, transition to a full-scale engagement and diffusion model to accelerate market penetration. Not every single distributor will join the journey. At least you'll have included them and given them the choice to get on board.

2 **Design and solidify your initial distribution engagement model.** Earlier in the chapter, I proposed several ways to engage with channel partners. Do you bypass, engage somewhat, engage fully, or delegate? Discussions and a strong commitment to the channel operating and engagement model are needed. Once that decision is made, manufacturers need to commit to the model by resourcing it the right way and by developing robust distribution and partnership strategies potentially including technology. First impressions matter, and distributors need support. In reality, many manufacturers lack the capabilities and resources to manage channel partners in the core business. Supporting subscription business models requires deep commitments.

> **Evolving channel strategies.** As face-to-face customer contact diminishes, manufacturers are re-thinking their channel strategies—both direct and indirect. With noted success in virtual selling, manufacturers will continue to increase their digital investments to stay in contact with their targeted customer base, while balancing the safety needs of their employees. Despite the rise of digital channels, manufacturers are not moving en masse to purely direct-selling models. Some manufacturers have their own e-commerce channels, while others prioritize distributors with full online capabilities. With direct channels, manufacturers are expanding enterprise programs and increasing efficiency with sales specialists and hybrid inside-sales

roles. (Sean Riley, Software AG global industry director for manufacturing & transportation; Riley, 2021)

3 **Develop a subscription marketing playbook.** Based on the entirety of this book, there are many things distributors will need to know. They'll rely on manufacturers to develop this Subscription 101 playbook (digital products catalog, subscription journey, value propositions, value pools, value maps, certifications, training materials, pricing strategies with promo and bundles) but also an operational handbook for the back office (customer success, invoicing, accounting, IT, etc.). Distributors also need help with their segmentation process, rules of customer engagement, what to offer and when to offer subscriptions, and business planning support. Remember that some channel partners will do this on their own and it will be a simple integration and support process. Others might require some hand-holding.

4 **Develop attractive distributor compensation models.** Channel partners are accustomed to making anywhere between 15 and 30 percent margins on their traditional core products and services. Should you decide to "bypass" them and pay a commission or the equivalent of a margin, be ready to fork over at least this amount to maintain the peace. Others might require a 50 percent margin to make it extremely attractive to get involved. This brings us back to the pricing discussion in section 3 of the book. Pricing your subscription on value and differentiation allows you to price high and to share value with your partners. If margins are low and the efforts to see the industrial subscriptions are high, little will happen. Compensation models must include not only a margin or commission but also incentives to scale, grow, and maintain. Important KPIs to consider include new-subscriber acquisitions and utilization, retention rate, and renewal rate. Utilization is a particularly important KPI for models like the cloud, which depend on recurring revenue. If customers aren't using a particular solution, they aren't likely to keep paying those monthly fees. So, vendors and channel partners need to ensure that there's a plan for tracking—and sustaining—utilization. Manufacturers should carefully consider the economics of their partners and develop a formula that gets the channel's continued attention. Early-pay discounts, back-end rebates, business development and marketing funds, and ad-hoc investments with the channel partner are all useful here. HP, for example, offers early-pay discounts, among other incentives, to sweeten the pot in a lower-margin category.

While channel incentives programs are growing in scope, complexity, and scale, 22% of global marketers already consider managing their channel partners to be one of their greatest challenges. Nonlinear ecosystem programs that offer extensive personalization by partner type and customer opportunity are replacing traditional tiered partner programs, and it is difficult to run incentives in an increasingly diverse, highly fragmented environment. To ensure that your incentives program and technology investments meet the needs of your expanding channel partner ecosystem, Forrester recommends you analyze the current partner program and determine gaps, add channel incentives to individual partner personas (IPPs), conduct an inventory of your current processes and technology, and make sure to work with a vendor that aligns with program requirements. (McBain, 2019b)

5 **Simplify your subscription model across the board.** You know the KISS principle. You need to keep things super simple. Product offers, pricing, administrative tasks, technology integration, access to performance data, visibility of inventory, and offers must be clearly explained. All unnecessary complexity must be handled up front or removed. It's all about making it easy for partners to sell a solution. Some good ways to do that: offer basic solutions with upgrade options; provide both "velocity" SKUs (popular configurations that distributors can stock in the software space). Channel partners will gravitate toward products that can be explained to customers in a compelling elevator pitch—not a 50-page synopsis. Remember that distributors already sell hundreds or thousands of SKUs. Now we're adding subscriptions and bundles on top of those.

6 **Make a strong commitment to the indirect model.** As mentioned, the manufacturer's long-term commitment to their subscription business model is important. You have to first clarify what's direct and what's indirect with digital innovations. Make it clear from the get-go whether you're going direct as well as with your partners. I see too many companies beginning with one model and changing it constantly based on how it's working for them, forgetting the potential impact to distribution. This is where both C-suites need to get involved and agree on the operating models and contracts. Both sets of executives must share their commitments to the long-term subscription joint strategy, including their support operating model, resource plans, and focus on future innovation. This is just the beginning of the journey. Subscription business models evolve fast, and innovations will be developed based on the success of the strategy. Working together on a data-driven strategy also enables distributors with data, future growth, and upselling and cross-selling opportunities.

Let's be clear. If you don't have great capabilities in managing partners today, you'll most likely struggle to convince them to join your subscription journey. Channel partners are partners indeed, but they're also customers with deep requirements. They'll have great expectations of your new subscriptions or when they must transition to the cloud, for example. Successful companies like Adobe and Microsoft have invested tremendously with resellers and partners to reach success.

One aspect I didn't discuss fully is the role of technology in partnership relationships. There's a whole ecosystem of technology focusing on partner management. Forrester publishes

the annual channel software tech stack infographic and blog that includes more than 100 companies competing across six categories for investment to improve partner relationship management (PRM), channel incentives and program management (CIPM), channel data management (CDM), channel enablement, channel finance, and through-channel marketing automation (TCMA). It's currently a $1.32 billion market, growing quickly and attracting significant interest from private equity investors (McBain, 2019a).

There are also licensing and entitlement technologies that can help with integrating IT infrastructure and packaging your subscription for efficient supply chains. I invited David DiMillo, formerly of Thales Software Monetization, to contribute an essay on how to best support channel partners with software sales.

 ## Lightning Strike: Best Practices for Selling Subscription Software through Channels

David DiMillo

It's common for companies to sell and distribute software, hardware, and services through a sales channel that leverages external partners. These channels are often structured in a multitiered fashion in which the vendor sells to a distributor, who sells to resellers, who in turn sell either to other resellers or to the end customer. The reseller ultimately serves as the intermediary between the vendor who produces the product or service and the end customer.

Having one or more partners between the vendor and the end customer presents its share of challenges for the vendor given the lack of visibility throughout the entire sales model. The vendor needs to ask itself these questions:

- We know our history of sales to our distributor, but how do we know how our products and service flow from the distributor and end up getting to the end customer?
- How do we know who the end customers are when our goods are sold through a channel?

Getting such insights can put the vendor in an ideal position to market directly to the end customer. Without that visibility, the vendor is flying blind.

The right IT tools can make a measurable difference to companies selling through a sales channel. In this section, we look at a platform developed by Thales that gives the vendor real-time insight into the flow of goods throughout their sales channel and allows the vendor to identify their end customers. For simplicity's sake, we discuss moving subscription software through the sales channel, but the model also applies to SaaS and PaaS subscriptions.

The channel model

We look at two sales channel models: the single-channel partner model and the multitier-channel model. We discuss the multitier model in detail since most of the concepts also apply to the single-channel partner model.

Single-channel partner. In this scenario, there's a single partner entity between the software vendor and the end customer. We refer to such partner as *resellers*. The model works as follows, working from the software vendor to the end customer (Figure 20.1):

1 The software vendor receives an order from a reseller. Either the reseller places the order on behalf of the end customer, such that the vendor knows who the end-customer is, or the partner does not identify the end customer at order time.
2 The end customer purchases software from the reseller.
3 The reseller helps the end customer install and/or configure the software.
4 The end customer either relies on the reseller for support or gets support directly from the software vendor.

Multitier channel. In this model, there are at least two corporate entities between the software vendor and the end customer (Figure 20.2). We refer to these entities as *distributors* and *resellers*. The model works as follows, working from the software vendor to the end customer:

1 The software vendor receives an order from a distributor who's buying in bulk. There's no end customer associated with the order in this case.
2 The distributor sells a portion of their in-stock software to a reseller either in bulk or for a specific end customer.
3 The reseller sells software either to the end customer or to another reseller.
4 The reseller helps the end customer install and/or configure the software.
5 The end customer either relies on the reseller for support or gets support directly from the software vendor.

Figure 20.1. The single-channel partner model.

Figure 20.2. The multitier-channel model.

Top challenges faced by software vendors
when selling through a channel
Selling and distributing software through either channel model presents challenges for the software vendor: managing time-based licenses and getting insight into the sales chain.

- **Time-based license management.** Software and services sold on a subscription basis present a challenge to the vendor. Subscription software and services entitle the end user to services for a specific period that usually begins on the purchase date. Having one or more channel partners between the vendor and the end customer can result in the subscription software beginning before the end customer receives access to the software. This not only can cause immediate end-customer dissatisfaction but also can present a revenue recognition issue if the vendor isn't giving the customer access to the software for the full subscription period.
- **Insight.** Having partners between the software vendor and the end customer can easily result in the vendor's not knowing the entities below the partner who placed the order. In a multitier model, the vendor knows who the distributor is but often nothing beyond that point. The distributor could sell the software to another reseller or to an end customer without the software vendor's knowledge. This results in the vendor having a lack of insight throughout the sales channel.

As the channel grows and involves more partners, tiers, and end customers, the challenges for the vendor increase. Figure 20.3 depicts a two-tiered model with multiple resellers and end customers. Even in this simplified model, you can see how the software vendor is removed from its end customers and how the challenges noted above become increasingly more difficult to manage as the channel grows.

Software vendor and channel partner needs
I've worked with many large companies who sell through a single or multitier channel. Their needs are commonly these:

- Allow distributors to purchase software in bulk with no customer specified on the order.
- Allow distributors to resell a portion or all of the software purchased in bulk to a reseller or to an end customer.
- Retain visibility throughout the sales cycle as far as the company and contact of the partner or end customer who purchases the software.
- The subscription start date must start when the end customer gains access to the software, not when the vendor sells to the partner.

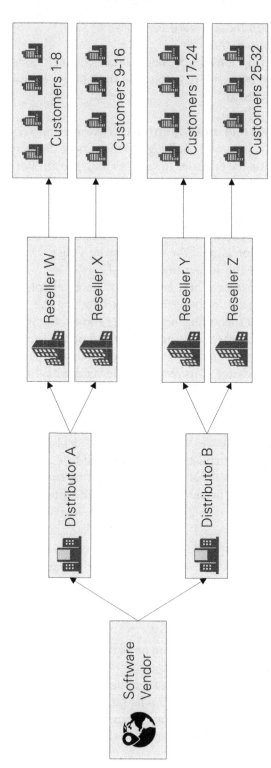

Figure 20.3. A multitier-channel model with multiple partners.

- Software resellers must have a way to manage software activation or provisioning on behalf of their end customers.
- Software resellers must have a view across their customer base as to who the end customers are as well as the deployment status of the software.

The last three challenges become difficult to manage in cases where the software requires license key activation or where the partner sells the vendor's SaaS-based solution.

The solution: A smart channel portal

As the most senior consultant for Thales, I was tasked with finding a solution for large customers that would meet the needs described above. Our company developed a smart portal and back-end system that met our customer requirements. The system I describe below is a standard offering from Thales, but there is nothing keeping a company from building a system like this on their own.

The partner portal has the following capabilities, among others:

- The portal and back-end licensing system allow the vendor to classify the purchasing entity as either a partner or an end customer. This is important because partners and customers have different needs, capabilities, and workflows.
- The vendor and system allow a distributor to purchase software without specifying the end customer.
- The portal is smart enough to understand when a subscription license has been sold and does not start the subscription clock until the software is sold to an end customer.
- The portal and back-end system allow distributors and resellers to "split and transfer" software entitlements to downstream entities.
- The distributor can log in to the portal and view the software they have in stock, meaning software not assigned to a reseller as well as software sold to resellers.
- Resellers can log in to the portal and view the software they have in stock and manage the software sold to end customers.

Let's look at an example of how software entitlement flows from the vendor to a distributor, from the distributor to a reseller, and then from the reseller to an end customer.

Step 1. The distributor purchases subscription licenses from the vendor in bulk (Figure 20.4). This step is straightforward, but note that the entitlement does not have a customer and lists the distributor as a partner along with the vendor's sales order number, parts ordered,

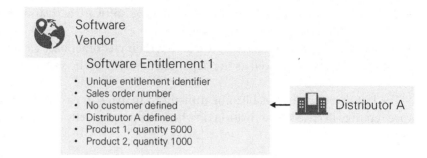

Figure 20.4. Distributor purchase of two software products in bulk.

quantities, and end dates. The distributor can log in to the portal and see the entitlement.

Step 2. The distributor sells a portion of its in-stock subscription licenses to a reseller. Let's look at the case where Reseller X buys 200 licenses of Product 1 and 100 licenses of Product 2 (Figure 20.5). The portal allows the distributor to split the entitlement by taking the purchased quantity and putting it in a new entitlement for Reseller X. The quantities on the original entitlement are decremented accordingly.

Note how the reseller entity gets defined in the vendor's portal, because the software vendor doesn't know who bought the licenses from the distributor. We look at this more closely in the next section.

Step 3. The reseller sells a portion of its subscription software stock to an end customer. Here, the reseller from the previous step sells 50 licenses of both

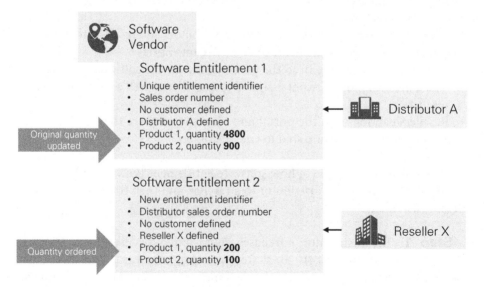

Figure 20.5. Distributor splits off licenses upon selling to a reseller.

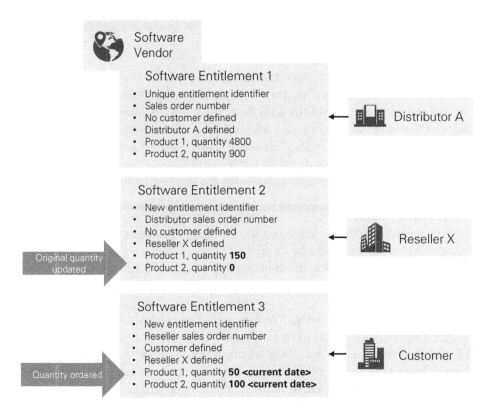

Figure 20.6. Reseller splits off licenses upon selling to an end customer.

Product 1 and Product 2 to an end customer. The reseller connects to the partner portal and executes a similar entitlement-splitting transaction in the portal.

During the split transaction, the reseller specifies the end-customer's account name and contact information as well as the products and quantities to split (Figure 20.6). The portal recognizes the software sold as a subscription and sets the subscription start date as the date sold. This ensures that the end customer can access the software for the duration of the subscription period.

Additional capabilities

In the simple examples above, the system meets all the needs the software vendor specified, including the end customer's company and contact information. Other capabilities offered are these:

- The portal allows Reseller X to log in and see the deployment status across all their customers. This includes the sale date, quantities, and end dates as well as the software that has been activated and the software available for activation.

- The portal also allows Reseller X to manage the license activation on behalf of the end customer if desired.

Managing reseller and end-customer names

Figure 20.3 shows that there are two partners sitting between the software vendor and the end customer in the workflow. The notion of allowing a partner to specify the reseller or customer to whom they've sold software raises an interesting challenge for the vendor: "How can I let a partner specify a reseller or customer when their corporate entity is not defined in our system?" I've worked with large software vendors who handle this challenge differently:

1 Use email address only.
2 Partner is required to define the sell-to entity as a customer or partner in the vendor's system prior to splitting.
3 Partner is free to define the downstream partner or end customer's company name and contact info on the fly.

Use email address only. Vendor 1 is a large technology company and designed the partner portal to rely on email addresses during the entitlement-splitting process. The reseller selects a button in the portal to indicate whether the purchasing entity is another partner or an end customer. In either case, the reseller specifies only the email address of the user purchasing the software. The vendor then has a routine that determines the company name based on the email address and then updates the entitlement accordingly with the company name.

Sell-to entity previously defined. Vendor 2 is a large tech company that requires its partners to define the entities to whom they are selling in the vendor's CRM. During the split transaction, the partner specifies the company name and vendor customer ID as well as the email address of the contact.

Free definition. Vendor 3 is a global technology company that does most of its B2B business through a multitier channel. The company sells many of its products in higher volumes than Vendor 2, so the notion of predefining the purchasing entity wouldn't work. Vendor 3's model allows distributors and resellers to specify a new company name during the splitting process on the partner portal. Here, a few rules keep the partner from entering erroneous data, but the partner is essentially free to define the company name as it sees fit.

In the first model, the vendor considers the email address to be the critical unique identifier, and the routine that determines the company name is sufficient. They're assured that the model will work given that email addresses are unique. The second model will yield the most accurate and complete customer data but can slow the purchasing process in high-volume scenarios. Vendor 3's model gives the partner latitude but can easily result in bad data.

Benefits summary

In conclusion, using the right technology can give you visibility through your entire sales channel:

- You can offer time-based subscription services through the sales channel.
- The right tools give your partner network a professional experience. Happy resellers sell more!
- Your company can scale faster through the use of a well-oiled channel partner network.
- You can assess the quality of your reseller network by understanding which resellers are doing the most business.
- And most importantly... you'll understand who your end customers and end users are so that your company can market additional services and support directly to them.

About David DiMillo

Dave DiMillo is currently the Sr. Director of Business Value Consulting at 6sense and is based in the Boston area. Prior to joining 6sense, Dave served as the VP of Solution Sales for Thales, where he built and led their strategic value-selling program. Dave also led Thales's consulting practice within its Professional Services organization and has firsthand experience helping large companies conquer their channel challenges. He can be reached at www.linkedin.com/in/daviddimillo/.

References

Baxter, A., Tordjman, K. L., Paizanis, G., & Robnett, S. (2021). *Don't let channel conflicts limit e-commerce sales.* Boston Consulting Group, June 29. www.bcg.com/publications/2021/mitigating-e-commerce-channel-conflicts

Horton, C. (2021). AVEVA steering partners toward recurring revenues. *Channel Futures,* June 25. www.channelfutures.com/new-changing-channel-programs/aveva-steering-partners-toward-recurring-revenues

McBain, J. (2019a). *Channel automation becomes table stakes for partnership success.* Forrester, October 22. www.forrester.com/blogs/channel-automation-becomes-table-stakes-for-partnership-success/

McBain, J. (2019b). *Time to rethink channel incentives and program management (CIPM)?* Forrester, April 1. www.forrester.com/blogs/time-to-rethink-channel-incentives-and-program-management-cipm/

Riley, S. (2021). A peek inside the crystal ball: Three manufacturing trends for 2021. *Smart Industry,* January 14. www.smartindustry.com

/articles/2021/a-peek-inside-the-crystal-ball-three-manufacturing
-trends-for-2021/

Trenka, J., Schmidt, A., Deryckere, K., & Barth, C. (2021). How the auto industry is revolutionizing its sales model. *Automotive News Europe,* March 24. https://europe.autonews.com/guest-columnist /how-auto-industry-revolutionizing-its-sales-model

21

Implications for Your Sales Operating Models

WHEN IT COMES TO subscription business models, we often focus a lot on technology and marketing. During the scaling phase of a subscription program, we identify pilot prospects and successfully deploy controlled experiments or proofs-of-concept to demonstrate the value of the subscription offer for both the vendor and the customers. So far, so good. Eventually, we must begin thinking about sales operating models once the subscription takes off, and we must manage a rich pipeline of prospects and pipelines. Getting to this phase is already a win. At that stage, I often hear things like "sales can sell anything" or "if this is given to all the salesforce, they will make a killing." That can't be further from the truth! My experience shows that selling subscriptions challenges the core of the sales operating model of any firm. Most companies face the following difficulties:

1 **The salesforce isn't interested because they're already stretched.** Right now, companies are growing and doing more with less. There are millions of open positions. It's not unexpected for sales teams to push back as they are required to grow the core while launching innovations.
2 **The salesforce doesn't believe the solution will work.** Have you done enough demos internally and shown successful pilot projects to your salesforce? Do they believe this is actually a viable and executable business models?
3 **The salesforce isn't incentivized to sell smaller recurring transactions.** In the industrial world, sales teams are compensated based on one-time sales and attached service contracts. Their commission plans are designed around these components. The subscription business economics is different. Sales transactions are possible smaller but last longer. There are also many more transactions over time. Have you complemented your

compensations plan to account for that? Have you modeled the transition to more recurring business models for your sales teams?

4 **The salesforce resists because of cannibalization.** This topic is often brought to the table. The concern is bigger if you haven't redesigned your segmentation process and shown the amount of overlap between segments. The sales playbook needs to account for segmentation and end-use prioritization. It needs to explain the rules of engagement with existing accounts that buy using an ownership model. Some worry about the J curve or swallow-the-fish pattern. That needs to be explained and modeled fully to address this fear.

5 **The salesforce isn't trained on the basics of the subscription go-to-market.** Many salespeople have never been exposed to recurring business models and consumption revenue streams. Lack of training means low adoption and slow scaling.

6 **The salesforce lacks the skills for strategic selling.** Selling subscriptions requires knowing the buying center and the various stakeholders involved in the purchasing and consumption decisions. For this approach, traditional transactional selling isn't efficient.

7 **The salesforce couldn't care less about digital and recurring.** Successful salespeople doing well selling one-time equipment or product offers couldn't care less about selling more recurring offers or upselling equipment sales with software or services. They focus on selling more of the same. What's in it for them?

8 **The salesforce doesn't see the value of the LTV of the accounts.** Because of the recurring nature of subscriptions, salespeople need to focus on retention and renewal to capture as much value over time. That's essential given the possible high cost of acquiring customers up front. Customer lifetime value is a critical concept in subscription business models, requiring a different type of sales process.

9 **The commercial process is designed for one-time transactions and relationships.** Fitting the sale of recurring revenues into a commercial process that's designed and focused on one-time transactions is tricky. We trust salespeople to follow the process. Therefore, the process needs to be flexible and adaptable.

10 **Sales leadership is not 100 percent on board.** If this is the case, your subscription plan is dead on arrival. Nothing will get done or sold. They must be the first to have full confidence that this is the right priority for the business.

Structural changes in your sales operation model

To prepare for scaling of your subscription business model, you need to think about these 10 situations ahead of time and design with them in mind. This means making structural changes in your sales operating model. It might require running multiple models at once for a while depending on how you organize your salesforce. There are critical differences to keep in mind between an ownership and a usership business model. They drive a need for significant operational and systems change across product development, sales, and marketing. For example,

- The marketing and sales functions must execute selling campaigns in an accelerated and agile fashion to attract new customers at scale. Remember that we're potentially reaching a much larger total addressable market. This can't be done without integrated marketing and sales automation engines.
- Free and limited trials play a strong role in customer acquisition, conversion, and adoption. In the subscription world, managing the sales pipeline actively is a must-do. This can't be done without a strong CRM system managed by a lead generation and sales operation team.
- A consumption business model requires much stronger collaboration between marketing, sales, and the back office because of the stronger role in data-driven lead generation. Sales velocity and quoting systems must work fast at scale.
- Subscription sales requires a tighter quoting cycle and quicker turnaround for customer inquiries, meaning that the CPQ systems and underlying quoting, pricing, and contracting capability must be streamlined and optimized.
- Subscription companies are increasingly rolling out self-service models and end-to-end e-commerce capabilities to streamline costs and maximize customer experience. Self-service must include online payment options.
- Sales organizations must redesign their sales playbook. They must balance a traditional transactional sales model with a new relationship management approach focused on customer lifetime value, long-term customer success, and fast adoption. Sales processes, compensation models, and talent management strategies need to evolve commensurately.

Eight recommendations for your subscription sales operating model

I propose eight recommendations for adapting your sales operating model and integrating it with your existing sales transactional model.

1 Design the proper sales organization. First, design the sales team properly. Who's going to sell the subscription portfolio? Do you adopt a generalist approach, meaning that all salespeople sell product, services, and subscription together, or a specialist approach, meaning only a few sales folks sell subscriptions? A third option might be to embed a subscription sales champion each time and use this person to stimulate subscription sales. Honeywell's Forge division has salespeople who specialize in selling digital services including subscriptions. There's no right or wrong approach. There's a need to adapt the process, the compensations, the training approach, and the rest of the steps for the organizational design you select.

2 **Conduct a talent capability assessment to evaluate your salesforce readiness to sell consumption-based models.** This is another must-do. Run a capability assessment of your current sales to gauge your sales readiness. Quickly identify the gaps in the team in order to boost the talent pool and design the right organizational development plans. Remember that selling subscriptions requires different skills and job descriptions. Work closely with human resources.

3 **Beef up the sales operations team and back office.** You might not have the right back office in place to support selling in the subscription world. Most SaaS companies will have sales development representatives qualifying accounts and passing them to the account executives. Customer success managers have a key role to play in retention and renewal of enterprise accounts. See the box below for more information about who does what.

The Bridge Group SaaS models, metrics, and compensation research (287 SaaS firms)

Each year, the Bridge Group publishes the results of a survey of SaaS companies on critical sales dimensions. Here are key statistics to keep in mind (Bridge Group, 2021):

- 68% of AE groups are supported by sales development teams.
- 51% of companies support the customer life cycle with at least three distinct sales roles—sales development reps, account executives, and customer success managers. *High-growth* companies are 2.5 times as likely to "triple specialize" as *laggards*.
- Median demos sit at five per account executive per week.
- Median on-target earnings are $158K with a 50/50 (base/variable) split.
- At 100% of quota, the median commission rate is 10% of annual contract value.
- When account executives are responsible for renewal and expansion revenue, we found that commission on renewals are either paid at the same rate (37% of respondents) or at a lower rate (55% of respondents) than new business. Expansion commissions, on the other hand, are much more likely to be paid at the same rate (85% of respondents) as new business.
- New SaaS sales representative average ramp time sits at 4.3 months.

4 Develop a parallel and/or dedicated commercial process. The new commercial process will be either dedicated to the new revenue model or integrated with the traditional sales process. Either way, there needs to be more information about the total addressable market, the priority end-uses, the ideal customer profile, the various personas we engage with, and the deal-making process, including pricing. Selling subscriptions is different; therefore, a dedicated sales playbook needs to be designed. That playbook integrates the roles and activities of the three critical functions: sales development reps, account executives, and customer success managers.

5 Design compensations systems focused on recurring business models. One overlooked growth lever is sales compensations and how they can drive growth at scale. Yes, money drives behavior. That's a must, but it shouldn't be the only focus. The combination of the right organizational design, the right job descriptions, the right key performance indicators, and the right compensation program can be powerful. Think of it as a holistic redesign. Going through the process of modifying sales comp forces you to crystallize your objectives into the two or three metrics that matter for your subscription business. Then it forces you to continuously communicate those objectives—in trainings, hiring conversations, manager one-on-ones, performance reviews, and quota-tracking tools. The key is to select the right metrics. ARR is one of them. Average contract value (ACV) is another good one. Price realization and win/loss ratio can be added, especially if you have high margins and need to value sell. Bringing new and reputable logos to the customer list is often selected as a key metric, especially in some industrial verticals when you need to show traction and use them as a reference. Finally, signing multiyear deals can be added to the basket of metrics. Compensations are often a point of contention internally. If you decide to have all salespeople sell subscriptions, it might be tricky to blend one-time and recurring metrics in one scheme. Sales reps will compare how much money they can make on both sides and make some choices. With a dedicated digital sales team, it's easier to design and execute. Don't forget to include the rest of the sales team in the incentive discussions. Sales development reps will have different metrics, and so will customer success managers.

Hilti, a Liechtenstein-based maker of power tools, fastening systems, and other construction and manufacturing products, aligned its salesforce's rewards with the core objective of increasing each customer's lifetime value. This means Hilti pursues a customer-centric strategy that views each one as a "partner," and the company seeks stable, sustained revenue growth from these relationships. As a result, the company applies an incentive system to motivate salespeople to nurture long-term customer relationships instead of boosting specific services through incentives. This motivates salespeople to continuously deliver value to customers and take extra efforts to retain them. This approach has fostered alignment between the service and sales teams, rewarded long-term partnerships, and created more value for the customers and the company. (Strempel et al., 2021)

6 **Train the salesforce on the basics of subscriptions.** You must think about designing a Subscription 101 handbook for sales, marketing, and operations, covering what it is, what success means, internal changes and interdependencies, roles and responsibilities, quotas/targets, value proposition of the subscription, pricing strategics and tactics, and so forth. This handbook must include sections on subscription economics (new KPIs, the J curve, the subscription P&L, the compensation implications), on customer journey and buying personas, on customer success, and on cross-selling and upselling when bundles are offered or products are augmented with software and services.

7 **Bring sales closer to pricing.** Sales needs to be involved in the design and execution of your subscription pricing. The sooner the better. They're your first line for testing and validating your pricing package, pricing model, and pricing structure. Listen carefully to the objections and the feedback. Letting sales share feedback and iterate with the pricing strategy helps a lot during the scaling process. They're much more familiar with the pricing playbook and have bought in to the project.

8 **Inject best practices into your sales operating model.** If your initial sales capabilities assessment shows serious gaps in your ability to launch and scale, it's important to consider bringing in sales professionals from the outside who've sold successfully in the B2B SaaS world or the service world. You have limited time to make a splash in your space before you're imitated. Use that time to ramp up and train. Use it to scale and capture the best logos in your industrial verticals. Similarly, embrace the best commercial practices that you can read in this book and in other reports. This has been done before, and there are no secrets or magic tricks. Your philosophy for how to design your subscription salesforce, shown in Point 1, will impact the rest of your operating model. You could begin with a decentralized approach having all sales reps sell subscriptions. If this doesn't work, you can quickly pivot to a centralized approach with a dedicated team. The key is speed and agility in making the pivot.

I invited two experts to share their experience in the subscription world as lightning strike essays. Alex Smith focuses on value selling in the world of subscription. John Porter discusses the need for value realization to support the scaling of subscription offers. I hope you enjoy reading them.

References

Bridge Group. (2021). *SaaS account executive report: Metrics and compensation research*. https://blog.bridgegroupinc.com/saas-inside-sales-metrics

Strempel, K., Karlsson, M. C., Lewis, T., Roth, P., Classen, M., & Friedli, T. (2021). *Industrial services: How to sharpen the go-to-market strategy*. Bain & Company, July 12. www.bain.com/insights/industrial-services-how-to-sharpen -the-go-to-market-strategy/

Lightning Strike: Getting Your Value-Based Price and Expanding Your Subscription Revenues

Alex Smith

Most B2B industries are transforming digitally and leveraging their data to develop innovative business models and, with that, delivering flexible subscription-based offers to these new services and solutions. OEMs that produce trucks or ship engines and computer servers are all moving toward delivering total solutions "as-a-service." *Selling these flexible subscriptions requires industrial companies to develop a key new capability: value-selling infrastructure.*

This trend began in the software industry, with Salesforce being the pioneer in software-as-a-service (SaaS); 20 years later, it's gaining traction in SKU-oriented companies as well. In industrial companies, to steer clear of the commodity trap, savvy commercial-excellence organizations are looking to transform from a SKU orientation to a solution orientation by packaging their product and wrapping in services, maintenance, support, upgrades, financing, monitoring, replenishment, and other value-add services. This enables businesses to create differentiation, increase margins, improve customer experiences, and itcreates long-term stickiness (if the promised customer success is realized). When done right, it's a win-win.

The SaaS industry quickly learned that business success, and true profitable growth, depends much more on the adoption of their solutions and renewals across their customer base than it does on acquiring new customers. When selling products, businesses cared if you were successful, but once a product was purchased, businesses shifted to focusing on the next sale in the pipeline. Every quarter, sales would reset to zero, and there would be a new quota number to achieve. But in this new evolution of selling SaaS and the establishment of annual recurring revenue (ARR) models, monetization models depend heavily on whether customers expand and renew, or not, based on the success and business value they see from their purchases.

The subscription business model is therefore all about customer retention. Leading SaaS businesses invest heavily in customer success in the form of onboarding, implementation, and advisory services to ensure ARR growth. As a result, the focus on new KPIs like customer lifetime value or, specifically, net dollar retention rate in the boardroom has forced a culture of focusing on where customer value lies.

While selling on value is an age-old concept, *the need for consistent and scalable value selling is amplified in the B2B subscription world.* Customer-centricity can no longer be aspirational—a deep understanding of how your customers get value from your solution, and how much value, is now critical to a subscription growth model. It's this structured understanding of customer benefits that allows for a measured land-and-expand approach in driving ARR growth.

A tremendous gap separates best-in-class and average players in subscription value-selling effectiveness, which means there's significant room for gaining competitive advantages by building a value-selling infrastructure capability.

Subscription value-selling at scale is hard: It requires the right blend of sales skill and effort supported by enablement infrastructure
Which mix is right for your business (Figure 21.1)?

A A high investment in sales skills, plus a high effort per opportunity. This model is suitable when you have a small number of high-margin deals and each needs a custom evaluation. Think of large public-sector infrastructure projects.

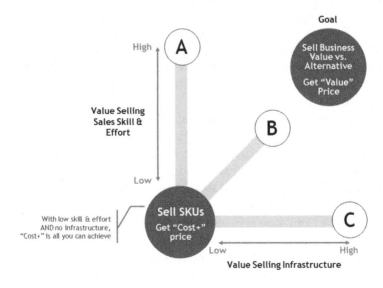

Figure 21.1. Scenarios by level of investment in value-selling skills and effort versus infrastructure.

B The fat middle that is not A and not C. Here, a salesperson is needed to communicate the value of the subscription, but there's a lot of repeatability to the message, and infrastructure is essential to make the salesperson efficient and the selling process scalable.

C A salesperson isn't necessary. The relationship between price and value is well established, understood, and built into customer self-service tools. The extreme example would be Google Adwords.

I expect most of you reading this will fall into the B zone. You have wide-ranging salesperson skills that year after year have wide-ranging results. The top salespeople can communicate and deliver a personalized value statement, but the bottom salespeople are more comfortable talking features and price, regurgitating the same content from the last customer meeting. In moving to selling in a subscription world, this difference is magnified.

COVID-19 has disrupted the typical B2B sales process for the long term, making the case for an investment in value-selling infrastructure stronger

In the software world, 89 percent of B2B SaaS companies have cited the pandemic as negatively impacting their sales teams' ability to sell effectively (O'Neill, 2020). Externally, prepandemic software selling relied heavily on in-person sales meetings and events; internally, enabling your sales team was based on in-person trainings and anecdotes gathered from sales team socializing. Because of COVID-related travel restrictions and budgetary constraints, the sales process is now increasingly virtual, a trend that McKinsey predicts will persist postpandemic. B2B subscription companies require new technologies that enable them to sell effectively in this new virtual sales cycle.

So, what does good value-selling infrastructure look like?

Evaluating your value-selling infrastructure maturity is the start to achieving your value-based price

To evaluate the strength and purposefulness of your value-selling strategy, put yourself in the shoes of a prospect and determine the likelihood of this statement in their words: "I understand what this will do for my business, and I am paying a price for that which I feel is fair, and that I can afford." If a prospective customer doesn't fully understand how your solution will help them and their business, they won't pay a value price no matter what you think your solution delivers.

Is your value-selling strategy consistent and scalable? Where does your commercial capability fit (Figure 21.2)?

B2B software companies that invested in their value-selling infrastructure have realized ARR growth from the following:

Figure 21.2. Value-selling maturity stages.

- 10 to 30 percent increase in average win-rate
- 20 to 45 percent reduction in sales cycle length
- 13 to 50 percent increase in sales reps hitting quota
- 33 to 50 percent reduction in new sales onboarding time
- 10 to 20 percent discount reduction
- 40 to 70 percent of customers increased solution scope[3]

As industrial organizations transform digitally and continue to codify their know-how, the companies that don't follow the trends of the SaaS industry will be the ones left behind.

References

O'Neill, P. (2020). *Continuous value management reporting will ensure customer retention success: The as-a-service business model increases value management importance.* Decision Link. Available at www.decisionlink.com/continuous-value-management -reporting-will-ensure-customer-retention-success/

About Alex Smith

Alex Smith is CCO and co-founder of cuvama. Alex has worked for 17 years in pre-sales, value selling across a wide range of B2B and B2C industries, including traditional wholesale distribution, financial services, and industrial

---

3   Mgpricing aggregated research on impact of value selling for B2B companies globally. Sources include Forrester, CSO Insights, IDC, Adobe, Sales Benchmark Index.

manufacturing. In addition to pricing, he has been part of and has led SaaS sales teams selling multimillion-dollar contracts. Alex's passion project now is helping fast-growth SaaS companies effectively communicate their value proposition and "get" their value-pricing potential across the land, renew, and expand phases of a SaaS subscription relationship. This know-how was codified, and formed the vision for the cuvama platform. Many years ago, Alex began life as a physicist getting his master's at Oxford University—but he doesn't remember much of that these days. He's an avid cyclist and lives in Manchester with his wife and two sons. Keep in touch with Alex via the web: Website: www.cuvama .com; LinkedIn: www.linkedin.com/in/alex-murray-smith/

 ## Lightning Strike: Value Realization to Help Scale Subscription Offers

John Porter

For a subscription-based business model to succeed, ongoing satisfaction, renewals, and expanded services are essential. This is where real subscription success occurs. It's also why net recurring revenue (NRR) has become such a critical measure of business health for many organizations. Recurring revenue is all about retaining, expanding, and growing customer relationships. As relationships in an as-a-service model are increasingly digital, making sure that every customer has a clear picture of the value that a product adds to their business is the most compelling way to demonstrate ROI and deepen relationships. This is the essence of customer value management (CVM) and why it delivers an important dimension as part of subscription model sales and customer success strategies.

Churn, attrition, and contraction are the greatest threats to a subscription business's success. The equation is straightforward: keeping customers and growing their use of a solution increases revenues and profitability. After all, the expense of recruiting new customers can add up quickly. Ensuring that existing customers have a clear sense of the value provided to them, how those results align with the value originally promised when they signed up, and that those measures of value are still relevant to their business is the most essential responsibility for anyone responsible for customer success within an organization. Depending on a company's size, this may be a dedicated team/individual. Or, in some organizations, it may be everyone who interacts with an account. For companies committed to CVM as business strategy, this is the value realization stage of the engagement.

Defining value with your customers
Before you can communicate value to a specific customer, you must know what value means for them. Each product and customer will have specific value drivers.

These might be reducing incidents, improving productivity, better using assets, offsetting costs, consolidating systems, and so forth. Most important is that the measures of value be relevant to their business. Typically, uncovering these drivers happens during the sales process as part of the business-case creation. Building a business-value case gives a salesperson a powerful way to elevate the conversation by speaking the language of business and financial value instead of features and generalized benefits. It ensures very personalized conversations because the value vectors are tailored to each company. This is where a software solution for CVM will be helpful.

To make creating and sharing business-value cases with prospects and value realization with existing customers truly scalable, companies need a centralized storehouse for value. One way to think about a CVM platform is as a complement to an existing CRM solution. Instead of just focusing on the front end of the customer journey, CVM is the bridge that helps close the deal and supports customer success in the renewal, cross-sell, and upsell process. Effective CVM tools should be accessible to any business user and shouldn't require extensive financial expertise or Excel capabilities. A good CVM platform allows salespeople to work directly with their prospects to identify a company's unique value drivers, input them into the system, and develop a tailored business-value case. The objective of the business-value case is to foster conversations about assumptions used in developing the model, stress-test the core value vectors across different departments or uses with the organization, identify other needs, and enable higher-level discussions about the results the prospect can expect. Once the deal is signed, this business case also becomes the baseline for measuring progress toward the promise of an offering.

The virtuous circle of value

A business case that focuses on higher-level financial value creates a different, more collaborative frame for the customer journey. Measurable objectives make all the difference in having meaningful value conversations with customers at every stage of the relationship. After the initial sale, the CVM platform and value more broadly are vital tools for calculating economic impact and proving the impact delivered before the next renewal cycle. Accessible insights include usage of the solution, results based on the value model built during the sales process, and qualitative opinions gathered by customer success throughout the relationship. CVM also gives champions within a customer organization the tools they need to share value gained from an investment with executives and others.

Having a real-time dashboard of value delivered can also make all the difference in retention and renegotiation. A defensive position during renewals is dangerous for a subscription business. Many procurement departments are looking for reasons not to renew. This can result in discounting or high churn rates. Leveraging value can help customer success teams bypass traditional procurement barriers and even provide opportunities for additional sales by sharing tangible ROI and value metrics that the client already identified as important and meaningful for their business.

Focusing on value enables companies to make the most of existing relationships and grow them based on a shared understanding of mutual success. Value is a proactive tool that can serve as a foundation for a lifetime relationship. Value can help ensure that subscriptions don't fall prey to staffing changes or wholesale budget cuts. Additionally, the more sophisticated the measurement and communication of the value provided, the greater the potential for additional sales or expanded use cases. With continuous communication of value delivered and regular, collaborative discussions about how needs have evolved and where programs (and use of subscription services) can grow and expand, customer interactions become moments of opportunity instead of times of fear of cancellation.

Value delivers bottom-line impact

According to DecisionLink research, focusing on value can help companies increase net recurring revenue (NRR) by 130 percent. Data shapes how customers assess their subscription relationships and the actions they take. One DecisionLink customer found that sharing value results with customers directly increased renewal rates. In situations where this information is not provided, renewals are less than 100 percent. When value insights are used, the renewal rate increases to 115 percent. According to Dimensional Research, the potential for value data to increase NRR and renewal rates is enormous, but only 18 percent of companies can provide the kind of value analysis their customers want. This is a key component of subscription business success that most companies can't deliver on. The missed opportunity is immense. Beyond NRR, companies should also be looking at customer lifetime value. The initial sale is a fraction of the potential. CVM can also be used to frame a vision of the added value that a company's subscription or add-on module or service could offer. Likewise, with a CVM platform in place, companies have the tools they need to automatically generate case studies, build ROI calculators based on aggregated customer value data, and integrate value earlier in the engagement process. With the increase in digital interactions, value-informed marketing lays a powerful foundation for value in the sales process, familiarizes prospects early on with a company's commitment to their success, and often serves as a powerful differentiator.

Value as a subscription success factor

CVM is the quantification of the value of each relationship that a company has. In a subscription business, this is the relational foundation that drives a shared future. By effectively quantifying the impact and value delivered by the subscription, every business conversation can be grounded in fact-based sales methodologies, personalized for each client. Most importantly, value is a tool that can be used at each stage of the relationship—from demand generation and prospecting to sales and ongoing customer success—to deepen commitments, strengthen loyalty, and build a shared, mutually dependent future.

About John Porter

John Porter is the first, and only, person to build an integrated platform for value management that aligns expectations, agreement, and realization of customer value across the entire customer journey. As CTO and co-founder of DecisionLink, John and his team have engineered more value solutions than any other company while helping to solve some of the most complex business modeling challenges for some of the largest companies in the world, including ServiceNow, DocuSign, Caterpillar, VMware, and CrowdStrike. John is an inventive technologist with incredible knowledge and enthusiasm about customer value management. He has served in numerous management and leadership roles across sales, product management, and customer success at eDocs, Siebel, Oracle, and SAP. More information is available at www.decisionlink.com/.

22

Scaling Your Subscription Business with the Support of Finance Teams

L AUNCHING AND SCALING A subscription business is a collective sport. You need great partnerships from a variety of internal functions. Of course, you know about sales, marketing, pricing, and customer success. But others are critical in building a powerful and scalable business. IT, legal, and finance functions can hold the keys to your success. This chapter focuses on how to bring the finance teams on board and how to turn finance experts into evangelists for your project.

My experiences in working with finance teams in scaling subscriptions business have been good and bad. Here's the bottom line. First, finance folks hold the key to profitability and cash. You can't do this without them. Second, you're responsible for bringing them on board. If they're not convinced of the sustainability of your subscription business models, they'll most likely object. Third, you must make the effort to work with them from the very beginning. I've worked with many organizations, and I often hear the following:

- "Finance will never go for it."
- "It's too risky for our finance teams."
- "The impact of cash flow is too big, and they'll kill the opportunity in gate review."
- "We need to make money right away to match the corporate objectives."

Do these sound familiar? As a Prosci® certified Change Manager, I want to bring forward some of the best practices for bringing finance teams on board. Here are six important considerations.

1 **Develop a "what's in it for me" (WIIFM) strategy as part of your change-management plan.** Get to know the motivations, objectives, and preferences of your main finance stakeholders. Prepare a plan to respond to their objections and their preoccupations. Having that ready can go a long way toward holding a dialogue with both parties in mind.

2 **Socialize the subscription business model with top management and high-level financial executives.** In any organization, you have powerful and influential executives. Some might sponsor your project. Others might open some doors for you. If you spend time socializing your subscription business models with these people, they can be influential in convincing middle management to meet with you and support your efforts. Think of it as infiltrating the matrix!

3 **Bring finance into the core right away during the design phase.** The sooner you can involve financial experts in the design of your subscription business model, the better it is for your scaling process. Ask for help from the very beginning, and involve these experts early so that they have skin in the game. Don't present something to the financial community that nobody's seen before. That's a rookie mistake.

4 **Develop scenarios and options to address and anticipate risks.** Understanding the risk appetite and the constraints of your core business might help in setting up presentations that include several scenarios and risk options. If cash flow is an issue right now in your business, presenting a 100 percent subscription business model as the only choice might not work. Present three options with different impacts on cash flow. I understand that presenting a subscription financial model with an up-front CapEx payment isn't really a SaaS or PaaS model. But it is what it is. You have to work within the financial constraints of your organization.

5 **Train finance teams on recurring business models and subscriptions.** Invite as many finance people as possible to your training on subscription business models, subscription pricing, and how to transition to a SaaS model. It's worth the time to have this community trained. You might be surprised by their lack of knowledge on these topics.

6 **Make them part of the success.** Create dashboards that include financial KPIs that blend traditional KPIs, such as margins and earnings before interest, taxes, depreciations, and amortizations (EBITDA), with subscription-related KPIs such as ARR, average contract value (ACV), and others. As you involve them in your ventures, they'll help you track success and will have more skin in the game.

Working on these six considerations can help you develop a great partnership with finance. You could argue that the same considerations might work for the IT and legal teams to a certain extent. They're equally important in the scaling of your subscription business models.

To strengthen my argument, I've invited two experts in the field to write lightning strike essays to help with the finance topic. Nizard Djemmali is CFO at NeoXam and has tremendous experience in the subscription world as a finance expert. Gunnet Bedi is SVP and General Manager at Relayr, and he addresses the topic of risks and finance in the world of EaaS. I thank them both for their contributions.

 ## Lightning Strike: Top Things Finance Teams Need to Know about Industrial Subscriptions

Nizard Djemmali

Swallow-the-fish effect and cash-flow impact:
Not the same for industrial companies with assets worth millions
Transitioning to a subscription business model will force your company to swallow the fish. Not a big deal... depending on the size of the fish. Industry businesses can face significant cash-flow needs because their activity is naturally capital-intensive. Working-capital needs, business seasonality, debt reimbursement may impair the cash situation if coupled with a subscription business transition which itself will require additional financing. Client retention and monetization over time will ensure cash recovery eventually.

Anticipation and pedagogy toward bank partners will be instrumental to ensuring the success of the transition without impairing the future of the company. One good thing to keep in mind is the need to also review any existing covenant obligations and negotiate them anew, taking into consideration the potential impacts of the transitions and the financials.

As-a-service models means services, which are far from products.
They also mean that margins should be higher than the cost
of enabling and servicing accounts
Shifting to as-a-service is not only a fancy fad any company should move toward. As-a-service means going beyond the product realm, which can already be complex itself. Companies willing to make the move need to consider adding new services to their portfolio and investing in those to optimize their value chain. New services may include, for example, data hosting, customer care, maintenance, usage insights, and so forth. However, the whole bunch of new services comes with new accountability and... new risks.

Adding up part or all those servicing costs implies the need to ensure that the fee paid by the user will cover, over a satisfying time range, the costs and ensure sufficient margin to the manufacturer.

Another thing to consider is that those costs must be continuously scrutinized through usage data provided by product sensors or by the user—provided that the latter is willing to share them with the manufacturer. Finally, risk to deliver a new scope must be assessed cautiously, as companies may, in order to lower it, need to massively invest in new skills, new people, and new partnerships, or even reassess their M&A strategy.

Risk of carrying assets on the balance sheets for PaaS and EaaS: New forms of financing are on the way

PaaS and EaaS stand apart because they carry significant assets on their balance sheet. As-a-service models are characterized by the fact that users don't purchase and own the product. They use the product, consume its features, and generally pay a price based on consumption. One benefit of this model is that users shift from a CapEx-like investment to an OpEx-like purchase, in this way lowering access to the products. This is great for companies willing to gain access to a bigger market, as it lowers the price-entry barrier. However, the downside for companies is that they don't get the immediate cash benefit of a one-off sell. This may conflict with capital needs to cover investments, infrastructure maintenance, and repairs or financing costs. To cover all obligations, companies may then need to diversify their activities and position themselves on all value bricks in order to capture most of the margins from their product usage. The opportunity to blend their offers, splitting revenue between a one-off entry fee and usage fees, can also be tempting but needs to be assessed cautiously in order not to offset the benefits of the as-a-service model.

Moving from product to subscriber has implications

Moving from a product-centric view to a subscriber-centric view is a tremendous change in paradigm.

First, companies change their focus reference. Previously, companies focused on their product, their features, their design, and so forth, and this served as a reference to benchmark against the competitive landscape. Think how convenient it is to compare two cars considering their top speed reached. But does one of the cars fit the usage its users expect? Is it necessary to reach a 180-mph top speed when taking five-mile trips in an inner-city circuit? You get the point. When companies change their focus to the subscriber, they focus on design no longer in terms of industrial performance but to fit a particular usage. Second, shifting from a product to a subscriber implies the introduction of a new variable: time! It's no longer about "sell and fly"; it's more about building a relationship with subscribers, following up on how the product solves their pains over time, getting continuous feedback from increased or decreased or even abandoned usage to feed the virtuous circle of the product and offer design.

New and blended metrics...but not only

What comes with a new business model? A brand-new set of key performance indicators. As said above, shifting to subscription business models will bring new considerations and a new way to look at operations. As time becomes a key variable, time-dependent KPIs may arise on the management landscape. Client lifetime value, time to recover subscriber acquisition cost, and so on will come on top of revenue, EBITDA, or net debt to fully assess company performance. Something else to consider is the need to align a whole organization around the new embraced business model. Management should make sure to organize the company by value generation clusters with identified responsibilities and accountabilities. Top management must ensure that each person in the organization understands their contribution to the transition and the key metrics necessary to assess the performance obligations.

Pricing based on cost leaves money on the table

Traditional businesses usually show the same pricing principles. Determine first the cost to design, craft, and sell the product and add to that a reasonable (marketwise) margin, and you'll be able generate enough cash to sustain your company and respect your commitments. Focusing on the usage and the true pains addressed by your solution won't let you take the full value of your client equity. In addition, it's not only short-term cash benefits that you downsize if you decide to focus only on classical pricing methodologies. It's about feeling, understanding, and eventually taking advantage of market trends to orient your company strategy and future market acquisition and monetization. Companies can spend lots of money trying to get strategic studies to "feel the market" where getting the flavor of the usage of your product can make you disrupt your own market and ensure your company's future.

Impact of recurring revenue on revenue recognition and ASC 606

For accounting and finance teams, new revenue accounting standards in a subscribed-relationship context require multisource environments, significant manual processing, and complexity handling. Managing this complexity will keep the teams awake at night. The change of perspective also adds complexity as one-off sells leave the stage to continuous selling and contract amendments (upwards or downwards) within the course of the year or even spread over multiyear arrangements. Delivering a continuous service to a client requires a deep analysis of all components of the client contract and continuous valuation of those components, from a dollar perspective, as well as a constant evaluation of the right timing to release the underlying revenue in the company P&L. The big change, if we simplify, is that we used to run this analysis once and for all, and now it needs to be performed continuously over the course of the relationship with the subscriber.

Mitigating the cannibalization impact between one-time sales and recurring sales

Organizations are skewed when transitioning from recurring sales to one-time sales. Indeed, it can always be tempting to return to old memories and apply the highest pricing or choose the best offer to enhance revenue impacts in order to improve the figures and show more favorable short-term financials. Especially if you're struggling to "swallow your fish." Therefore, in most transitioning businesses, trade-offs can generate offer cannibalization and, even more, organization misalignment. Management of companies undergoing this change must strongly focus on the change and team alignment. Don't hesitate to align teams' compensations to push new offers, but don't forget that all business is good business and that teams selling old offers must not be penalized. Change will eventually come; it will take time, and you need to keep your team motivation at high levels to ensure the success of your transition.

"As-a-service" means large numbers of smaller invoices. Can your financial systems and accounting teams handle the traffic?

Changing business models, business paradigms in fact, requires more than just the will to do so. While considering the changes involved, managers often focus on these concerns:

- the necessity to review the company's offer
- the need for new jobs that would reflect new responsibilities
- pricing reshuffles
- et cetera

However, transitioning from one-off deals of tens of thousands of dollars to usage-based deals (sometimes thousands-of-cents deals) introduces a new necessity to handle numerous transactions and fully revamp information system infrastructures. Indeed, past or current accounting software is often designed to rely on industrial traditional accounting constraints to deliver current normalized financial aggregates. They tend to face difficulties when shifting from accounting backward-looking statements to forward-looking usage-based financial indicators. Fortunately, a bunch of new actors can now natively solve those pains. We mentioned above the transition from a product-centric to a subscriber-centric view. This enhances the necessity to know your customer and put them at the center of your information system map. Finally, we should emphasize the need to train finance team people on new indicators, business concepts, or even new company valuation concepts and benchmarks. You see the point here. Don't neglect team training and change-management efforts while transforming your business. For the sake of your company and your teams.

About Nizard Djemmali

Nizard Djemmali is CFO at NeoXam, a leading software company providing financial solutions for the buy-side and sell-side. Nizard has been through companies shifting to the subscription economy and has been responsible for managing those transitions such as information system transformation, team training, and offer revamping. linkedin.com/in/nizard-djemmali-47302aa, www.neoxam.com/

 ## Lightning Strike: Using Insurance and Financing Strategies for De-risking Your EaaS Transition in Manufacturing

Guneet Singh Bedi

Equipment-as-a-service (EaaS) is a subscription business model in which equipment is provided for a fee that also bundles together maintenance, spare parts, installation, consumables, value-added services, and in some cases even outcome (SLA/uptime/performance) guarantees. By moving toward providing a service, industrial companies can create a stable and resilient recurring revenue base, ensure better outcomes for their end customers, and capture more of the lifetime value chain through value-added services.

EaaS offers numerous benefits, but it also creates many new risks. When it comes to risk, adopting a new business model goes through the following stages: identifying potential risks, getting comfortable with them, and eventually turning them into strengths. There's another appealing aspect of embracing innovative models—competitors in the market are still risk-averse, which generates additional advantages for early adopters. It's essential to create a bulletproof strategy to reap the benefits and avoid financial risks.

Below are four practical tips that include elements of specialty insurance and financing offers:

- See risk as a performance enabler and as creating value
- Find the right partner to mitigate or insure against risk
- Just like a college education, it always needs more financing than you thought
- Think of EaaS not as standard leasing (or pure CapEx to OpEx) but as much more

See risk as a performance enabler and as creating value
Usually risk in business is seen as something to be eliminated, a complication that hinders a company's efforts to deliver products or services. However, there's another point of view that reflects the history of innovation—the economist

Robert Merton, mentioned by *Harvard Business Review,* argues that companies create value by managing risk better than their competitors.

In the context of EaaS, by bundling hardware, software, and services into one solution, industrial companies can fully benefit from reliable data and insights. Use the EaaS business model to create value with value pools that will help minimize your customer's risk. For example, if unplanned downtime is catastrophic in your industry, assume this risk yourself as a manufacturer or service provider within the EaaS offer. In return, provide equipment uptime and reliability guarantees and capture this value pool with higher and more predictable revenue. If equipment performance is the critical value pool, then include outcome/performance within your EaaS offer and address your customers' risks.

Find the right partner to mitigate or insure risk

Relying on lifetime revenues means that you reap the benefits of the EaaS model over a few years and need to manage potential risks so that they become strengths. Specialty insurance possibilities exist through many companies, among them my parent company, Munich Re:

- **Completion warranty.** Making machines smart is the basis for ensuring higher uptime guarantee and higher performance. Yet it's a challenging process that involves deep expertise and careful orchestration. You can insure delivery of interoperable IIoT solutions with smart-connected assets.
- **Business outcomes warranty.** Business outcomes (e.g., operational efficiency gain, maintenance cost reduction, zero-unplanned downtime) warranty is a unique approach to minimize risks for both manufacturers and end customers. Can extend to cover loss of income.
- **Retrofit warranty.** Sometimes an original manufacturer's warranty becomes void in the process of IoT deployment. There are also potential risks when buying back equipment that was at the customer side for retrofitting purposes. A retrofit warranty minimizes the risks for the manufacturer and provides a way to guarantee the performance of older equipment. For service providers, you avoid taking the extra risk of voided warranties and machine failures when retrofitting old machines.
- **Equipment breakdown insurance.** This covers costly physical and financial damage that can result from an equipment breakdown and in some cases can also cover property damage, business income, extra expense, expediting expense, and perishable goods. With an IoT solution, it can be a key differentiator for EaaS offers.

Risk minimization enables organizations to rethink their business models and future-proof their business. Identifying potential risks, getting comfortable with them, and finally turning them into opportunities is one key advantage of EaaS and can help you gain a competitive edge. Choose a partner familiar with EaaS and services business models so that they understand the complexity involved.

Have additional sources of financing in the initial period

> Upgrading our production environment is extremely reliant on the payment method we can obtain. Each phase might cost around €1 million, and we quickly recover those costs, but until that point, there's a real impact on cash flow. Traditional financiers do not provide appropriate mechanisms for this kind of project as they do not understand how our operations function. (Spanish machine manufacturer, Siemens report on Industry 4.0 quotes)

Plan for the worst-case scenario with a conservative lens on how initial investment will affect liquidity and restrict financial flexibility. If you need less investment and if EaaS adoption happens faster, you can use this to accelerate your commercial ramp-up. Although the EaaS model offers stability and business growth in the long run, it requires a significant commitment in its adoption phase. Choosing to go down that road with a partner makes it easier for businesses to bridge the gap. There's only one condition: companies must be willing to share the benefits of the achieved business outcomes and help with cost coverage and capabilities up front.

EaaS isn't standard leasing—It's much more

The standard leasing triangle is not EaaS, and leasing is just one example of numerous financing opportunities. In a standard leasing triangle, the manufacturer sells its assets by transferring ownership to the financing company. The financing partner then offers a leasing contract to the end customer. Although it's simple, it doesn't capture the numerous advantages of EaaS for the manufacturer and the end customer, such as machine uptime backed by IIoT, higher machine performance with maintenance included, low monthly payments when not in use, and tailor-made pricing. In the case of EaaS financing, a firm can make use of the leasing-plus model as a basis by adding value-added services to it. A third-party provider finances the equipment or production system, makes it available to the end customer, and ensures that operational and maintenance services for the equipment are in place. This allows the end customer to pay only one invoice—either through a rental lease model or standard lease-plus model. For the manufacturer mentioned before as an example, the end customers do not require an off-balance solution.

There are also numerous advantages for manufacturers: the servitization model multiplies the lifetime value of the equipment and gives suppliers control over the lifetime quality of their products. It stabilizes revenues and captures life-cycle revenues. Relying on lifetime revenues means that the manufacturer needs to secure the performance with, say, higher performance guarantees. For service providers, the so-called brownfield approach is also possible in the case of EaaS buy-back financing. The financing partner is buying back equipment and retrofitting it with the right availability, performance guarantees, and all O&M included in a pay-per-use price. End customers see up to a 15 percent lower TCO, and their interests are aligned with those of the manufacturer or service provider who offers EaaS.

Because of the unique nature of the EaaS model, there's no one-size-fits-all solution. Find a strong partner to guide in finding the financing model that best fits needs. In the industrial world, there are no off-the-shelf solutions with differences in size, capabilities, and needs. One thing's for sure: transforming to a EaaS model is a big leap for every company and requires a tailored approach.

About Guneet Singh Bedi

Guneet Singh Bedi currently serves in Relayr's management team as CRO & SVP/GM. Relayr (https://relayr.io) is Munich Re's Industrial IoT and Equipment-as-a-Service division and has taken dozens of companies through this journey. Guneet is a seasoned technology executive with experience and demonstrated successes in global technology companies across enterprise software, IoT applications, and computer networking. He has held various roles at Cisco Systems, Symantec Corporation, Oracle Corporation, and Telelogic AB (acquired by IBM). Guneet has lived in various cities in the US, India, and Europe and in his spare time is passionate about mentoring CXO's of early-stage startups. Guneet received a BE in Computer Engineering from National Institute of Technology, India, and an MBA from the Kellogg School of Management, Evanston, Illinois.

SECTION 5

INDUSTRIAL SUBSCRIPTION EXAMPLES

23

A Review of Subscription Offers and Pricing in Industrial Markets

By Emilie Saule

RECURRING REVENUE MODELS, SUCH as subscriptions, are generating new opportunities for industrial companies. Subscription revenue models have benefits on both sides, offering greater financial stability for companies and convenience for customers.

This shift from a CapEx (capital expenditure) to an OpEx (operational expenditure) model is, most of the time, made possible through the use of new technologies such as IIoT, big data analytics, cloud computing, and so forth. Thanks to these technological evolutions, industrial companies can introduce new digital services (e.g., data analytics) and shift their current offerings to new business models (e.g., equipment-as-a-service; EaaS).

Methodology

To better understand the new recurring revenue models in industrial markets, we studied 100 subscription offerings from major industrial companies worldwide. The industrial companies we researched are evolving in various industries (manufacturing, transportation, health care, agriculture, construction, etc.). For our research, we gathered public information from corporate and media websites such as brochures, press releases, and articles. The research was focused on B2B (business-to-business) offerings in industrial markets. We excluded B2C (business-to-consumers) offerings. We also did not focus on pure digital players.

We studied a variety of subscriptions from diverse industrial markets and various offer types such as IaaS (infrastructure-as-a-service), PaaS (platform-as-a-service), SaaS (software-as-a-service), and EaaS (equipment-as-a-service).

Our objective was to understand how those offerings were structured, from the market problem and service description to the packaging and pricing model. Next, we analyzed the results to see the trends and identify good practices for subscription offerings in industrial markets.

We selected the 25 best offerings that are good examples to look at for their structure, clarity, and/or transparency

Statistics

Of the 100 industrial subscription offerings we studied, 68 percent are SaaS, 16 percent are EaaS, 12 percent are PaaS, and 4 percent are IaaS (Figure 23.1). Of these, 52 percent are structured as a "digital bundle," combining hardware, software, and support in a single subscription, and 30 percent are offered as "services on top of a product," offering a digital service on top of equipment. We believe that some industrials still struggle to value their new digital services and that they are offering them free of charge, usually to win a major deal.

In terms of transparency, 55 percent communicate on the offering structure, describing the options included in each tier (package or bundle); 47 percent also describe the pricing model, explaining the type of subscription, duration, metrics, and so forth (Figure 23.2). However, only 28 percent disclose the actual price.

We noticed a lack of transparency on the offering packaging and pricing model in some industries, such as aerospace and defense.

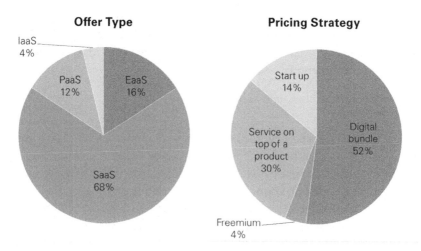

Figure 23.1. Offer types and pricing strategies.

Figure 23.2. Transparency.

Observations and good practices

Offering definition

Everything begins with a good offering. It needs to answer to a clear market problem and meet customer needs. This requires a very good understanding of the market, with strong customer insight.

We noted different approaches to the development of new digital offers. Some companies build on their current offerings using their existing assets, some create new divisions with new assets, and others rely on partners, such as digital pure players and startups.

The use of partners is good for quickly growing in the digital and for leveraging already established resources, organization, and tools (e.g., TRUMPF and Relayr, Siemens and Mendix). Most of the known successes have been achieved through partnerships, in various forms. Partnerships seem key to success in digital.

User benefits and value-proposition description

A good offering always begins with a good description. It's important to describe the market problems it solves and, then, the offering itself:

- How does it work?
- What's included in the subscription?
- Who are the users?
- What are the user benefits and value proposition?

The key is to ensure that the value proposition is clear and can be understood quickly. A frequent mistake is to overwhelm prospective customers with too much information. Sometimes, there are too many offerings. In other cases, there are too many options (stand-alone features, "add-ons," etc.). It could be difficult to understand the differences between them and the benefits of each offer.

Investing in marketing/communication is key, as it allows a clear understanding by prospective customers. A short video, a clear schema, and/or other visual representations will improve the clarity of the offer.

It's also important to use the right nomenclature for the offering. We've seen many companies using "PaaS" for offers that are closer to a SaaS model. PaaS is most often built atop an IaaS platform to reduce the need for system administration. It allows customers to focus on application development instead of infrastructure management. SaaS offers ready-to-use, out-of-the-box solutions.

The description of the value proposition is very important. As the baseline for the customer negotiation, it must highlight the savings or increased value delivered to the customer. Adding examples of prospective savings (real achievements if possible) will make it more powerful: it needs to demonstrate a clear return on investment.

The value proposition and benefits need to be communicated per end users. For example, benefits might not be the same for operators and for executives. The offer needs to convince customers at all levels. Most of the time, several decision-makers are included in the purchasing process (procurement, marketing, engineering, etc.). A good understanding of the buying center and role of each function will help to reach the right audience.

Another good practice is to have customer testimonies. Few customers would want to be the launch customer (perceived as the crash test). Customer testimonies make the offer real and more reliable. It helps reassure future customers and allows illustrating the value proposition. It also drives interest (*if my competitor's using it, it might be useful for my company too*).

Digital pure players are more advanced in their subscription business models (e.g., Amazon, HubSpot). They are good examples to look at in order to benchmark on the value-proposition definition.

Offering structure and pricing model

Subscription offerings need a clear packaging and pricing model. Offering too many options might be difficult to follow and scale.

To define a good offering structure, it's important to have a good understanding of the market segmentation and identify needs and price sensitivity for each segment.

Most of subscription offerings are structured around a good/better/best approach with several tiers (packages) targeting different customer segments. With an offering packaging strategy using bundles, each bundle needs to be clear and differentiated from the others.

Sometimes, the first bundle is offered free of charge and customers must pay if they want additional features. This is called the freemium approach. Under a freemium pricing strategy, the free bundle must only include very basic features. Features generating the highest value should not be included.

Bundles usually include many components (hardware, software, support, etc.). Some companies failed to capture the value of each component of the package. It's important for the sales team to know how to sell each component.

We also noticed that many companies are offering a "custom" bundle, sometimes called enterprise, where customers can customize their options according to their needs. This is a good option, with a less rigid pricing, mainly targeting customers that are less price sensitive. However, the right organization needs to be in place to support it. It might increase the work order to track all different pricing structures and thus costs. The billing will be more complex, especially without the right support tools.

In terms of metrics used for the pricing, the most common are

- per number of users
- per number of connected devices
- per company type (with increased number of users, connected devices, features or support)

Our recommendation is to use metrics that make sense for the targeted customers. Metrics need to be aligned with the value delivered. "Per user" doesn't always make sense.

In studying the offerings, we noticed changes in the pricing structure of some of them. It has evolved over the months/years. Pricing isn't a one-time exercise. It requires a dynamic approach. It's important to anticipate those evolutions at the beginning. It will be difficult to justify a higher price without major evolutions in the service offered.

We also noticed that some companies offer automated renewal in the contract. This is a good practice, as it reduces the risk of reopening the negotiation at the end of the contract.

Some companies still struggle in valuing their new digital services and tend to offer them free of charge. This is probably one of the biggest mistakes in trying to sell new services. Once something is offered for free, it's very difficult to go back and value it. Many industries still face a big challenge in valuing their services because of a lack of maturity in the market but mainly in the organization itself. It remains a challenge for them to present and defend the value proposition.

Conclusion

Adopting and implementing new subscriptions business models is a challenge for industrial companies. Many had focused on hardware and equipment for decades. In some cases, they were offering services for free, as a concession to win deals. Now that there's a major price erosion in most markets, industrials need to shift their value pool and develop their service offerings.

A big challenge they face is implementing the right organization. All teams within the organization need to adapt and transition to subscription: the sales force needs to be trained in how to sell, the legal team needs to establish a specific contract frame, the accounting team needs to collect the recurring revenue, and so forth. Industrial companies need to change how they're operating today and have a new organization in place to support those offerings, with the right people and the right tools.

About Emilie Saule

Emilie Saule is a Digital Partner at the Thales Digital Factory, supporting Thales business units in their digital transformation. She specializes in Pricing and Digital Services. Emilie has eight years of experience in the industrial and service sector working with companies like Thales and Daher. Emilie joined Thales in 2018, first as a Pricing & Value Coach, supporting Marketing and Product Managers in the value proposition and pricing definition. Then, she moved into a Digital Services Product Line Manager position within the Avionics Business Unit. She holds a master's degree in Marketing and Innovation from Toulouse School of Management. She is certified in Value-Based Pricing. She can be reached on LinkedIn.

Top 25 Subscription Models from Industrial Companies

24

Case Study 1

3M

Division:	3M Commercial Solutions
Region:	Worldwide
Offer Name:	Visual Attention Software
Link to Subscription:	www.3m.com/3M/en_US/visual-attention-software-us /pricing-sign-up/
Subscription Category:	Digital bundle
Public Pricing Info?	YES

Statement of customer & market problem
- "3–5 seconds. That's about all the time you get for your design to be noticed or lost in the shuffle."
  Source: www.3m.com/3M/en_US/visual-attention-software-us/ (08/12/20)

Offer description (technology)
- Visual Attention Software analyses your designs, using algorithms that simulate what people see during the first 3–5 seconds of viewing.
- Upload your design and use VAS via web, mobile app or Photoshop plugin.
  Source: www.3m.com/3M/en_US/visual-attention -software-us/features/ (08/12/20)

Value proposition of the subscription offer
- VAS helps increase client confidence, simplify approvals, and gain consensus on visual priorities.
  Source: www.3m.com/3M/en_US/visual-attention-software-us/ (08/12/20)

Stated customer benefits
- Use the results to confirm that you have achieved your visual goals, or to guide revisions.
- VAS makes it easier to know when the work is ready to present to your client.
- Use VAS as many times as needed to analyze alternate layouts.

Source: www.3m.com/3M/en_US/visual-attention-software-us/ (08/12/20)

Subscription packaging
- Subscriptions are for individual use only, and on one device at a time.
- Group subscriptions are available for teams of 20 or more people.
  Source: www.3m.com/3M/en_US/visual-attention-software-us
      /pricing-sign-up/ (08/12/20)

Subscription pricing model
- Subscription per month or per year.
  Source: www.3m.com/3M/en_US/visual-attention-software-us
      /pricing-sign-up/ (08/12/20)

Subscription pricing structure
- $49 per month or $588 per year.

VAS Subscription Options

Source: www.3m.com/3M/en_US/visual-attention-software-us
      /pricing-sign-up/ (08/12/20)

Case Study 2

ABB

Division:	Electrification
Region:	Europe
Offer Name:	ABB Ability Electrical Distribution Control System (EDCS)
Link to Subscription:	https://new.abb.com/low-voltage/launches /abb-ability-edcs
Subscription Category:	Service on top of a product
Public Pricing Info?	YES

Statement of customer & market problem
- "Your plant is like your body, it needs to work perfectly to be really powerful. Thanks to ABB solutions and management services, monitoring the correct energy consumption and avoiding losses and waste."
  Source: https://new.abb.com/low-voltage/launches/abb-ability-edcs
  (05/04/20)

Offer description (technology)
- ABB Ability Electrical Distribution Control System is the innovative cloud-computing platform that monitors, optimizes, controls and predicts the condition of electrical distribution systems.
  Source: https://eu.marketplace.ability.abb/en-US/apps/22677 /edcs---predictive-access# (05/04/20)

Value proposition of the subscription offer
- For end users: save up to 30% on operational costs.
- For consultants: increase the value of projects by 15%.
- Facility managers: take action in 1 minute, anywhere, anytime.
- Panel builders: connect the panel to the cloud in 10 minutes.
  Source: https://new.abb.com/low-voltage/launches/abb-ability-edcs
  (05/04/20)

Stated customer benefits

Monitor	Optimize	Predict	Control
Discover plant performances any time, anywhere	Collect thousands of data, analyze information and take your decision	Supervise the system health conditions and predict next maintenance actions	Implement your strategy and reach the goal

Source: https://new.abb.com/low-voltage/launches/abb-ability-edcs (06/20/20)

Subscription packaging

Tiered pricing per number of devices:

- Small Tier (15 users, 1 plant, 5 devices)
- Medium Tier (15 users, 1 plant, 10 devices).
- Large Tier (15 users, 1 plant, 30 devices).
- Extra Large Tier (15 users, 1 plant, 90 devices).

Customers can select some "add-ons" for additional users, plants, devices or features.

> *Source: https://eu.marketplace.ability.abb/en-US/apps/22677 /edcs--predictive-access# (05/04/20)*

Subscription pricing model

- Packages: 5-month trial period, then a subscription per year.
- Add-ons: One-time payment or subscription per year depending on the option.

> *Source: https://eu.marketplace.ability.abb/en-US/apps/22677 /edcs---predictive-access# (05/04/20)*

Subscription pricing structure

- 5 Tiers:
  - Tier S = 460 euros per year
  - Tier M = 980 euros per year
  - Tier L = 1,664 euros per year
  - Tier XL = 2,836 euros per year
- Add-ons
  - Unlimited users = 299 euros, one time
  - 10 extra devices = 350 euros per year
  - Intelligent alerts = from 573.75 euros to 1,498.75 euros per year, depending on the selected tier.

> *Source: https://eu.marketplace.ability.abb/en-US/apps/22677 /edcs---predictive-access# (05/04/20)*

Case Study 3

BAE Systems

Division: Financial Services

Region: Worldwide

Offer Name: NetReveal

Link to Subscription: www.baesystems.com/en-financialservices/platform/deployment-options

Subscription Category: Digital bundle

Public Pricing Info? NO

Statement of customer & market problem

- Faced with increasing transactions, evolving regulations, growing number of payment channels, customer friction, investigation challenges and strengthening privacy regimes, financial crime and fraud, investigators are under pressure to make more confident intelligence-led decisions.
  Source: www.bloomberg.com/press-releases/2019-04-15/bae-systems -launches-major-update-to-its-netreveal-platform (05/16/20)

Offer description (technology)

- BAE Systems provides financial crime, risk management and fraud detection and prevention across Banking, Financial Markets, and Insurance via the NetReveal Platform.

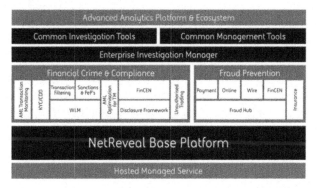

Source: www.baesystems.com/en-financialservices/platform /netreveal-platform-overview (05/16/20)

Value proposition of the subscription offer

- NetReveal enables Financial Institutions to benefit from lower total cost of ownership across their compliance and fraud teams with a single solution.
  Source: www.bloomberg.com/press-releases/2019–04–15/bae-systems -launches-major-update-to-its-netreveal-platform (05/16/20)

Stated customer benefits

- Smarter
    - Profiling and detection against data that commonly takes hours to process, now gets processed within 30 minutes.
- Faster
    - Advanced analytics with machine learning improve operational performance by driving fewer false positives.
    - Routine tasks are automated to enable investigators to focus more on high value work.
    - Real-Time Detection Engine helps institutions keep pace with evermore sophisticated criminals across digital channels.
- Intelligence-Led
    - Entity-based investigations deliver efficiency improvements of 20–30% on average by streamlining multiple detections into a single alert dashboard.
    - Interactive lists also provide actionable information to adjudicate alerts effectively.

Source: www.bloomberg.com/press-releases/2019-04-15/bae-systems
-launches-major-update-to-its-netreveal-platform (05/16/20)

Subscription packaging

- NetReveal platform and applications can be configured and deployed on premise, in a hybrid-cloud or full-cloud scenario.
- Deployments can be fully private or private in a multi-tenant environment.
- 3 packages are offered:
    - Foundation Edition
    - Enhanced Edition
    - Advanced Edition

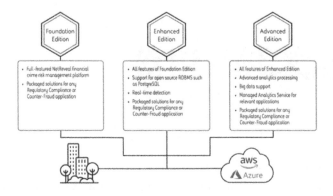

Source: www.baesystems.com/en-financialservices/platform
/deployment-options (05/16/20)

Subscription pricing model
Not disclosed.

Subscription pricing structure
Not disclosed.

Case Study 4

ForeFlight (A Boeing Company)

Division:	Corporate
Region:	Worldwide
Offer Name:	ForeFlight, Intelligent Apps for Pilots
Link to Subscription:	https://foreflight.com/pricing/business
Subscription Category:	Startup
Public Pricing Info?	YES

Statement of customer & market problem
- ForeFlight has been phenomenal with all that it provides for the safe operation of our aircraft.—Mark Palmer, CEO X8 AVIATION
- Using the own-ship position on the ground is invaluable for avoiding runway incursions.—Paul Simpson, VP Flight Operations Mountain Air Cargo
  Source: https://foreflight.com/solutions/business-aviation/ (05/18/20)

Offer description (technology)
- ForeFlight delivers all-in-one affordable technology to keep pilots informed and organized and your entire flight department in sync.
  Source: https://foreflight.com/solutions/business-aviation/ (05/18/20)

Value proposition of the subscription offer
- "With faster and more accurate answers, ForeFlight Business Performance can literally pay for itself after just one mission."
  Source: https://foreflight.com/solutions/business-aviation/ (05/18/20)

Stated customer benefits
ForeFlight makes aviation safer, easier, and more efficient for thousands of business jet operators:
- Plan smarter.
- Empower your pilots.
- Save money.
- Never miss a meeting.
- Safer, more efficient flight operations.
- Better weather visualization for better decision making.
  Source: https://foreflight.com/solutions/business-aviation/ (05/18/20)

Subscription packaging
ForeFlight is targeting 3 customer segments:
- Individuals
- Business
- Military

Packages and pricing are disclosed only for Individuals and Business (not for Military).

For Business plans, 2 packages are offered:

- Business Pro
- Business Performance

Business Performance offers additional features for "flight departments that want to fly with the best."

Source: https://foreflight.com/pricing/business (05/18/20)

Subscription pricing model
- Subscription per year per licensing (with a minimum purchase of 2 licenses).
  Source: https://foreflight.com/pricing/business (05/18/20)

Subscription pricing structure
- Business Pro: $200 per year per license (minimum of 2 licenses).
- Business Performance: $300 per year per license (minimum of 2 licenses).
- Discounts are available with the purchase of 5 licenses or more.
- "Add-ons": synthetic vision (+$25), checklist (+$25), logbook (+$50).
- One Geographic Region is included (United States, Canada, or Europe), additional region available as "add-on" (+$100).
  Source: https://foreflight.com/pricing/business (05/18/20)

Case Study 5

Bosch

Division:	IO
Region:	Worldwide
OfferName:	Bosch IoT Suite
Link to Subscription:	https://aws.amazon.com/marketplace/pp/B07HY7KLCP
Subscription Category:	Digital bundle
Public Pricing Info?	YES

Statement of customer & market problem
- On their website, Bosch describes market problems per market segment. For Connected Office Buildings–

What drives the shift toward connected office buildings?

Enhanced efficiency	Better utilization of space	Greater user comfort, convenience, and satisfaction
IoT-enabled solutions can harmonize building use and equipment utilization, for example, by orchestrating heating, air conditioning, and ventilation systems. Integrated energy management boosts efficiency and saves money otherwise spent on energy and electricity.	Building space is an increasingly scarce and therefore expensive commodity, especially in conurbations. If managers can get a good picture of office and meeting room occupancy, they can adapt their utilization plan accordingly, often without having to rent additional space.	Users expect more from a building these days. Their demands can be met with smart solutions, for example, automated systems to monitor and regulate air quality and IT-assisted booking options for parking spaces or desks.

Source: https://bosch.io/industries/office-buildings/ (06/20/21)

Offer description (technology)
Bosch IoT Suite provides all functionalities needed to build IoT applications:
- Reliably connecting and managing devices, sensors, and gateways.
- Providing secure access management.
- Creating digital representations of physical devices.
- Visualizing all data from diverse sources within one dashboard.
- Executing firmware update and software rollout processes.
- Managing and analyzing IoT data.
  Source: https://bosch.io/iot-technology/ (05/20/20)

Value proposition of the subscription offer
- Reduced costs.
- Increased revenue (increased efficiency, new business opportunities, etc.).

Stated customer benefits
- Bosch describes the customer benefits per market segment.

For Energy Management–

How companies benefit from energy management

Make the most of flexibilities

Compensate for volatilities with manageable flexibilities.

Electromobility

Smooth out peak loads caused by electric vehicle charging.

Reduce CO2 emissions

Manufacture in a predictive and sustainable way.

Source: https://bosch.io/industries/energy-management/ (05/20/20)

Subscription packaging
- 1 free plan and 2 subscription offers (Started Plan and Standard Plan).

Feature	Free Plan	Starter Plan	Standard Plan
Telemetry data processing	✓	✓	✓
Event processing with guaranteed delivery	✓	✓	✓
Event storage time	60 seconds	30 minutes	24 hours
Command & control message handling	✓	✓	✓
Supported protocols	HTTP, MQTT, AMQP 1.0	All supported protocols (HTTP, MQTT, AMQP 1.0, LoRaWAN)	All supported protocols (HTTP, MQTT, AMQP 1.0, LoRaWAN)
Device identity and credential management	✓	✓	✓
Per-device authentication and authorization	✓	✓	✓
Support for gateway based scenarios	✓	✓	✓
Included devices	10	100	Unlimited
Included number of messages	100,000	1,500,000	1,000,000,000
Included device connection time (minutes)	50,000	500,000	500,000,000
Additional capacity with a 'pay-as-you-grow' pricing	-		✓
SLAs	No SLAs	SaaS Service Level Agreements ⟳	SaaS Service Level Agreements ⟳

Subscription pricing model
- Subscription per month.
- Depends on the number of units used.
- Service credit in case of deviation of availability (set at 99.5%).

Deviation of Availability	Service Credit in %
1% - 1.99% below the agreed Availability	1% of the total monthly usage fee
2% - 4% below the agreed Availability	2% of the total monthly usage fee
> 4% below the agreed Availability	An additional 0.5 % of the total monthly usage fee for each next percentage point (1.0 %) of reduced availability

*Source: https://developer.bosch-iot-suite.com/legal/saas-service-level
-agreements/ (05/20/20)*

Subscription pricing structure
- Starter Plan $155 per month (average).
- Standard Plan $1450 per month (average).

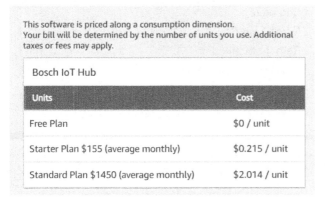

This software is priced along a consumption dimension.
Your bill will be determined by the number of units you use. Additional taxes or fees may apply.

Bosch IoT Hub	
Units	**Cost**
Free Plan	$0 / unit
Starter Plan $155 (average monthly)	$0.215 / unit
Standard Plan $1450 (average monthly)	$2.014 / unit

Source: https://aws.amazon.com/marketplace/pp/B07HY7KLCP (05/20/20)

Case Study 6

Des-Case

Division: Corporate

Region: North America

Offer Name: Remote Monitoring

Link to Subscription: www.descase.com/remote-monitoring/

Subscription Category: Digital bundle

Public Pricing Info?   YES

Statement of customer & market problem
Not communicated.

Offer description (technology)
- Des-Case offers a Remote Monitoring solution allowing to monitor a variety of assets.
- It includes:
  - Sensors
  - Software
  - Lubrication experts

Source: www.descase.com/remote-monitoring/ (10/20/20)

Value proposition of the subscription offer
- Cost savings vs. traditional cost of asset monitoring.

How many assets do you need to protect?
Minimum of 10 assets required for We Monitor™ package

| 10 | 20 | 30 | 40 | 50 | 60 | 70 | 80 | 90 | 100 |

Traditional costs (includes breathers and inspection costs)	$10,898
We Monitor™ costs	$8,388
We Monitor™ costs with promo applied	$8,388
Total Savings	**$3,559**

Additional value as a We Monitor™ subscriber

Training licenses	+$30,000
Connected hardware	+$11,653
Lubrication experts, data analyst and local support	+$41,600

Source: www.descase.com/remote-monitoring/ (10/20/20)

Stated customer benefits

 Peace of Mind
Know your assets are protected and monitored by our lubrication experts.

 Holistic Monitoring
Ensure successful lubrication of your critical assets by monitoring the lubricant's health, cleanliness and RH level. Edge gateways included.

 Cartridge Replenishment
When the breather spends on a subscribed asset we'll order and ship a replacement at no cost to you.

 Program Sustainability
Maintain your program, regardless of changes in team personnel, with over $30,000 worth of continued lubrication best practices training and consulting.

 Personalized Reporting
Not just a canned report. Our lubrication experts continually monitor your assets to provide reporting and solutions unique to your conditions.

 Workforce Efficiency
Lean on our team so your millwrights and mechanics will have more time to complete more tasks on time.

Source: www.descase.com/remote-monitoring/ (10/20/20)

Subscription packaging

3 subscription plans:
- "You Monitor"; access to the platform, self-analysis.
- "We Monitor"; access to the platform with enhanced features, analysis provided by experts and specific tools.
- Enterprise; customer plan for companies with more than 100 assets.
  Source: www.descase.com/remote-monitoring/ (10/20/20)

Subscription pricing model

- "You Monitor"; subscription per month per asset, 2-year agreement, billed quarterly.
- "We Monitor"; subscription per year, billed annually.
- Enterprise; custom plan for 2-year agreement, billed quarterly.
  Source: www.descase.com/remote-monitoring/ (10/20/20)

(continued next page)

Subscription pricing structure

- Subscription packages starting at $34.95 per month, per asset.
- Free 3-month trial period.

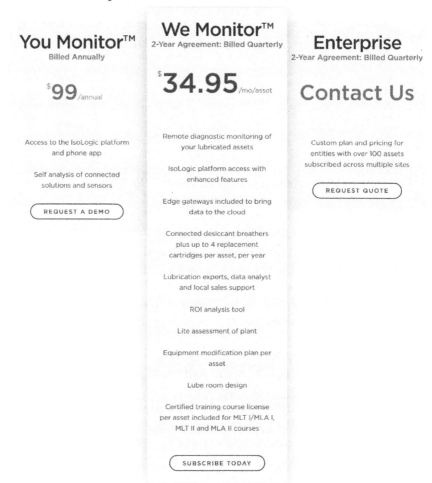

Source: www.descase.com/remote-monitoring/ (10/20/20)

Case Study 7

Enlighted (A Siemens Company)

Division:	IoT Applications
Region:	United States
Offer Name:	Advanced Lighting Control
Link to Subscription:	www.enlightedinc.com/system-and-solutions /iot-applications/light/
Subscription Category:	Startup
Public Pricing Info?	NO

Statement of customer & market problem
- "It gave me complete flexibility to control all of our lighting systems and reduced energy usage up to 90%." Lewis Meline, Agilent Technologies
  Source: www.enlightedinc.com/system-and-solutions/iot-applications/light/ (10/18/20)

Offer description (technology)
- Enlighted delivers advanced Lighting Control System.
- Built on the leading IoT architecture, the system consists of a network of LED lights and patented sensors, connected to an advanced analytics platform.
- Data is collected 65 times per second to monitor environmental and occupancy changes and adjust lighting in real-time.

Source: www.enlightedinc.com/system-and-solutions/iot-applications/light/ (10/18/20)

Value proposition of the subscription offer
Enlighted demonstrated total lighting energy savings of:
- 88% across a range of space types, sizes, and geographies, in over 328 U.S. installations.
- 50% of the energy savings came from switching to LED lighting, and an additional 38% came from intelligent lighting control.

- Occupancy data can integrate with building management systems, providing additional energy savings of 35% or more.
Source: Enlighted Advanced Lighting Controls Brochure (10/18/20)

Stated customer benefits
- Simple to install and program.
- Improve overall light quality.
- Increase energy savings by 85% or more.
- Lower lighting maintenance costs by up to 25%.
- Collect large volumes of data for lighting and IoT applications.
- Task tuning, occupancy monitoring, daylight grouping and harvesting.
- Color temperature and intensity adjustments.
- Retrofits to LED lighting + smart sensors paid for by energy cost savings.

Capabilities	Enlighted One	Enlighted Connected	Enlighted IoT
Motion and Switch Groups	✓	✓	✓
Daylight Harvesting	✓	✓	✓
Scheduled Lighting		✓	✓
Energy Reporting & Optimization		✓	✓
Overrides & Automated Demand Response		✓	✓
Aire		✓	✓
Environment Data & Lighting Controls API		✓	✓
Building Management System Integration		✓	✓
Where & Space Applications			✓
Location & Occupancy APIs & Beaconing			✓
Future App & API Ready			✓

Source: www.enlightedinc.com/system-and-solutions/iot-applications/light/
(10/18/20)

Subscription packaging
Three Configuration Options:
- Enlighted One
- Enlighted Connected
- Enlighted IoT
Source: Enlighted Advanced Lighting Controls Brochure (10/18/20)

Subscription pricing model
Not disclosed.

Subscription pricing structure
Not disclosed.

Case Study 8

Fujitsu

Division:	Scanners
Region:	United States
Offer Name:	Scanner Subscription Services
Link to Subscription:	www.fujitsu.com/us/about/resources/news/press-releases/2019/fcpa-20190131.html
Subscription Category:	Digital bundle
Public Pricing Info?	YES

Statement of customer & market problem
Not communicated.

Offer description (technology)
- Scanner Subscription Services by Fujitsu is a "scanner-as-a-service" business model.
- Fujitsu's partners can combine their cloud and on-premise solutions.
- This cloud-ready solution provides an easy pay-by-month package.
It includes:
- FUJITSU fi-7300NX Document Scanner with NX Manager.
- Advanced Exchange Warranty.
- Free Shipping (both ways).
- Priority customer support line for setup and support.
  Source: Scanner Subscription Services by Fujitsu FAQ's (05/04/20)

Value proposition of the subscription offer
- Low upfront investment breaks costs down into manageable payments.
- Minimizes financial risk to the customer.
  Source: https://fujitsuscannerstore.com/cg01000-295001/ (05/04/20)

Stated customer benefits
- Convenient pay by month document scanning solution.
- Affordable low monthly cost with reduced risk to the customer.
- Easy to implement.
- Fewer approvals for purchase due to low monthly price.
  Source: Scanner Subscription Services by Fujitsu FAQ's (05/04/20)

Subscription packaging
Not disclosed.

Subscription pricing model
- Minimum term is 6 months, thereafter payments are auto renewed on a monthly basis.
  Source: www.fujitsu.com/us/microsite/subservices/ (05/04/20)

Subscription pricing structure
- Monthly subscription pricing starts at $59.95 (including shipping) per month.
  Source: www.fujitsu.com/us/about/resources/news/press-releases/2019 /fcpa-20190131.html (05/04/20)

Case Study 9

Heidelberger Druckmaschinen AG

Division:	Printing
Region:	Worldwide
Offer Name:	Heidelberg Subscription
Link to Subscription:	https://news.heidelbergusa.com/heidelberg-subscription/
Subscription Category:	Digital bundle
Public Pricing Info?	NO

Statement of customer & market problem
- Sheet prices are falling.
- Can only be compensated by extreme levels of productivity.
  Source: www.youtube.com/watch?v=fxp3FFC5SOc (05/19/20)

Klampfer Group became one of the first customers to sign a subscription contract with Heidelberger in April 2018:
- "Makeready times have dropped by an average of over 21%, printing speed has increased by approximately 5% on average, and paper waste is down an average of 19%. The end result is that Klampfer is saving around 110,000 waste sheets every month alone, which equates to an actual paper saving totaling some 60,000 sheets. Productivity as a whole has risen by approximately 13% on average."
  Source: https://whattheythink.com/news/97718-one-year-after-signing
  -heidelberg-subscription-verdict-klampfer-group-positive/ (05/19/20)

Offer description (technology)
What Heidelberg Subscription includes:
- Printing equipment.
- Prinect workflow.
- Automated process.
- Saphira consumables.
- Performance consultancy.
- Service support.
  Source: www.heidelberg.com/global/en/services_and_consumables
  /subscription_1/subscription_1.jsp#_ (05/19/20)

Value proposition of the subscription offer
- Maximize productivity and profit without the burdens of equipment ownership.
  Source: www.piworld.com/article/heidelberg-digital-subscription
  -business-model/ (05/19/20)

Stated customer benefits
- Pay as you print.
- Heidelberg provides the machines, workflow, consumables, expertise, and services.
  Source: https://news.heidelbergusa.com/heidelberg-subscription/ (05/19/20)

Subscription packaging
- Monthly subscription based on customer needs.
- The first step is to arrive at a cost-per-page charge that reflects how much productivity the shop stands to gain.
  Source: www.piworld.com/article/heidelberg-digital-subscription-business -model/ (05/19/20)

Subscription pricing model
- Cost-per-sheet charges are a monthly base fee.
- An additional impression charge for production in excess of the monthly base fee.
- Five-year life of the agreement.
  Source: www.piworld.com/article/heidelberg-digital-subscription-business -model/ (05/19/20)

Subscription pricing structure
Not disclosed.

Case Study 10

HELLER

Division:	Machines & Solutions
Region:	Worldwide
Offer Name:	HELLER4Use
Link to Subscription:	www.heller.biz/en/machines-and-solutions/heller4use/
Subscription Category:	Digital bundle
Public Pricing Info?	NO

Statement of customer & market problem
- Shorter innovation cycles, growing material and component variety as well as constant cost pressure are posing significant challenges to enterprises aiming to remain competitive.
  *Source: www.heller-us.com/home/news/article/heller4use-nutzungsmodell
  -fuer-neue-flexibilitaet/ (05/09/20)*

Offer description (technology)
- Built on top of the Siemens MindSphere Platform, HELLER4Use enables customers to use machines in accordance with current requirements at variable costs, ensuring maximum flexibility.
- Machine data are collected, evaluated and provided to a digital billing system.
- Customers benefit from extremely efficient machines without any capital commitment.

What this means for you:

Pay-per-Use model for a flexible machine pool	Highest possible machine availability through all-round carefree support	Certainty for your cost calculation
You decide which orders the machine will process and how long you use the machine.	Your process your orders and HELLER guarantees service and maintenance.	Apart from a monthly basic charge, you will incur costs only when the machine is running and earning money.

*Sources: https://new.siemens.com/global/en/company/stories/industry/heller
-appsolute-efficiency.html,
www.heller-us.com/home/news/article/heller4use-nutzungsmodell
-fuer-neue-flexibilitaet/ (05/09/20)*

Value proposition of the subscription offer
Source: www.heller.biz/en/machines-and-solutions/heller4use/ (05/09/20)

Stated customer benefits
- Flexibility for additional orders.
  - Increase your machine capacity to suit exactly the volume required.
- Security for your costing.
  - You only pay for the time the machine is actually producing.
  Source: www.heller.biz/en/machines-and-solutions/heller4use/ (05/09/20)

Subscription packaging
- HELLER4Use offers a unique subscription based on customer usage (pay-per-use).
  Source: www.heller.biz/en/services/financing/ (05/09/20)

Subscription pricing model
Heller is offering several pricing models for their customers
- Pay-per-use model.
- Customers decide which orders the machine will process and how long they will use the machine.
- Carefree support and insurance for lost machine hours.
- Customers will incur costs only when the machine is running and earning money.

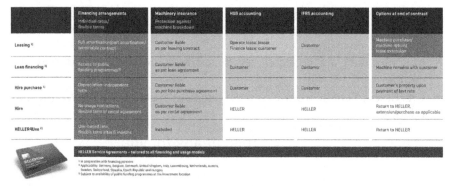

Source: www.heller.biz/en/services/financing/ (05/09/20)

Subscription pricing structure
Not disclosed.

Case Study 11

Hilti

Division:	Engineering Software
Region:	Worldwide
Offer Name:	PROFIS Engineering Suite
Link to Subscription:	www.hilti.com/content/hilti/W1/US/en/engineering/software/hilti-software/structural-engineering/profis-engineering-suite.html#nav/close
Subscription Category:	Digital bundle
Public Pricing Info?	YES

Statement of customer & market problem
- "I'm looking forward to creating customized template files our office can share online to address common anchorage situations we encounter every day." David Hackney, Structural Engineer at Hollis and Miller
  *Source: www.hilti.com/content/hilti/W1/US/en/engineering/software
      /hilti-software/structural-engineering/profis-engineering-suite
      .html#nav/close (05/09/20)*

Offer description (technology)
- PROFIS Engineering Suite cloud-based anchor design software enables automatic and advanced calculating, easy specifying and integrated BIM modeling.
  *Source: www.hilti.com/content/hilti/W1/US/en/engineering/software
      /hilti-software/structural-engineering/profis-engineering-suite
      .html#nav/close (05/09/20)*

Value proposition of the subscription offer
- Save time.
- Improve efficiency.
  *Source: www.hilti.com/content/hilti/W1/US/en/engineering/software
      /hilti-software/structural-engineering/profis-engineering-suite
      .html#nav/close (05/09/20)*

Stated customer benefits
- Improve accuracy with automatic load transfers.
- Reduce design time from 1 hour to 10 minutes.
- Increase efficiency in design and accelarates project schedules.
  *Source: www.hilti.com/content/hilti/W1/US/en/engineering/software
      /hilti-software/structural-engineering/profis-engineering-suite
      .html#nav/close (05/09/20)*

Subscription packaging

- 2 plans: standard and premium (offering extended capabilities).

PROFIS Engineering Suite	Standard	Premium
Anchor Design:		
ACI 318 and CSA A23.3 Design	✔	✔
Post-installed anchors	✔	✔
Cast-in anchors	✔	✔
Base Materials:		
Concrete	✔	✔
Concrete-Over-Metal-Deck	✔	✔
Masonry	✔	✔
Productivity Features:		
Project Sharing		✔
Customizable Reports		✔
Multiple load combinations		✔
Load Engine		✔
Base Plate Design Type:		
Rigid anchor Load Distribution	✔	✔
AISC Design Guide 1		✔
Component Based Finite Element Analysis (CBFEM)		✔
Weld and stiffener design		✔
Integrations with 3rd party Analysis Software:		
Import Loads from Excel		✔
RISA Connection		✔
STAAD.PRO		✔
ROBOT		✔
ETABS		✔
SAP 2000		✔
Output:		
Item Number	✔	✔
BIM/CAD Export		✔
REVIT Plug-in		✔
TEKLA Plug-in		✔
Smart Design Tools:		
Smart Base Plate Selector	✔	✔

*Source: www.hilti.com/content/hilti/W1/US/en/engineering/software
/hilti-software/structural-engineering/profis-engineering-suite
.html#nav/close (05/09/20)*

Subscription pricing model
- Standard plan = Free
- Premium plan = Subscription per month or per year (price reduction with the per year model)
- 3 types of license for the premium plan:
  - Standalone license
  - Floating license (only 1 user access at a time)
  - Enterprise license
- 30-day trial period.

  Source: www.hilti.com/content/hilti/W1/US/en/engineering/software
  * /hilti-software/structural-engineering/profis-engineering-suite*
  * .html#nav/close (05/09/20)*

Subscription pricing structure
- Standard plan = Free
- Premium plan =
  - Standalone license = $25/month or $240/year
  - Floating license = $35/month or $360/year
  - Enterprise license = price based on company size

  Source: www.hilti.com/content/hilti/W1/US/en/engineering/software
  * /hilti-software/structural-engineering/profis-engineering-suite*
  * .html#nav/close (05/09/20)*

Case Study 12

John Deere

Division:	John Deere Construction and Forestry Division
Region:	US and Canada only
Offer Name:	JDLink™ Ultimate
Link to Subscription:	www.deere.com/en/our-company/news-and-announcements/news-releases/2019/construction/2019apr16-jdlink-discount/
Subscription Category:	Freemium (during 5 years for new equipment)
Public Pricing Info?	YES

Statement of customer & market problem
- "I cut $20,000 of idle time out in just one year. That's less hours on the machine over it's lifetime. That's less fuel we have to purchase." Kevin Van Bree, Birmam Excavating Ltd.
  Source: www.deere.com/en/construction/construction-technology/jdlink-telematics/ (05/01/20)

Offer description (technology)
- JDLink lets you track your machines, which machines are working and if they are working properly and to their utmost productivity and efficiency.

Features

- Five years standard with most new construction equipment purchases
- Updated JDLink website
- Geofence
- Machine grouping
- Alert escalation logic
- Dealer data services/third party access

- Distance traveled
- Engine hours
- Maintenance tracking
- JDLink mobile app
- Equipment utilization and engine load levels
- Fuel consumption
- Operator productivity indicators

- Payload and trip counter for ADTs
- Tire pressure monitoring
- Diagnostic trouble code alerts
- Remote diagnostics and programming capability
- Dual mode satellite option
- On-demand updates
- Curfew

Source: www.deere.com/en/construction/construction-technology/jdlink-telematics/ (05/01/20)

Value proposition of the subscription offer
- Customers can estimate the return on investment with the "JDLink ™ ROI Estimator."
- The return on investment estimation is intended to demonstrate the value of using JDLink—maximize asset, fuel and warranty utilization and reduce service trips.

Total Annual Savings

$ 14047.55

Return On Investment (ROI)

221%

Payback

4 Months

Total Annual Savings

- Fuel
- Maintenance
- Repairs
- Service Trips

Source: www.deere.com/en/construction/construction-technology /jdlink-telematics/ 05/01/20)

Stated customer benefits
Improve Productivity.
- Put the right machine on the job.
- Ensure proper operation.
Improve Uptime.
- Enable remote diagnostics and programming.
- Easily track maintenance.
- Quickly act on alerts.
Improve Daily Operating Costs.
- Prevent theft.
- Track overall fuel consumption and idle time.
- Track time and fuel spent on jobsite.
  Source: www.deere.com/en/construction/construction-technology /jdlink-telematics/ (05/01/20)

Subscription packaging
- JDLink Ultimate and JDLink Ultimate dual.
- The value added of JDLink Ultimate dual" is to offer a dual communication system (cellular + satellite).
  Source: www.deere.com/en/forestry/forestry-technology/jdlink-telematics/ (05/01/20)

Subscription pricing model
- 5 years standard with most new construction equipment purchase.
- Annual subscription.
- In 2019, consolidating of the subscription structure for a simpler offering. Tier pricing has been eliminated and customers can purchase up to three years of a subscription.

Source: www.deere.com/en/our-company/news-and-announcements
/news-releases/2019/construction/2019apr16-jdlink-discount/
(05/01/20)

Subscription pricing structure
- In 2019, pricing reduction to make this solution even more affordable.
- JDLink Ultimate = $200 per year
- JDLink Ultimate dual = $630 per year

Source: www.deere.com/en/our-company/news-and-announcements
/news-releases/2019/construction/2019apr16-jdlink-discount/
(05/01/20)

Previous Tiers Pricing (2015):

Description	List Price	MDP	DISCOUNT %
JDLink Ultimate - 1 Year			
Tier 1 (1 Unit) (Individual)	$600.00	$462.00	
Tier 2 (2-10 Units) (Small)	$510.39	$393.00	14.935065%
Tier 3 (11-24 Units) (Medium)	$450.65	$347.00	24.891775%
Tier 4 (25-74 Units) (Large)	$389.61	$300.00	35.064935%
Tier 5 (75+ Units) (Xlarge)	$300.00	$231.00	50.000000%
JDLink Ultimate Dual - 1 Year			
Tier 1 (1 Unit) (Individual)	$780.00	$600.60	
Tier 2 (2-10 Units) (Small)	$690.39	$531.60	11.488511%
Tier 3 (11-24 Units) (Medium)	$630.65	$485.60	19.147519%
Tier 4 (25-74 Units) (Large)	$569.61	$438.60	26.973027%
Tier 5 (75+ Units) (Xlarge)	$480.00	$369.60	38.461538%

"Ultimate Dual Satellite" will be $180/year more than
Ultimate in each tier with the same level of discounts.

Per year price in the pre-paid **5 Year Option** is subject to
machine discounting = **$365**

Source: https://slideplayer.com/slide/16768618/ (05/01/20)

Case Study 13

Kaeser Compressors

Division: Corporate

Region: Worldwide

Offer Name: Sigma Air Utility

Link to Subscription: www.kaeser.com/int-en/products
                              /sigma-air-utility-operator-model/

Subscription Category: Digital bundle

Public Pricing Info?   NO

Statement of customer & market problem
- BASF Coatings User Story: energy management and contracting have been well worthwhile for the company, with confirmed annual savings of some €30,000.
  Source: https://us.kaeser.com/compressed-air-resources/references/success -stories/compressed-air-contracting-for-basf.aspx (05/06/20)

Offer description (technology)
- "With the SIGMA AIR UTILITY operator model, you will secure a reliable supply of compressed air tailored to your needs. Instead of investing in a complete compressed air station, all you pay for is the compressed air you actually use."
  Source: www.kaeser.com/int-en/products/sigma-air-utility-operator-model/ (05/06/20)

Value proposition of the subscription offer
- Estimated annual energy reduction of 28.5%.
- The yearly energy savings pays for at least 40% of the total annual compressed air supply cost.
- Customers assessed additional savings in maintenance and overhead costs.
  Source: Industrial SPP Partner Teaming Profile—Kaeser Compressors, Inc. (05/06/20)

Stated customer benefits
- No compressed air worries.
  - From the analysis of your compressed air needs to the machines and service.
- From fixed costs to variable costs.
  - Investments in a compressed air system are no longer needed.

- A system scaled to your needs.
  - Adjust your compressed air supply to your needs.
  Source: www.kaeser.com/int-en/products/sigma-air-utility-operator-model/
      (05/06/20)

Subscription packaging
- A fixed basic price that covers an agreed quantity of compressed air.
- When larger amounts are needed, a fixed price applies for the additional quantities used.
  Source: www.kaeser.com/int-en/products/sigma-air-utility-operator-model/
      (05/06/20)

Subscription pricing model
- A subscription per month.
- All prices remain in effect for the entire duration of the contract.
  Source: www.kaeser.com/int-en/products/sigma-air-utility-operator-model/
      (05/06/20)

Subscription pricing structure
Not disclosed.

Case Study 14

KCF Technologies

Division: Corporate

Region: Worldwide

Offer Name: SmartDiagnostics

Link to Subscription: www.kcftech.com/smartdiagnostics/

Subscription Category: Digital bundle

Public Pricing Info?   NO

Statement of customer & market problem
- Reactive maintenance processes inherently lead to unplanned downtime and lost production, inefficiencies that cost the U.S. economy as much as $2.5 trillion per year (as estimated by the DoE Industrial Technologies Program).
- Just a 1% improvement in global pump performance would provide over a half-million additional barrels of oil per day—that's $19 billion per year.
  Sources: www.kcftech.com/smartdiagnostics/,
  www.kcftech.com/smartdiagnostics/industries/oil-gas.html,
  www.kcftech.com/smartdiagnostics/industries/power-generation
  .html (05/05/20)

Offer description (technology)
- A predictive maintenance system for pumps, motors and other rotating industrial and commercial equipment.
- It was designed from the outset as an affordable, integrated suite of products that puts predictive maintenance within practical reach of medium and small operations.

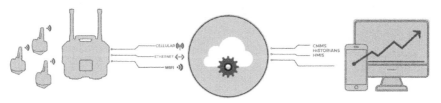

IOT PLATFORM

A comprehensive machine health network gathers all relevant asset health data across plant.

ADVANCED ANALYTICS

Cloud-based analytics predict machine health and share actionable insights.

ENTERPRISE SOFTWARE

User-friendly software connects with plant infrastructure, makes workflow suggestions to extend asset life, and automatically generates work orders.

Source: www.kcftech.com/smartdiagnostics/ (05/05/20)

Value proposition of the subscription offer
- Eliminate 80% of unplanned downtime.
- Optimize machine reliability.
- Implement machine vibration monitoring in their plants.
- Increase production by 25%.
- Triple bottom line profit.
  Source: www.kcftech.com/ (05/05/20)

Stated customer benefits
- Inexpensive and easy to install.
- Shows more data at a lower cost.
- Allows maintenance teams to more efficiently use their time and schedule maintenance activities.
- Reaches places more traditional monitoring methods cannot.
- Real-time continuous remote monitoring.
  Source: www.kcftech.com/ (05/05/20)

Subscription packaging
Not disclosed.

Subscription pricing model
Not disclosed.

Subscription pricing structure
Not disclosed.

Case Study 15

Lockheed Martin

Division: CDL Systems

Region: Worldwide

Offer Name: VCSi Software

Link to Subscription: www.lockheedmartin.com/en-us/products/cdl-systems/vcsi.html

Subscription Category: Service on top of a product

Public Pricing Info? YES

Statement of customer & market problem
Not communicated.

Offer description (technology)
- VCSi Ground control station software platform designed to provide command and control unmanned systems and their payloads.
- VCSi Software provides a command control solution for operators during mission planning, launch and recovery, mission operations and post flight analysis.

Features
- Multi Vehicle Control.
- Payload Control.
- Spatial Awareness.
- Software configuration.
- Notification Center.
- Mission Planning.
  Source: www.lockheedmartin.com/en-us/products/cdl-systems/vcsi.html (05/09/20)

(continued next page)

Value proposition of the subscription offer

Source: www.lockheedmartin.com/en-us/products/cdl-systems/vcsi.html
(05/09/20)

Stated customer benefits
- Assemble the capability that you require, while only purchasing the components you need.
- Plug-in architecture and detailed Software Development Kit (SDK), allowing you to include custom capabilities specific to your needs.
- Dockable panels make it easy for you to customize, organize, and save layouts. This enables VCSi to run effectively on a laptop or expand across several monitors.
Source: www.lockheedmartin.com/en-us/products/cdl-systems/vcsi.html
(05/09/20)

Subscription packaging
- Core licenses:
  - 4 tiers (1–10 licenses, 11 to 25 licenses, 25 to 50 licenses and 50+ licenses).
  - Access to minor updates until 1 year from date of purchase.
  - Availability of basic email technical support until 1 year from date of purchase.
- Development license:
  - 2 tiers (1 to 50 licenses, 50+ licenses).
  - Extend basic support and access to regular, minor updates beyond the initial one year period.
  - Full Software Development Kit (SDK) access.
- Options:
  - Additional modules are available to tailor different use cases. Modules are priced separately from the Core VCSi license.

- Additional technical support, customization, and/or module development available via a separate service contract based on our hourly rate (set at $200 per hour based on January 2019 pricing).

Source: Lockheed Martin CDL Systems Software Products Price List (05/09/20)

Subscription pricing model

- Core licenses = one-time fee per license (tiers pricing, depending on the number of licenses), perpetual licensing.
- Development licenses = subscription fee per year per license.

Source: Lockheed Martin CDL Systems Software Products Price List (05/09/20)

Subscription pricing structure

CORE LICENSE PRICES

Quantity	Discount	Price
1-10	-	$15,000 USD
11-25	10%	$13,500 USD
25-50	20%	$12,000 USD
50+	Please call	Please call

DEVELOPMENT LICENSE PRICES

Quantity	Discount	Price
1-50	-	$2,500 USD (annually)
50+	Please call	Please call

Source: Lockheed Martin CDL Systems Software Products Price List (05/09/20)

Case Study 16

Michelin

Division: Corporate

Region: Worldwide

Offer Name: EFFITIRES

Link to Subscription: https://news.michelin.co.uk/michelin-solutions-launches
                             -effitires-with-fuel-commitment-at-cv-show-2015/

Subscription Category: Digital bundle

Public Pricing Info?   NO

Statement of customer & market problem
Not communicated.

Offer description (technology)
- Michelin solutions' EFFITIRES™ comprehensive tyre management pro-gramme.
- It combines outsourced tyre procurement and expert tyre management with a commitment to saving fuel.
- To be eligible for this offer customers must have equipped at least 70% of theirfleet with a telematics system and commit to fitting vehicles covered under the contract with energy-efficient Michelin tyres.
  Source: https://news.michelin.co.uk/michelin-solutions-launches-effitires
  -with-fuel-commitment-at-cv-show-2015/ (05/09/20)

Value proposition of the subscription offer
- Strong fuel saving. In the event of the contractual savings not being attained, Michelin solutions will reimburse the operator for the unrealised savings on a pro rata basis.
- Extend tyre life.
- Increase uptime.
  Source: https://news.michelin.co.uk/michelin-solutions-launches-effitires
  -with-fuel-commitment-at-cv-show-2015/ (05/09/20)

Stated customer benefits
- Allows customers to create value while focusing on their core business.
- Include services of a dedicated team of business support personnel, auditors and technicians.
- 24-hour roadside assistance for tyre-related breakdowns, with a promise to arrive on the scene within 2 hours of receiving a call-out.
  Source: https://news.michelin.co.uk/michelin-solutions-launches-effitires
  -with-fuel-commitment-at-cv-show-2015/ (05/09/20)

Subscription packaging
Not disclosed.

Subscription pricing model
Several models are offered:
- Price-per-mile deal (pay per use model) based on a 3-year agreement was signed by Go-Ahead.
- Price-per-vehicle was signed by Abbey Logistics.
  *Sources: https://news.cision.com/michelin-solutions/r/michelin-solutions
        -go-ahead-with-effitires--extension,c2087888,
        https://news.michelin.co.uk/michelin-solutions-launches
        -effitires-with-fuel-commitment-at-cv-show-2015/ (05/09/20)*

Subscription pricing structure
Not disclosed.

Case Study 17

Rolls-Royce

Division: Aircraft Engine
Region: Worldwide
Offer Name: CareServices
Link to Subscription: www.rolls-royce.com/products-and-services/civil
                          -aerospace/aftermarket-services.aspx
Subscription Category: Service on top of a product
Public Pricing Info?   NO

Statement of customer & market problem
- Engines are critical to customer's operations and their complexity and safety-critical nature makes maintenance and repair costly and time consuming.
- If an engine is unusable or out-of-service, it can have a significant impact in terms of disruption to flights, resulting in lost revenue and reputational damage for customers.
  *Source: www.rolls-royce.com/media/our-stories/discover/2017/totalcare.aspx
  (05/06/20)*

Offer description (technology)
- Real-time data monitoring of engines using sophisticated telematics offers agility to both Rolls-Royce and its customers.
  Source: https://amindsolutions.com/portfolio/recycle-bank-2-2/ (05/06/20)

Value proposition of the subscription offer
- Predictable engine maintenance costs.
- Reduces acquisition costs.
- Through TotalCare, the service intervals between engine overhauls can be extended by around 25%. This is of significant value to customers.
  *Sources: https://amindsolutions.com/portfolio/recycle-bank-2-2/,
           www.rolls-royce.com/media/our-stories/discover/2017/totalcare.aspx
           (05/06/20)*

Stated customer benefits
- Customers enrolled benefit from higher aircraft residual values as well as predictability and control of maintenance costs.
- Removes the burden of engine maintenance from the customer and transfers the management of associated risks to Rolls-Royce.
  *Sources: https://amindsolutions.com/portfolio/recycle-bank-2-2/,
           www.rolls-royce.com/media/our-stories/discover/2017/totalcare.aspx
           (05/06/20)*

Subscription packaging
- Different offering per market segment (airlines, lessors, business aviation).
- Designed to suit customers' needs at every stage of the engine lifecycle.
- Comprising various core and optional services, in the CareStore customers can select from a broader scope of Service Solutions.

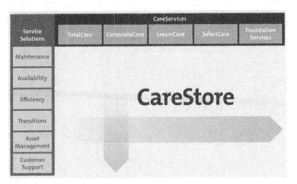

Source: www.rolls-royce.com/products-and-services/civil-aerospace
/aftermarket-services.aspx (05/06/20)

Subscription pricing model
- Charged on a fixed $ per flying hour basis.
- 10-year subscription basis.
  Source: https://amindsolutions.com/portfolio/recycle-bank-2–2/ (05/06/20)

Subscription pricing structure
Not disclosed.

Case Study 18

Saint-Gobain

Division:	Homly You
Region:	France
Offer Name:	Homly You
Link to Subscription:	https://pro.homly-you.com/pro
Subscription Category:	Startup
Public Pricing Info?	YES

Statement of customer & market problem
Not communicated.

Offer description (technology)
- 3 applications:
  - Tolteck, a solution for quote and billing management.
  - Cap Renov+, a solution to assess energy efficiency.
  - Simplebo, a solution to create a turnkey website.
  Source: https://pro.homly-you.com/pro (05/09/20)

Value proposition of the subscription offer
- Homly is offering tailored solutions to help you develop your business.
  Source: https://pro.homly-you.com/pro (05/09/20)

Stated customer benefits
- Tolteck
  - Gain time: create quotes and bills in 5 mins.
  - Simple management of work: integration and automated updates of the database.
  - Bring information and quoting everywhere with you: Tolteck works online or offline.
- Cap Renov+
  - Help your customers to identify heat losses in their home.
  - Advise them on the different technical solution and prospective savings.
  - Establish a global economic assessment to facilitate decision-making.
- Simplebo
  - Creation of a website in only 7 days.
  - Simple and cost-effective solution.
  - Google referencing and domain name to value your brand.
  Source: https://pro.homly-you.com/pro (05/09/20)

Subscription packaging
- Users can subscribe to each solution as a standalone subscription or can choose from between 4 different packages:
  - Essentiel (Essential)
  - Energie (Energy)
  - Gestion (Management)
  - Integral (Complete)
- Tolteck is included in both "Gestion" and "Integral."
- Cap Renov+ is included in both "Energie" and "Integral."
- Simplebo is included in all packages.

Subscription pricing model
- Subscription per month or per year.
- 30-day free trial.
  Source: https://pro.homly-you.com/pro (05/09/20)

Subscription pricing structure
- Standalone subscription
  - Toltek: €25/month or €228/year, no engagement.
  - Cap Renov+: €15/months or €165/year, no engagement.
  - SimpleBo: €49.90/month or €548.90/year, no engagement.
- Packages
  Sources: https://pro.homly-you.com/pro,
  https://pro.homly-you.com/pro/cap-renov (05/09/20)

	Essentiel	Énergie	Gestion	Intégral
Tarifs mensuels	29 €HT	34 €HT	44 €HT	49 €HT
Tarifs annuels	319 €HT	374 €HT	484 €HT	539 €HT

Case Study 19

Sandvik

Division:	Digital Manufacturing Solution
Regions:	US, UK and Sweden
Offer Name:	Prism
Link to Subscription:	https://makewithprism.com/
Subscription Category:	Startup
Public Pricing Info?	YES

Statement of customer & market problem
- "Finding skilled CNC operators is almost impossible. It's a risk to have these expensive machines and nobody who can operate them. With modern solutions, we can attract younger people."
  Source: https://makewithprism.com/prism-is-what-the-industry -was-missing/ (05/04/20)

Offer description (technology)
- Prism from Sandvik delivers easy-to-learn, touch-based CNC programming for 2.5D parts.
  Source: https://makewithprism.com/prism-is-what-the-industry -was-missing/ (05/04/20)

Value proposition of the subscription offer
- Increase machine utilization.
- Reduce programming costs.
- Address the skilled labor gap.
- Leverage the knowledge of trusted industry experts.
- Reduce human error.
  Source: https://makewithprism.com/ (05/04/20)

Stated customer benefits
- Prism can be operated from anywhere, no need to wait for the machine to be available.
- Also comes with built-in recipes, which speeds up programming and removes the guesswork.
- Helps to bridge the gap between office and workshop by improving communication between.
  Source: https://makewithprism.com/prism-is-what-the-industry -was-missing/ (05/04/20)

Subscription packaging
- Only one subscription.

Subscription pricing model
- Subscription per month with a 30-day free trial.

Subscription pricing structure
- $149 per machine per month.

Case Study 20

Schindler

Division:	Service Maintenance
Region:	Worldwide
Offer Name:	Schindler Ahead
Link to Subscription:	www.schindler.com/us/internet/en/service-maintenance /schindler-ahead.html#button
Subscription Category:	Service on top of a product
Public Pricing Info?	NO

Statement of customer & market problem

- An office building saved 37.5% on its elevator phone line:

Building Type	Class A office building in Williamsburg, VA with a Schindler Ahead connected elevator
Problem	Customer incurred an extra monthly cost for the analog emergency telephone line in the elevator
Solution	Schindler's DigitalAlarm 4G wireless solution replaced the elevator's analog phone line at a lower cost per month
Results	Customer realized a **37.5% annual cost savings** for the elevator phone line by replacing the elevator analog phone line with Schindler DigitalAlarm

*Source: www.schindler.com/us/internet/en/service-maintenance
/schindler-ahead/solutions/office-building.html (05/06/20)*

Offer description (technology)

- Schindler Ahead connects elevators and escalators with cloud platform, powered by GE Predix.

Source: Schindler Ahead Brochure (05/06/20)

Value proposition of the subscription offer
- For Building Managers:
  - Increase the value of your building by connecting to the Internet of Things.
  - Cost-saving solutions with service guarantees and removal of phone line.
- For Facility Managers:
  - Better cost predictability to help stay on budget.
- Passengers:
  - Reduced waiting times and increased reliability lead to gains in the passenger experience.

  Source: Schindler Ahead Brochure (05/06/20)

Stated customer benefits
- Schindler is providing customers with the real-time insights, predictive analytics and proactive communication they need to make data-driven decisions about their portfolios.

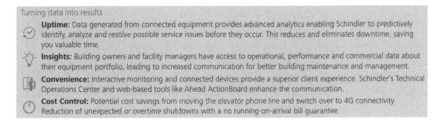

Turning data into results

Uptime: Data generated from connected equipment provides advanced analytics enabling Schindler to predictively identify, analyze and resolve possible service issues before they occur. This reduces and eliminates downtime, saving you valuable time.

Insights: Building owners and facility managers have access to operational, performance and commercial data about their equipment portfolio, leading to increased communication for better building maintenance and management.

Convenience: Interactive monitoring and connected devices provide a superior client experience. Schindler's Technical Operations Center and web-based tools like Ahead ActionBoard enhance the communication.

Cost Control: Potential cost savings from moving the elevator phone line and switch over to 4G connectivity. Reduction of unexpected or overtime shutdowns with a no running-on-arrival bill guarantee.

  *Sources: www.schindler.com/us/internet/en/service-maintenance/schindler
  -ahead.html#button,
  Schindler Ahead Fact Sheet (05/06/20)*

Subscription packaging
- 3 packages
  - Connect
  - Enhanced
  - Premium

(continued next page)

	Connect	Enhanced	Premium
Ahead ActionBoard	+	+	+
ActionBoard Mobile	+	+	+
Real-Time Notifications	+	+	+
24/7 4G Remote Monitoring	+	+	+
Data Analytics with GE Predix	+	+	+
Future Ready with Over-the-Air Updates	+	+	+
ActionBoard with HealthCheck and Next Level Notifications		+	+
Guaranteed Elimination of Running on Arrival Billable Calls Never get an unexpected running on arrival bill again		+	+
Elevated Support Professional (ESP) Real-time support from Schindler's team of experts		+	+
Dedicated VIP Service Number Get an exclusive number that provides priority service			+
Concierge Service Call Assessment			+
Customizable Digital Solutions Tailored solutions to meet custom service needs			+

Source: www.schindler.com/us/internet/en/service-maintenance/schindler-ahead/solutions.html (05/06/20)

Subscription pricing model
Not disclosed.

Subscription pricing structure
Not disclosed.

Case Study 21

Schneider Electric

Division: Corporate

Region: Worldwide

Offer Name: EcoStruxure

Link to Subscription: https://ecostruxureit.com/

Subscription Category: Digital bundle

Public Pricing Info?   NO

Statement of customer & market problem
- Business owners who need their equipment running, even when they are away from their business.
  Source: https://ecostruxureit.com/ (05/06/20)

Offer description (technology)
- Cloud-based software and app to optimize energy operations and maintenance management.
  Source: https://ecostruxureit.com/ (05/06/20)

Value proposition of the subscription offer
- Increase business continuity by up to 10% and reduce your energy bill by up to 5%.

  Flückiger Electricité: Customer Story Key Figures

  +8% operational efficiency for Flückiger Electricité

  Over 10,000 assets under preventative maintenance services

  Reduced unnecessary downtime at customer's sites by over 10%

  *Sources: www.se.com/ww/en/work/products/product-launch
  /ecostruxure-facility-expert/subscriptions.jsp,
  www.se.com/ww/en/work/campaign/life-is-on/case-study
  /fluckiger-electricite.jsp (05/06/20)*

Stated customer benefits
- Gain a better understanding of energy usage and costs.
- Use multi-site comparison to easily identify poor performing sites.
- Save time by avoiding manual logging and spreadsheets.
- Offer opportunity to promote a sustainable image.
  *Source: https://shop.exchange.se.com/en-US/apps/38617
  /ecostruxure-facility-expert---energy-subscription/overview
  (05/06/20)*

Subscription packaging

4 subscriptions with different features:

- Free
- Operations
- Energy
- Smart Power

Features	Free	Operations	Energy	Smart Power
QR code creation	✓	✓		✓
Asset status and map localization	✓	✓		✓
Asset log history and reference document library	✓	✓		✓
Maintenance plan and task reminders	✓	✓		✓
Task manager features (ex. task assignment, notifications)	✓	✓		✓
One-click intervention reports	✓	✓		✓
Collaborative features (ex. chat, information sharing)	✓	✓		✓
Alarms for threshold and status changes		✓		✓
Preconfigured alarms for Schneider Electric assets (LV/RF)		✓		✓
Custom alarms for 3rd party assets		✓		
Data trending on assets. T°C, running hours, voltage, current		✓		EO assets
Energy consumption: max, usage, zone, meter			✓	✓
Power demand and power factor monitoring			✓	✓
Alerts for over-target energy consumption			✓	✓
Multi-site comparisons, consumption aggregation			✓	✓
Energy site performance vs. standards			✓	✓
Monthly scorecards			✓	Optional
Cost monitoring - Energy cost			✓	Optional
Energy kiosk			Optional	Optional

*Source: www.se.com/ww/en/work/products/product-launch
/ecostruxure-facility-expert/subscriptions.jsp (05/06/20)*

Subscription pricing model

- Subscription per month.
- Automatic renewal of subscription at contract expiration date.
- 12-month bidding period.

    *Source: www.se.com/ww/en/product/SVSFE0002/ecostruxure-facility
    -expert%2C-energy/?range=63106-ecostruxure%E2%84%A2
    -facility-expert (05/06/20)*

Subscription pricing structure

Source: www.slideshare.net/DamienChardonnereau
/ecostruxure-facility-expert-building-maintenance-20-is-here
(05/06/20)

Case Study 22

Siemens

Division:	Software
Region:	Worldwide
Offer Name:	Mendix
Link to Subscription:	www.mendix.com/pricing/
Subscription Category:	Startup
Public Pricing Info?	YES

Statement of customer & market problem

- "Mendix enables iterative, collaborative development. The developer and a business person can sit together, bounce ideas off each other, build workflows, design and easily hone applications on-screen." Brad Kendrick, Vice President, IT, Texas Life
Source: www.mendix.com/ibm/ (05/06/20)

Offer description (technology)

- Everything you need to design, build, integrate, test, deploy and manage enterprise apps at scale.
- No UI design skills required. Anyone can create engaging, high value apps that run on any device.

Visual modeling and building blocks speed up time-to-market.

Collaboration tools align Business and I.T. across the app-dev process.

Embedded governance gives you control, even at high scale.

Source: www.mendix.com/the-mendix-difference/ (05/06/20)

Value proposition of the subscription offer

- Increase revenue with smart apps to introduce new products and services leveraging IoT, Machine Learning and Big Data.
- Build multi-channel apps infused with cognitive delivering a great user experience to improve customer engagement.
- Build smart apps to improve operational efficiency and increase employee productivity.
- Migrate legacy applications to the cloud, reducing cost and improving compliance.
Source: www.mendix.com/ibm/ (05/06/20)

Stated customer benefits
- Build smart apps 10x faster with Mendix on IBM Cloud.
  Source: www.mendix.com/ibm/ (05/06/20)

Subscription packaging
- Free editions.
- 3 plans offering additional features and support.
  - Single app
  - Professional
  - Enterprise
  Source: www.mendix.com/pricing/ (05/06/20)

Subscription pricing model
- Free trial period.
- Pay what you need per month (billed annually).
- Monthly cost based on a 3-year commitment.
- Limited up to 50 internal or 500 external users.

Compare plans

Deployment Options	Free Edition	Single App	Professional	Enterprise
Public Mendix Cloud [2]	✓	✓	✓	✓
On-premises				✓
Private Cloud (IBM, SAP, Azure, AWS, Public)				✓
Development & Deployment Environments	Free Edition	Single App	Professional	Enterprise
Number of Environments [3] (Testing, acceptance, production)	1	2	2	3
Dedicated Application Container and Database		✓	✓	✓
Automated Backups		✓	✓	✓
Horizontal Scaling [4]				✓
Failover				✓
Support for Continuous Integration & Deployment				✓
Reliability & Support	Free Edition	Single App	Professional	Enterprise
Uptime Guarantee		99.50%	99.50%	99.95%
Support [5]	Community	Gold	Gold	Platinum

Source: www.mendix.com/pricing/ (05/06/20)

Subscription pricing structure

Source: www.mendix.com/pricing/ (05/06/20)

Case Study 23

SKF

Division:	Services and Solutions
Region:	Worldwide
Offer Name:	Condition Monitoring
Link to Subscription:	https://servicesandsolutions.promo.skf.com/acton /media/26359/rotating-equipment-performance
Subscription Category:	Service on top of a product
Public Pricing Info?	NO

Statement of customer & market problem
Not communicated

Offer description (technology)
- SKF Condition Monitoring uses condition detection systems and sophisticated data processing algorithms to detect, analyze and warn about incipient damage on rotating equipment.
  Source: https://servicesandsolutions.promo.skf.com/acton/media/26359 /rotating-equipment-performance (10/10/20)

Value proposition of the subscription offer
- Increase the reliability of operations.
- Lower maintenance costs.
- Lower total cost of ownership.
  Source: https://servicesandsolutions.promo.skf.com/acton/media/26359 /rotating-equipment-performance (10/10/20)

Stated customer benefits
- Identify areas for improvement by assessing and benchmarking.
- Avoid unplanned downtime by detecting and diagnosing impending machine failures.
- Use the right tools and services for maintaining machines day-to-day.
- Leverage our technologies and expertise to solve problems.
  Source: https://servicesandsolutions.promo.skf.com/acton/media/26359 /rotating-equipment-performance (10/10/20)

Subscription packaging
Not disclosed.

Subscription pricing model
- Flexible supply or performance-based contracts.

- No additional information disclosed.

Subscription pricing structure
Not disclosed.

Case Study 24

Thales

Division:	Soarizon
Region:	Worldwide
Offer Name:	Soarizon
Link to Subscription:	www.soarizon.io/features-pricing
Subscription Category:	Startup
Public Pricing Info?	YES

Statement of customer & market problem

> ❝ SOARIZON is the best platform for operational planning available on the market. It is incredibly intuitive and comprehensive. All of the operational planning is in one place, which streamlines the process and helps you access all of the right information, which is a huge advantage.

- **Ben Shirley, Head of Training, HELIGUY.com**

Source: www.soarizon.io/ (05/07/20)

Offer description (technology)

SOARIZON is a drone management platform, including:
- Live Weather Data.
- Aviation Data.
- Live NOTAM Data.
- Customer & Technical Support.
- Secure, GDPR Compliant Platform.
- Comprehensive Mission Planning.
- Collaborate With Others.
- 3D Mapping.
  Source: www.soarizon.io/ (05/07/20)

Value proposition of the subscription offer
Not communicated.

Stated customer benefits
- Helps plan, fly and track safe and compliant drone missions anywhere in the world.

- No need to use multiple apps to plan drone missions, everything can be done through one platform.

Source: www.soarizon.io/ (05/07/20)

Subscription packaging
- "Good," "Better," "Best" approach.
- 3 subscription plans:
  - Soarizon Go, 5 missions per month. Possibility for "add-ons" (3D mapping, extra missions).
  - Soarizon Go+, unlimited missions.
  - Soarizon Enterprise.

Source: www.soarizon.io/features-pricing (05/07/20)

Subscription pricing model
- Soarizon Go: free.
- Soarizon Go+: subscription per month.

Source: www.soarizon.io/features-pricing (05/07/20)

Subscription pricing structure

Source: www.soarizon.io/features-pricing (05/07/20)

Case Study 25

TRUMPF

Division:	Corporate
Region:	Worldwide
Offer Name:	Pay-per-part
Link to Subscription:	www.trumpf.com/en_INT/company/presse /global-press-releases/press-release-detail-page/release /pay-per-part-trumpf-and-munich-re-plan-new-business -model-for-the-manufacturing-industry/
Subscription Category:	Digital bundle
Public Pricing Info?	NO

Statement of customer & market problem
- "With the Pay-per-Part approach, I have TRUMPF and Munich Re on my side, helping me to work toward my larger goals of higher productivity and greater efficiency." Customer Andreas Riguzzi, Riguzzi Gruppe AG CEO
  Source: www.hsbconnectedtechnologies.com/en/industrial-iot/pay-per -part-en.html#1324446584 (03/08/21)

Offer description (technology)
- TRUMPF Group is offering an innovative service for laser cutting machines.
- Use a full-service laser machine without having to buy or lease any equipment.
- Customers pay a previously agreed price for each cut sheet metal.
- The project will commence with a learning phase whose length is to be agreed.
- TRUMPF Group has collaborated with Relayr which provides the data analysis for the financing model.
  Source: www.trumpf.com/en_INT/company/presse/global-press-releases /press-release-detail-page/release/pay-per-part-trumpf-and-munich -re-plan-new-business-model-for-the-manufacturing-industry/ (10/10/20)

Value proposition of the subscription offer
- Increase their production capacity without massive up-front investments.
- Enable the acquisition of new customers.
  Source: www.trumpf.com/en_INT/company/presse/global-press-releases /press-release-detail-page/release/pay-per-part-trumpf-and-munich -re-plan-new-business-model-for-the-manufacturing-industry/ (10/10/20)

Stated customer benefits
- Make production processes more flexible and react faster to market changes.
- Access to the latest automated laser cutting technologies without the need for massive investment.
- Thanks to the planned performance guarantee, customers will also be insured against the financial impact of potential production downtime.
  Source: www.trumpf.com/en_INT/company/presse/global-press-releases
  *   /press-release-detail-page/release/pay-per-part-trumpf-and-munich*
  *   -re-plan-new-business-model-for-the-manufacturing-industry/*
  *   (10/10/20)*

Subscription packaging
- The offering includes fully automatic laser cutting machine, a storage system, TRUMPF's production know-how, and the necessary service components, as well as equipment maintenance and the required raw materials.
  Source: www.trumpf.com/en_INT/company/presse/global-press-releases
  *   /press-release-detail-page/release/pay-per-part-trumpf-and-munich*
  *   -re-plan-new-business-model-for-the-manufacturing-industry/*
  *   (10/10/20)*

Subscription pricing model
- Pay per use.
- Flexible monthly payment.
- Monthly fee is calculated based on the orders actually produced.
  Source: www.hsbconnectedtechnologies.com/en/industrial-iot/pay-per
  *   -part-en.html#1324446584 (03/08/21)*

Subscription pricing structure
Not disclosed.

The Author

Stephan M. Liozu (www.stephanliozu.com) is a pricing evangelist who has widely promoted value, pricing, and monetization for the past 10 years. He is the Founder of Value Innoruption Advisors (www.valueinnoruption.com), a consulting boutique specializing in industrial, digital, and value-based pricing. He is also an Adjunct Professor & Research Fellow at the Case Western Research University Weatherhead School of Management. Stephan holds a PhD in Management from Case Western Reserve University (2013), an MS in Innovation Management from Toulouse School of Management (2005), and an MBA in Marketing from Cleveland State University (1991).

Stephan holds the following certifications:

Value Black Belt—VBB (DecisionLink, 2021)

Certified Platform Design Toolkit Facilitator (PDT, 2020)

Certified IoT Professional (IoT-Inc., 2019)

Certified Black Hat Coach (Thales, 2018)

Certified Pricing-to-Win Shipley Instructor (2017)

Business Model Innovation Coach (Strategyzer, 2016)

Certified Innovation Leader—GIMI/IXL (2014)

Master Customer Value Modeler (CVM®, 2013)

Prosci® Change Management Certification (2013)

ThinkBuzan® Licensed Instructor—iMindMap® (2012)

Certified Pricing Professional (CPP) (2009)

Certified Facilitator for DDI Learning Systems (2009)

Breakthrough Thinking (Gap International ECC 2007)

Six Sigma Green Belt (2007)

Over the past few years, Stephan has published academic articles in the *Journal of Revenue & Pricing Management, Business Horizons, MIT Sloan Management Review,* and *Industrial Marketing Management.* He has also written many articles on strategic pricing issues for the *Journal of Professional Pricing.* Stephan sits on the Advisory Board of the Professional Pricing Society and Leverage-Point Innovation.

Over the past 10 years, Stephan has edited or published 11 other pricing books:

Pricing: The New CEO Imperative (VIA Publishing, 2021)

B2G Pricing: Best Practices in Business-to-Government Pricing Strategies (VIA Publishing, 2020)

Pricing Strategy Implementation: Translating Pricing Strategy into Results (Routledge, 2019)

Monetizing Data (VIA Publishing, 2018)

Value Mindset (VIA Publishing, 2017)

Dollarizing Differentiation Value (VIA Publishing, 2016)

The Pricing Journey (Stanford University Press, 2015)

Pricing and Human Capital (Routledge, 2015)

The ROI of Pricing (Routledge, 2014)

Pricing and the Sales Force (Routledge, 2015)

Innovation in Pricing: Contemporary Theories and Best Practices (Routledge, 2012 & 2017)

All books are available on Amazon.com. Please connect on LinkedIn or contact through the website at stephanliozu.com.

Made in the USA
Monee, IL
14 June 2022